THE
MAKING
OF
FOREIGN
POLICY

EAST AND WEST

Kurt London

Institute for Sino-Soviet Studies

The George Washington University

J. B. LIPPINCOTT COMPANY

PHILADELPHIA   NEW YORK

To Archibald M. Woodruff

Preface

In 1949, the first edition of my book *How Foreign Policy Is Made* was published. A second, revised edition followed in 1950. In the Foreword I stated that the book's purpose was to investigate the machinery by which foreign policies are evolved, formulated, and applied and that a correct appraisal of such policies was difficult, if not impossible, without an appreciation of the apparatus governments use to develop their principles and objectives.

When the book first appeared, literature on this subject was scant and the traditional historical approach to the making of foreign policy was still prevalent among political scientists and students of world affairs. As the book became recognized for its new approach and scope, its audience increased, particularly among students of international relations.

When a new revision was suggested, therefore, I agreed. I had not looked at the book for a long time, however, and when I finally did, having already undertaken the obligation of revising it, I realized that mere revision would not suffice. Its approach to the making of foreign policy I still considered sound. In particular, the role of the communist states, which has thoroughly changed the character of international relations, was focused correctly. But during the fifteen years that had passed since I wrote the book, new problems had arisen and old ones had to be reevaluated in their light.

V

Thus, instead of revising what I had written at the end of the forties, I wrote a virtually new book. My purpose, however, has remained unchanged—namely, to examine the policy machinery of representative states in the East and the West and, in so doing, to analyze its ramifications for the end product—foreign policy— without attempting a critique of finished policies. By machinery I mean not only the purely technical and organizational instrumentalities of policy and decision making but also many other aspects which influence formulation and implementation of policies. Not nearly enough attention has been paid to these vital aspects of foreign relations. This approach was germinated and stimulated during many years of government service in the field of foreign affairs and by an even longer preoccupation with the problems of international communism and its disintegrating effect upon the relations of nations.

I am greatly indebted to the U.S. Department of State, the British Embassy in Washington, and the French Ministry of Foreign Affairs in Paris for providing me with the newest available material pertinent to the subject of this book. No such cooperation was forthcoming from the communist camp, as was to be expected. Fortunately, ample material became available to me, and the charts of the pertinent Soviet and Communist Chinese Government organizations are from reliable sources.

I am grateful for the substantive, technical, and moral support received from members of the Institute for Sino-Soviet Studies and from my editor, John Bernheim of the J. B. Lippincott Company. My wife, Jean, as often before, gave me her unflinching editorial support. Miss Dorothy A. Owen and Miss Patricia Comanduras provided me with a fair copy of an almost illegible manuscript, and I appreciate their efforts on my behalf.

KURT LONDON

The George Washington University
Washington, D.C.
October 1, 1964

Contents

Introduction

THIS BOOK IS ABOUT foreign policy, its meaning and its making. Since foreign policy vitally influences relations among nations, or groups of nations, it may be called the father of all things in international affairs. Indeed, the fate of the world depends upon wise foreign policy.

A country's foreign policy determines its course of action toward other nations. It consists of short-range measures and long-term programs, all designed to carry out the objectives of a foreign policy for, obviously, every such policy has goals and purposes. On the whole, foreign policy reflects the sum total of those principles which have grown out of a nation's history, beliefs or ideologies, power potential, and its cultural predilections.

The fundamental policy objectives of every sovereign nation are the preservation of territorial integrity, the maintenance of political and economic independence, and the attainment of as high a living standard for the population as conditions permit. These are, of course, minimal requirements, essential for the continuation of national life. They are therefore premises rather than objectives. Beyond these requirements, a nation's foreign policy seeks to formulate and achieve its aims in accordance with historic aspirations, its political philosophies, and its physical potential.

Before the atomic age, war was an indication of the failure of

1

policy or of attempts to execute policies at any price. One of the great changes in policy consideration is realization of the impracticality of such an approach in the nuclear age: In a nuclear conflict there would be little difference between victor and vanquished. For this reason, even local wars, which occur mainly in the non-Western-aligned areas, are being conducted with circumspection lest they escalate into large-scale war in which the use of nuclear weapons could hardly be avoided.

Foreign policy, to be realistic, must be developed on the basis of certain facts of political life, not only within but outside the nation. In the following chapters, we shall first observe those factors which contribute to foreign policy inside a nation, keeping in mind the differences between Western-aligned and communist states. Next we shall investigate the foundation of foreign policy, namely, intelligence, which must provide vitally needed information about the outside world, friend or foe, and without which policies are meaningless.

These factors constitute the ABC of foreign relations. Having surveyed them, we must consider the three prime aspects of the foreign policy machinery: its originating organs, the technique of its formulation, and the ways of its implementation. This will be done on a comparative basis where necessary; many features are universally accepted, but others will differ in the West and in the East. But since, in general, aspects of international relations have changed so radically in the twentieth century, some thoughts concerning the nature of these changes must serve as an introduction to what should become a new approach to the meaning and making of foreign policy.

BACKGROUNDS OF CONFLICT

The causes of World War I are commonly attributed to conflicts between the economic interests of the great competing European powers. However, in the course of the war, the belligerents found the traditional issues of territory and markets superseded by the issue of freedom versus domination. During the Great Armistice, 1918-1939, the increasing effect of the political religions of Communism, Fascism, and Nazism further reduced the significance of economic conflicts as causes of war. Competition for foreign markets became a marginal issue, communist claims to the contrary; instead, the far more fundamental problems of the relationship between state and individual had to be faced again; also, the ideological confrontation between inimical political philosophies had to be clarified. Even the war between the United States and Japan, whose origin was supposedly devoid of ideological conflicts, soon began to show evidences of more than economic differences when Japanese imperialism claimed leadership over all Asia under the principles of the racial and divinely pre-ordained superiority of *Hakko Ichiu*.[1]

The participation of the Soviet Union on the side of the Western Allies in World War II created much popular confusion and postponed a struggle between two camps which did not become clearly defined until 1947 when the Stalinist campaign in Europe became virulent. Misconceptions of Chinese Communism also added to the ideological confusion while, on the other hand, the apparent toleration by the democracies of such fascist disciples as Marshal Pétain of France and General Franco of Spain—a strategic expedient for the hard-pressed Allies during the first years of World War II—still disturbed the politically unsophisticated in the West.

After the war, public opinion in the Western democracies was inclined to assume that military victory over the Axis would bring the solution of almost all major problems and that unfinished business could then be negotiated with ease and goodwill. This attitude reflected some misconceptions of the totalitarian "isms." Many Western statesmen before the war had been

---

[1] A mystical Japanese conception, meaning that the peoples of the world should be brought under one "roof." Former Foreign Minister Matsuoka once stated: "Japan should take over management of the continent on a large scale, propagate *Hakko Ichiu* . . . and then extend it all over the world." (Cf. K. London, *Backgrounds of Conflict*, New York: The Macmillan Company, 1945, 91 ff.)

inclined to regard the writings of Hitler and Mussolini as the demonstrations of political maniacs which, they assumed, had little or no practical importance. The writings of Marx, Lenin, and Stalin, which had been available for years, had aroused the attention of malcontents rather than politicians or even academicians. Indeed, the collected communist writings which could have provided a mine of information and clues to Soviet policy and strategy were often overlooked by the men who should have studied them most. Meanwhile, the Soviet leaders, strengthened through victory and the awareness of their vastly increased power and ignoring the war-weariness of their people, accelerated their plans for ideological conquest.

Thus World War II did not act as a catalyst, unifying the victors and solidifying peace through the establishment of the United Nations. On the contrary, the immediate postwar era saw an open split between the wartime allies, more or less along ideological lines, which resulted in the formation of the opposing blocs of nations. The Soviet Union was no longer the only "socialist" country but had in its camp the East European satellites, then Communist China, and finally the Asian satellites. Moreover, a host of emergent nations in Asia and Africa, with their newly acquired sovereignty, sought to straddle political demarcations. It is a truism that the world is no longer composed, as before World War I, of a pluralistic system of states. Rather it has developed into essentially three distinct groups— the communist, the anti-communist and the neutralist nations. Within each of these groups, there are considerable differences in political concepts and beliefs. But each group nevertheless has in common a basic approach to world affairs.[2]

The major powers in the anti-communist group represent parliamentary democracy strongly opposed to reducing the individual to a mere cog in the state-party machinery even though some smaller Western nations, for example Portugal and Spain, have

---

[2] The Sino-Soviet dispute is no proof to the contrary. Even if Moscow and Peking should split the international communist movement, their ideological fundamentals and political goals remain basically identical.

discarded popular representation and rule by authoritarian devices.

The communist nations, on the other hand, are united in their determination to end what they call "imperialism." They also have internal divergencies. Conflicting interpretation of Marxism-Leninism, which has led to a dispute between the Soviet Union and Communist China, is a telling example. Nevertheless, the members of the "socialist commonwealth" still have in common the conviction that communism is the wave of the future and that it will ultimately prevail. They share a hatred of "imperialism" and an obsession with conquering the earth for communism with a minimum of risks.

The neutralist nations, most of them new and untried, are preoccupied with their own problems. They want to consolidate their newly won sovereignty and develop their national character in dignity. They also want to achieve rapid economic development so as to attain political viability. While the anti-communist nations are primarily concerned with the preservation of their way of life and therefore assume a basically defensive stance, and the communist bloc seeks to shatter this tradition and supersede it with its own system of values, the neutralist, nonaligned states, though differing vastly from each other in background and resources, are wary of becoming involved in what they regard as a power struggle between East and West. They are trying to deal with both, but they are concerned about what they believe to be the former colonial powers' neo-colonialist economic domination and they are becoming suspicious of communist efforts to interfere with the free development of their new nationhood or already well entrenched political systems.

It is easy to realize that political differences no longer can be resolved through economic agreements as nineteenth-century political observers believed, for economic philosophy is but a manifestation of political creeds. In an age of ideological conflicts, politics and economics are but different sides of the same fabric; a change in economic principles reflects a related change in political beliefs. Hence moral suasion no longer can be expected to achieve compromise. It is in the nature of a dogma to remain unalterable, whereas democratic rationalism allows for adjustments. The search for compromise remains a prominent characteristic of democracy, which exercises it internally and tries to apply it externally. This worked so long as there existed governments that shared this basic approach. But when in a contracting world a large component of states no longer regards itself as part of the traditional family of nations and shuns compromise or when the most that can be achieved are day-to-day working agreements, the foundation of world politics is shaken.

It will be asked whether the quest for international organization does not indicate humanity's inherent desire for compromise and genuine peace—not mere coexistence while the "ideological struggle" continues unabatedly. We know, of course, that the League of Nations was a failure, despite its valiant efforts. The United Nations certainly has shown more promise, but its effectiveness as a world parliament has suffered on occasion when many member states exploited the UN for their own purposes rather than for common ideals. Without overlooking its successful actions to preserve the peace (e.g. in the Near East) or furthering human welfare in its specialized organizations, the UN, with all its potential, has suffered mainly from the inability of the Security Council to take a lead in the pursuit of peace. The presence of communist delegates prevents concerted action, and if action is taken by technical default of the communist members as was the case in the Korean war, participation by other member nations, except the United States, may be limited.

INTERNATIONAL LAW IN A DIVIDED WORLD

There can be no doubt that individual men have been far more successful in legally institutionalizing relations with their fellow men than have communities with other communities or, in modern times, nations with other nations. During millennia of slow, painful growth, life has produced a body of usages, taboos, and laws the authority of which man usually accepts because he considers them essential for his own protection. However, he has accepted the laws of his own community only. He has refused to be guided by the laws of outsiders who did not share his taboos. Nevertheless, his laws have changed through evolution and revolution. Laws are effective only when they can be enforced.

The laws and customs determining the relations between groups or nations, although achieving quite definite shape and substance in the course of the past centuries, differ from the laws pertaining to individuals in that they are non-enforceable. This does not mean international law is an illusion. Indeed, there are many instances testifying to the fact that some of its practices have become firmly accepted and that the covenants on which it is based or the usages that helped to evolve the covenants have become part of many national laws.

Apart from private international law, which deals with litigations between citizens or firms of different countries, most disputes between nations (public international law) are of a political rather than a legal nature. They are justiciable, as a rule, unless they constitute fundamental conflicts between national interests or, worse, between political ideologies. Political and ideological disputes are, in most cases, nonjusticiable for there is no way to enforce the law except by armed intervention. Legal rights and political differences frequently overlap. For this reason international jurists have felt that since legal disputes may well be political in nature, the difference between justiciable and nonjusticiable conflicts should be explained by the existence or absence of law.[3] Absence of law, in the international realm, would make treaties and agreements virtually useless. It is at this point that the makers of foreign policy are of necessity affected by the governments, the countries they are concerned with, and by the extent to which a nation will subordinate its sovereign rights to international law.

International law can be considered an attempt to help adjust

[3] L. Oppenheim, *International Law* (H. Lauterpacht, ed.) New York: Longmans, Green and Co., 1944, Vol. II, 4 ff.

a nation's interests to those of other nations. In this sense, it is in part the foundation, in part the aim, of foreign policy. To what degree it may be justiciable, therefore active, will depend on foreign policy decisions. The interpretation of international laws, treaties and agreements, like their creation, is subject to the consent and good faith of the contracting parties. Any nation which believes that it must renounce a treaty or disagree with its interpretation, renders the law nonjusticiable, or passive, for all. The passion for sovereignty is still strong enough to break the law of nations; a "re-examination of international law would involve an alteration of the traditional notion of sovereignty."[4] Under the concept—or pretext—of sovereignty, international law remains subject to the consent of those for whom it was created and to whom it is to be applied. If one of these parties sees fit to break the law, there is little other nations can do, other than to apply diplomatic or economic pressure, launch a propaganda campaign or wage a war.

Most laws stand or fall on their interpretation and the effectiveness of their execution. Moreover, every law is interpreted according to prevailing social and political concepts. Thus governments in the orbit of Judeo-Christian civilization—or a civilization akin to it—understand the principles of international law in similar terms, divided though they may be with regard to their national interests. Violations of the law of nations have occurred from time to time, but on the whole, international law and its concepts are respected not only for ethical reasons but because mutual accommodation is a matter of self-interest.

The emergence of political religions or ideologies, which led to the establishment of totalitarian states, has largely eliminated this common ground and therefore caused serious difficulties for the development, recognition, and strengthening of international law.

[4] P. C. Jessup, *A Modern Law of Nations*, New York: The Macmillan Company, 1948, 6 ff.

IDEOLOGY AND FOREIGN POLICY

Ideology is more than a device to be exploited cynically to generate motivational power for a party or people. As a strong force, it has contributed to the division of the world during the twentieth century. It is more than an instrument of opportunism. Ideology is a kind of political religion. Ideological faith and the hope for the future it has stimulated among the underprivileged accounts for the development of what we call the communist bloc or, as it is termed, within the Iron Curtain countries, the "socialist camp," "world socialist system," or "socialist commonwealth of states." Communist ideology alone could not have achieved this development: It needed the combination of Marxist-Leninist doctrine with the modern technology of communication, which made possible the worldwide promotion of militant revolutionary trends.

It is by no means certain whether foreign policy made by communist governments is *national* foreign policy as we understand it or *international communist* foreign policy. This would seem to be one of the key questions to be considered by all free world statesmen in policy-making positions.

The danger of misinterpretation begins with the fundamental question: What is the communist objective? Political experts agree that the long-range communist intention is the spread of communism throughout the world, but they disagree over the nature of the driving forces behind this ultimate goal. Is it nationalist Soviet or Chinese imperialism or is it the inevitable consequence of the communist gospel? Do the major communist powers pursue their foreign policies as nation-states, i.e. in their own interests, or do they act primarily as leaders of and trustees for the international communist movement?

Many political observers in the West seem to believe that Marxism-Leninism is merely a tool for the expansionism of Soviet or Communist Chinese national self-interests. Since the communist states have maintained the trappings of a nation-state and since many of their policies seem to indicate national rather than international preoccupation, insufficient attention is given to the actual motives behind these policies. The cloak of tradition hides the body of revolution. For example, many students of diplomatic history have been led to identify czarist Russia's policy aims with those of Soviet Communism by the similarity of such shared strategic goals as warm water outlets, security against attacks from Western-Central Europe, domination of Eastern and Southeastern Europe, the quest for a Middle Eastern sphere of interest and influence in the Far East.

There is no denying that some of the outward manifestations of communist foreign affairs resemble those of non-communist countries. This is to be expected; it provides a suitable blind in a world in which nineteenth-century traditions of international relations still affect institutions and customs. But it is dangerous to conclude from their temporary adoptions of pre-revolutionary diplomatic habits or from their continuation of traditional policy objectives that communist policy makers are basically playing the old political power game.

Whether, or to what extent, ideology determines foreign policy is a matter of widespread controversy. Many decision makers and political analysts seem to believe that ideology is used to justify policies and actions instead of being shaped by it. Historical parallels are cited and reiterated. Social changes in Eastern Europe are taken as indications of a declining or eroding doctrinal position. Most of all, the apparent contradictions between theory and practice and the end of Stalinist monolithic communism are cited as proof that, in the USSR at least, the era of revolutionary convictions is past, though it is admitted that it still exists in Communist China.

This pragmatic approach fails to take into account the intricacies of Marxist-Leninist scholasticism. It forgets that communist ideology is a "guide to action," not a textbook giving specific answers to specific questions. It disregards the fact that the belief of the Soviet leaders in the ultimate triumph of communism has not changed; where they differ from the past, they have adjusted their methods to new conditions. It is conceivable that the Chinese Communist leaders, dogmatic as they are, will undergo similar adjustments in the decades to come.

Finally, it may be ventured that whatever disillusionment with ideology exists is concentrated on domestic issues. In international affairs, in the communist view of the outside world, in problems of economic or military strategy beyond the Iron Curtain, the changes are not essential ones and, as has been pointed out by a foremost Sovietologist, the Kremlin's foreign policy has shown remarkable continuity since Stalin.[5]

THE NUCLEAR STALEMATE AND FOREIGN POLICY

Another element of great import has hampered the style of policy makers: the existence of nuclear weapons and the means of delivering them quickly through rockets.

Foreign policy not only determines a course of action toward other nations; to be meaningful, it must have productive objectives; it must strive for positive achievements for the nation for which it is formulated. In former days, when war was considered a "continuation of policy by other means," as Karl von Clausewitz, the Prussian strategist, put it, it was feasible to let military action decide what the diplomats could not agree upon. Since nuclear weapons have become a part of the military arsenal of the members of the "nuclear club," military action is no longer the last resort for decision. What would happen to the human race during and after a nuclear war with hydrogen weapons is, of course, speculative. We do not know whether human life would be virtually destroyed or whether such a holocaust would leave any chance for recovery of a decimated world population. All we have to go by are the two relatively crude atomic bombs dropped on Hiroshima and Nagasaki in 1945 so as to

---

[5] Marshall D. Shulman, *Stalin's Foreign Policy Reappraised*, Cambridge, Mass.: Harvard University Press, 1963, *passim*.

hasten Japan's surrender. The effects were devastating but they did remain local. Obviously, an explosion of hydrogen weapons would vastly increase the radius of damage and produce a much deadlier fall-out; moreover, it is reasonable to assume that a mutual attack with hydrogen weapons would render meaningless the concept of military victory or defeat. There would be no victors, only survivors. The purpose of the initial attack would fail as a result of retaliation.[6]

This situation nullifies once and for all Clausewitz's theory, certainly in the event of global war and most likely in local wars that could escalate into world conflicts. Communist governments seem to be proceeding on the erroneous assumption that "national liberation wars" are in a special category of wars that can be fought without nuclear involvement. The Western alliance views the prospect of a communist take-over of the third world countries in Asia, Africa and Latin America as intolerable; local wars started in these areas would almost certainly spread to the centers which organized them, in which case escalation into full-scale world war would be the logical result.

This situation presents a dilemma for policy makers, both East and West. The coincidence of the nuclear with the ideological age presents further complications. Western leaders, with the possibilities of hot war diminished, are facing total cold war waged on all fronts of human endeavor. They are finding it difficult to create effective counter measures. Their traditional training and modes of thought were limited to an intellectual setting appropriate only to their own state of mind, but outdated by the revolutionary events which have produced the disorder of contemporary world politics. Communist leaders must determine among themselves whether Lenin's dictum that wars are inevitable so long as imperialism exists is still applicable. Khrushchev, at the Twentieth Congress of the Soviet Communist Party in 1956, made it clear that he did not think so and re-interpreted Lenin, declaring that "war is no longer fatally inevitable." Mao Tse-

[6] See also Herman Kahn's controversial book *On Thermonuclear War*, Princeton, N.J.: Princeton University Press, 1961.

tung, on the other hand, maintains that Lenin's thesis is still correct and, while acknowledging the greater destructiveness of nuclear weapons, holds it to be an act of cowardice to attempt communist conquest through peaceful coexistence.

As for the concept of peaceful coexistence, Khrushchev has said: "The policy of peaceful coexistence is, as far as its social content is concerned, a form of intense economic, political and ideological struggle between the proletariat and the aggressive forces of imperialism in the world arena."[7] There is no reason to believe that his successors will reject this view.

FOREIGN POLICY IN A DIVIDED WORLD

A workable foreign policy can never be static. In formulating policies, it is necessary to keep in mind that international conditions, like human life, are subject to constant change and that to build a policy on the basis of the *status quo* is an illusion that can only lead to disappointment, if not disaster. For nations, like human beings, are born, grow through a period of adolescence, become mature and—as history demonstrates—more often than not disintegrate. Maintenance of a *status quo* is unnatural and can lead to premature death. On this small globe there are few isolated issues. Problems of international relations are interconnected and rarely can one issue be considered in a vacuum. In other words, foreign policy has become intercontinental policy and as such is indivisible.

In an era which has seen the emergence of so many new nations it is important to remember that the birth of a nation is

[7] From Khrushchev's report to the Moscow Conference of 81 Communist parties, January 6, 1961. However, it should not be forgotten that Lenin, in his *Imperialism - the Highest State of Capitalism* (1916), explained this "inevitability" in terms of wars between the imperialist powers for colonies. It was only after the death of Lenin that the "inevitability" concept was used for conflicts between socialism and capitalism as well. See Frederick S. Burin, "The Communist Doctrine of the Inevitability of War" in the *American Political Science Review*, Vol. LVII, No. 2, June, 1963.

coincidental with the establishment of its territory and the recognition by other powers of its political independence. Recognition may not be global but once a new nation exists, lawfully or not, it is a factor to deal with. The process of growth may begin inside the newly drawn boundaries and aim at consolidating the nation's political, social, economic, military, and cultural status. But this process need not be completed before the new nation begins to look beyond its frontiers. Once consolidated, its government may feel that future security depends on the achievement of objectives such as the forging of alliances and the accessibility of natural resources or markets for its own products. It will then proceed to formulate its policy accordingly. Smaller nations are scarcely in a position to pursue military ventures or the export of ideologies; their policy can be "dynamic" only to a limited degree. President Nkrumah of Ghana may have found that it is easy enough to chart a dynamic course in international relations, but that it is quite another matter to steer it. For the execution of a plan depends, first, upon internal support and second, upon the attitudes of other nations whose policy may provide either for measures to check the advance of would-be usurpers of their national interests or for inducements toward obtaining the new nation's allegiance to specific alignments.

Traditionally, every sovereign nation tries to maintain a minimum but aims at a maximum of security and prosperity. Between these extremes, its policy must maneuver. Adjustments to changed conditions may be only apparent and tactical; it may, if less dogmatically conceived, develop alternative solutions while still remaining in the framework of the national goals. However, for conditions in the post-revolutionary, post-nuclear age, this would seem to be too simplistic an approach. For nations are not nation-states only but symbols of ideologies.

One of the decisive elements on which to base foreign policy concepts is power. It has two aspects: first, the extent to which national power can be generated and expended; second, the estimation of such power not upon actual (absolute) values but in terms of relative values. In other words, a statesman must know his own resources and potential and then compare them with those of other nations in order to arrive at a realistic estimate of relative power. It would be wrong, however, to assume that power can be "balanced" in the manner of the nineteenth century, when the conclusion and dissolution of political alliances was a dominating factor in international diplomacy. Remnants of this political game may still be found when "alignment preferences are based on specific and limited interests."[8]

Even these remnants are dying out because agreements between individual powers—the "super powers" excepted—are made to meet specialized interests of the contracting parties which would not automatically reach into the sphere of broader political implications. Such more important issues can no longer be solved by a single nation but must have concurrence of the group of nations to which it belongs. In the era of blocs and camps, not even a powerful country can dispense with the support of its allies. Clearly, the power-balancing chess game which so intrigued the diplomats of past centuries no longer applies and no policy maker in his senses can engage in it.

The balance-of-power concept has been replaced with the mutual deterrent of nuclear weapons, sometimes called the balance of terror. In addition there is "peaceful competition," which refers to a race between East and West in economic, technological, and social welfare achievements. This competition between the camps, and especially between the United States and the Soviet Union, has assumed great significance in the struggle for the favor of the third world. Increasingly, policy formulated in the West or in the East, not only in Washington and Moscow, but also in London, Paris, Bonn or Peking, takes into account relations with Latin America, the Middle East, or Black Africa and the non-communist Asian countries. Evidently, foreign policy anywhere in the world can no longer be based exclusively on national interest. The professed desire of the communist regimes to ensure a coordinated policy of the countries belonging to the

---

[8] Morton A. Kaplan, editor, *The Revolution in World Politics*, New York: John Wiley & Sons, 1962, p. 432.

socialist commonwealth (which has suffered some setbacks since the development of polycentric communism after the Twentieth Congress of the Soviet Communist Party in 1956 and the Sino-Soviet dispute) may be more deceptive than the trend of cooperation among Western or third world governments. It has different, rather sinister motives which cannot be objectively discerned in the West and the neutralist areas. A universal tendency toward groupings of more or less like-minded states appears to be speeding the process of international association and no leader, whether he be Charles de Gaulle or Mao Tse-tung, can arrest it.

To be sure, there are, in the world today, strong nationalist currents. We must, however, be careful to differentiate between nineteenth- and twentieth-century nationalism. In the previous century, nationalism was based upon the historical development of the nation-state which had then reached its zenith. Territorial, linguistic, religious, and cultural traditions had developed specific, distinguishable traits in the citizens of a nation which they were willing to defend—or even expand—to the death. This nationalism was self-centered and more often than not blind to the needs and feelings of other nations. The idea of an international community which developed after World War II was not yet present, a fact which contributed to the failure of the League of Nations.

It is significant that in our time nationalism is strongest in countries which are either new or have been under foreign tutelage for long periods of time. Feelings for newly acquired sovereignty and independence are running high; in many countries, true nationalism is not yet possible since they have not yet developed the common culture, historic traditions, and social homogeneity that are the foundations of nationalism. At the same time, the nationalism of the old, established states has mellowed to the degree that they recognize that the rugged nation-individualism of old is hopelessly outdated. Indeed, we must face the fact that the nation-state, as we knew it, is on the decline.[9]

[9] *The Mid-Century Challenge to U.S. Foreign Policy, Special Studies Project I*, New York: The Rockefeller Brothers Fund, Doubleday & Co., Inc., 1959, 48 ff.

The reasons for this development may lie in the upheavals caused by two destructive World Wars within one generation. More specifically, they are the result of differing political philosophies and the arrival of a new technology which has obliterated previous concepts of war and peace and created the new grey area of the cold war and large, ideologically divided, blocs of countries.

For policy makers, this situation is fraught with complexities, by no means limited to Western statesmen. The communists have their share of troubles, as the Sino-Soviet dispute demonstrates. While the rationale for this controversy is the doctrinal rather than power-political struggle, the central issue is the quickest way to destroy "imperialism." Methodology in doctrine corresponds to tactics in foreign policy, and there is at present no agreement on tactics in the socialist camp. Moreover, the communists must decide whether a "war of national liberation" in the former colonial and semi-colonial territories—a thesis which has been part of the ideology since the twenties—is indeed practicable. The Soviet leaders have professed this doctrine without, however, being overtly aggressive; the Chinese Communist leaders, on the other hand, conduct themselves most aggressively but without following their words with deeds—with the exception of the struggle with Tibet and the border dispute with India. Both Moscow and Peking have unquestionably been involved in Laos and Vietnam.

The uncommitted leaders, aligned with neither East nor West, want to deal with both sides. They frankly acknowledge their desire to obtain economic and military aid from both East and West while declining to bind themselves to any one group. They want none of colonialism or neo-colonialism of which they accuse the West—and in some instances the East as well. They doubt the usefulness of the free enterprise system in the capitalist states but they are just as wary of Marxism-Leninism. They are apprehensive lest the acceptance of Marxism-Leninism deliver them to outside rule or, at least, to a communist-type of neo-colonialism, and they probably view Cuba's dependence upon the USSR in this light. The uncommitted leaders prefer to create their own ideology, readily applicable to the particular conditions in their countries.

The Western allies and their friends in Latin America, the Middle East, and Asia obviously are also facing a variety of problems which will force them to revise their traditional approach to international relations and require an overhaul of the foreign policy machinery and processes. They cannot temporize as they did for so many decades. In the past, a benevolent fate often saved them from the need to commit themselves. There was no apparent need to formulate long-range policy. During the period between wars (1918-1939), it became clear that the traditional way of striving for some immediate, narrow national interests, while hoping for an even better future, no longer worked. Since virtually all statesmen of this period were traditionalists, neither the establishment of a Bolshevik regime in Moscow nor the social earthquakes elsewhere were regarded as seriously upsetting the ancient order of foreign policy making. Even World War II did not immediately contribute to a badly needed, thorough revision of the concept of international relations. Statesmen were too deeply rooted in diplomatic history of the nineteenth century to see the need for a complete overhaul of the substance and organization of foreign policy and even the best of them could not tear themselves away from the credo of the 1815 Congress of Vienna.

One reason for this phenomenon may have been their failure to take seriously the secular religions of the twentieth century. They did not look upon these aggressive ideologies as the crucial factors in the East-West struggle; they were slow to recognize the growing importance of the third world; they did not conceive of the world as an interconnected unit, nor did they admit that local issues cannot be taken out of the context of world politics. By implication, short-range policy decisions became increasingly insufficient to cope with a changed distribution of forces.

Moreover, as we shall see later in greater detail, modern communication systems have rendered obsolete much of the traditional diplomacy while, on the other hand, diplomacy, could it retain its former flexibility, has never been needed more than now. The effect of propaganda has perverted both policy making and the actions of professional negotiators. The borderline between internal and external politics, always nebulous, has disappeared and made the concept of foreign policy as total as war.[10] As a result, national foreign policy must embody a country's over-all political, economic, military, technological and social goals, its traditions and psychological attitudes, its educational level and motivation—in short its philosophy of life and the universe.

On the other hand—and here is the greatest dilemma—the policy maker's long-range vision must be supra-national rather than national. There is an inherent contradiction in this aspect: The men who make the decisions are expected to meet the demands of their own nation and yet, if they comply without regard for the rest of the world, they will fail as national leaders. The ideal policy maker in the nuclear age is a man who represents the interests of his country without losing sight of the forces at work beyond his borders. The rise of a nationalist in the classical sense, such as Charles de Gaulle, is no proof to the contrary. His usefulness to France's new internal stability is undeniable, but his grandiose visions of France as a first-class world power are unrealistic in view of France's natural limitations in comparison with more powerful states. Thus he is unlikely to become the leader of nations he aspires to be and, being a nineteenth-century nationalist, he is outdated by the movement of events. In contrast, it may be said that, ever since Franklin D. Roosevelt, the U.S. Presidents, as chief decision makers, have had the interplay of forces and powers well in mind.

PREMISES FOR FOREIGN POLICY

There is an unalterable foundation to every nation's foreign policy which reflects its character and aspirations. It is this foun-

[10] For an analysis of these problems, see chapter 10 of K. London, *The Permanent Crisis*, New York: Walker & Co., 1962.

dation that cannot be compromised except in defeat. Only its diplomatic "superstructure," to use a Marxian term, allows for flexibility of political strategy, tactical adjustments and alternatives, permitting it to maneuver and negotiate.

In developing his policies, no statesman can afford to overlook certain basic factors, premises which determine the scope of his planning and his courses of action. These factors are partly measurable in scientific terms, partly consist of imponderables full of uncertainty and, as has been indicated before, must be weighed against what is known of similar factors prevailing in other nations, whether friend or foe.

The first group of premises comprises conditions arising from a nation's physical, economic, and human geography, its commitment to history and tradition or ideology and the status of its technology. The second group involves the internal conditions of a country, its domestic, economic and military policies, its public opinion and pressure groups. The third group is concerned with such intangibles as the "national mind" and national morale, important factors in the propaganda battle between the blocs. Finally, the meaning of nuclear weapons and the conquest of space are new elements which tax the decision maker's imagination and compel him to integrate political with military and technological strategy, requiring the collaboration of practically the entire government apparatus.

Add to these premises the comparatively novel situation in which national interests are no longer the sole yardstick of foreign policy. This is not to deny that they exist but, in the broad world view, they have become a "static concept;"[11] they can no longer be the decisive issues of international relations. In other words, the policy maker, while having in mind the good of his country, cannot exclude from his calculations foreign interests, especially those of his friends; to a degree, his policy must be conceived as a cooperative proposition at least within the group of states to which his country belongs.

[11] G. Modelski, *A Theory of Foreign Policy*, New York: Frederick A. Praeger, 1962, p. 71.

To ensure clear understanding of these complexities, it will be necessary to examine these factors briefly. They are all part of an integrated whole, and only for the sake of systematic discussion have they been separated into different categories.

1. The Elements of National Power

IN THE PAST, relations among nations were governed by their relative power. The strengths and weaknesses of a country's position in the concert of nations appeared to depend on territorial size and location, accessibility for military and economic purposes, climatic conditions, transportation and communications facilities, manpower, industrial potential, and natural wealth. But in the nuclear age, not all these factors remain equally important. The ideological and technological developments of the first half of the twentieth century have already brought about changes in the international power structure that cannot be explained solely in traditional terms. In a period of transition neither the conventional nor the revolutionary concepts of international relations are quite acceptable. Increasingly, intangibles must be weighed against appearances. We can no longer measure power in visible terms only. Nor can we leave unrecognized the growing tendency of polarization—the creation of blocs consisting of like-minded nations which eventually may supersede the nation-state system in favor of a multi-national aggregate under leadership that is ideologically motivated. Most of all, the technological revolution of the twentieth century has created entirely novel conditions which have upset the traditional aspects of power relations and thereby forced policy makers to reappraise the new situation on the threshold of the twenty-first century.

PHYSICAL GEOGRAPHY

Among the inescapable elements influencing or determining the formulation of national foreign policy are the size, location, and nature of the territory; accessibility and character of frontiers; climate, density, and character of the population; natural resources, capacity and know-how of industrial production; transportation facilities and the general educational and technological level. These factors, however, are of limited significance unless they are compared with similar factors in other nations. Yet it must be remembered that some of these elements are no longer as critical as they were prior to the nuclear, jet, and missile age while others, formerly regarded as minor, have increased in importance.

Great nations acquired much of their power because geographic location gave them a dominant strategic position, access to sea lanes or intercontinental transport routes. Inevitably, nations with such advantages found themselves endowed with influence of more than local character, provided that their internal conditions permitted an intelligent and orderly organization of such privileges. We are thinking here of nations with a fairly large territory, having at their disposal ample manpower and natural resources. But size alone does not make a nation great: A vast land such as prerevolutionary China with its hundreds of millions of inhabitants was never a great power. Nor was the Ottoman empire. In both cases, the weaknesses of social and industrial organization prevented the governments of these countries from marshaling their potential strength. On the other hand, European great powers, as we knew them prior to World War II, were much smaller than the American or Eurasian territories of the United States and the Soviet Union; yet they were able (with the additional resources of colonies) to increase their natural resources and so develop such a degree of industrial and military efficiency that they became world powers in fact and formulated their foreign policy accordingly.

Regrettable though it may be, the smaller countries no longer lead an entirely independent political life. They must eventually decide—if they have the freedom of decision—with which group of nations they wish to join forces. The pluralism within the three main groups of nations complicates such decisions and at times appears to jeopardize the unity of the respective camps. In the West, the divergency of views between Great Britain and France has produced a crisis in the North Atlantic Treaty Organization (NATO) and the Common Market which has little chance of being settled while President Charles de Gaulle continues to influence French policy. In the communist orbit, the Sino-Soviet dispute has caused Albania to side with Peking and to be outlawed by Moscow; it will also be recalled that Yugoslavia, after being expelled from the Cominform in 1948, stayed outside the Soviet bloc although remaining a communist state. Both Yugoslavia's and Albania's actions were favored by their geographic location: They are not contiguous to the USSR, and a joint Soviet-satellite action would have constituted a serious risk of general war.

The small western European states knew they had little chance to withstand the onslaught of communist forces without joining the anti-communist alliance. Their predilection for the West was natural since, by tradition and attitude, they belong to its culture complex. But they also counted on the West's proclaimed principle of equality among all nations, large and small. A similar assurance was given by the USSR, but the satellite experience suggested that such promises could not always be trusted. Stalin indicated a contempt for small nations and believed they should entrust their fate to the leadership of the great countries. There has been no evidence that Stalin's successors disagree with his view.

The "different roads to socialism," first announced at the Belgrade meeting between Khrushchev and Tito and later codified at the Twentieth Congress of the Soviet Communist Party in Moscow, appear to have restored some internal independence in the Eastern European countries. It remains to be seen whether this new principle has affected the Soviet view on the role of the small nations.

In the third world area, the desire of the many small states to associate is logical. If it were not for the obstacles created by extreme nationalism or egocentrism, an alliance betwen African or Middle East states would be natural. With the surrender of a small portion of sovereignty for the common good, the political and economic importance of cohesive state systems would enhance the power and influence of all participating countries. The attempts being made through such bodies as the Organization of American States are noteworthy and may well be emulated by groups of states in other parts of the globe.

Against the assertions of the West and the East that proclaim the equality of all nations, stands the United Nations Charter, which clearly implies that only the big powers are in a position either to conduct or prevent large-scale wars and therefore must be granted special consideration. The organization of the UN Security Council is the logical result of this reasoning: Only the big powers are permanently represented; the six seats filled by elected representatives of the smaller member states are occupied for a period of not more than two years.[1]

The significance of size, however, has decreased as old established principles have been revolutionized. Upheavals produced by the introduction of new techniques of communication and weapons development have affected political positions. The sway of totalitarian ideologies has led to many changes in the relative power potentials. Nevertheless, in the realm of physical geography, the topographical character of an area remains important—even in the age of rockets. Accessibility to sea lanes, influence of topography on transportation, and the location of industrial centers and natural resources have retained significance.

The nature of frontiers (mountainous, wooded, flat-open, coastal) has traditionally conditioned a country's political position. From time immemorial, easy access has enticed aggressors

[1] At the inception of the UN, the "big" nations were the United States, the United Kingdom, France, the USSR, and China. After the Communist conquest of the Chinese mainland, Nationalist China, now limited to Taiwan (Formosa), has remained a member of the Security Council, the Peking regime not having been accorded membership by the General Assembly.

to embark on expansionist ventures. The central European plains are a classical example. This does not mean that natural obstacles have prevented attackers from trying to overcome all roadblocks; in ancient times, Hannibal crossed the Alps against enormous odds and succeeded in reaching the northern Italian plain. But such obstacles have given pause to aggressors and frequently persuaded them to forego their dreams of conquest.

Within a country, hilly and wooded areas can serve as a redoubt for both military and industrial bastions or as bases of resistance in the event of enemy invasion and occupation. On the other hand, they can impede internal economic development. Navigable rivers have both military and economic aspects. They might slow down, at least temporarily, an enemy's advance and they can facilitate the economical transportation of goods. They also further agricultural production and, in some instances, can be valuable in the production of electric power. Coast lines have the double advantage of being an outlet to the sea lanes and a natural defense.

Yet, in an era of jets, missiles, atomic submarines, nuclear developments and space exploration, all these considerations lose much of their former importance and are no longer necessarily decisive political-strategic factors. Still, in the period of transition from the electronic to the nuclear age there are exceptions. The vast reaches east of the Ural mountains and some Mongolian-Chinese areas bordering Soviet Central Asia are difficult targets even with the capacities of modern weapons. Moreover, Moscow and Peking have organized a large industrial decentralization program—in contrast to the heavy concentration of accessible American and European industries—which impedes the selection of vital targets as well as the delivery of weapons. Nor does the Soviet frontier, the longest national borderline in the world, afford "easy access to the seas or, with some exceptions, to contiguous lands."[2] Thus in both China and

[2] N. D. Palmer and H. C. Perkins, *International Relations*, Boston: Houghton Mifflin Co., 1957, p. 45.

Russia it is size rather than topography which, at present, is still strategically significant and must be considered by statesmen as a political reality.

The Western Hemisphere is separated from the Orient and the Occident by two great oceans; theoretically, it is shielded by the Arctic in the north and the Antarctic in the south; the United States in particular is bordered on the north by friendly Canada and on the south by more or less friendly Latin American nations. Yet, America is accessible to jet planes via the polar route and vulnerable to missile attack. It is almost certain, of course, that nuclear warfare would be as damaging to the Eurasian Communist powers as to Europe or the Western Hemisphere. Fall-out can impair or destroy life regardless of climate, frontiers, or geophysical conditions.

POLITICAL GEOGRAPHY

During the nineteenth century, the concept of geopolitics was developed by British, Swedish, and German geographers and political scientists. It was somewhat compromised when the German Professor Karl Haushofer tried—unsuccessfully—to influence Hitler's foreign policy by geopolitical conclusions which were essentially those of the British geographer Sir Halford Mackinder—namely, that the Eurasian land mass be looked upon as a "heartland", i.e. the geographical focus of power on earth.[3] If Russia and Germany were allied, Haushofer reasoned, the littoral powers' strategic position would be greatly weakened. Had Hitler agreed, had he allied himself with the Soviet Union, the face of the world might look different today. After the communist victory in China, the alliance between Moscow and Peking in 1950 again presented a terrifying menace to the Western world and, indeed, to all countries outside the communist orbit. The heartland seemed to have shifted east but, in view of

[3] *The Geographic Journal*, Vol. XXIII, No. 4, London, April 1904.

the division of Germany, had gained rather than lost: China was much larger and a littoral power as well.

Mackinder, in 1919, broadened his 1904 concept and added Africa to his Eurasian pivot area which thus became a "world island" and, he wrote: "Who rules the world island, commands the world."[4] Later, in 1943, he reiterated his "heartland" idea but suggested as counterbalance the North Atlantic powers.[5] Six years later, this prophetic view came to pass with the establishment of NATO.

How valid are these concepts now that the combination of ideological and technological revolutions is changing pre-atomic concepts of national power? No longer is it sufficient to look at a nation's territory from the point of view of general location, size and topography, its access to the sea, and relations with other countries. The one-time dynamics of geopolitics is about to become a historic phenomenon. Modern communications systems have opened up the remotest corners of the globe. Political ideologies have led to strange alliances which seem to mock national interests and disregard distances. Mackinder's theory had its roots in a world of traditional forces, with traditional land and sea powers. The growing significance of air power seemed to have escaped him. The development of jets and missiles which compelled military strategists to develop new approaches to modern warfare has of necessity changed the political map as well.

"Once the barriers of oceans, mountains and deserts are easily and speedily surmounted, once distance is conquered, every country's political position—including its geographic location—must be re-evaluated by its leaders."[6] As the twentieth century enters its last third, geopolitics can no longer be of great help to the policy maker.

[4] Sir Halford Mackinder, *Democratic Ideals and Reality*, New York: Henry Holt & Co., 1919, reprinted 1942.

[5] Cf. Mackinder, "The Round World and the Winning of the Peace," *Foreign Affairs*, New York, July, 1943, No. XXXI.

[6] K. London, *op. cit.*, p. 62.

ECONOMIC GEOGRAPHY

The quantity and quality of a nation's natural resources, the degree of its industrial and technical skills, the availability of manpower, and the ability to feed itself are politically and strategically significant. Once he has made an estimate of his country's relative economic strength, and realized what it means in terms of national security, the policy maker will know how far he can go in either enforcing or reducing his aspirations. However, a comparison between East and West economic assets and potentials, between capitalistic and socialistic economies, is not meaningful. Capitalism supports a free-wheeling, competitive consumer economy with the profit motive prevalent and the countervailing elements of supply and demand regulating the volume of production and consumption. The classical socialist economy is strictly planned, has few private sectors, and channels resources and labor according to political needs. Its fluctuations are controlled; and while it deprives the consumer of much-needed goods, not to mention luxuries, while it forces him to live in perpetual austerity, it has no depression cycles such as occur with unfortunate regularity to uncontrolled free enterprise economies. Since the objective of the socialist state in the social ist commonwealth is the establishment of a communist society in which the "material-technical base" would guarantee a high level of economic accomplishment, planning for an indefinite period must concentrate on investments that would further this objective regardless of the requirements of individual citizens.

One might describe the "socialist" economy, as practiced by communist-ruled governments, as a war economy of sorts. Ther is a continuous "struggle" for the achievement of goals; if politically expedient, priorities are assigned to certain sectors of the economy to the disadvantage of others; the cold war against "imperialism" is ever present, if not directly, then indirectly because the long-range objectives incorporate the communist strategy of conquest. Democracies and even authoritarian regimes such as those in Spain or Portugal do not engage in this type of "struggle" except in war time.

And yet, in communist as in capitalist economies, there are some aspects of national economy that must perforce be considered by policy makers and strategists: The more balanced a country's economy, the stronger is its position. Theoretically, in a balanced economy industrial and agricultural production are about evenly matched, creating a condition in which the state's own natural resources and industrial capacities furnish all the commodities required and in which the combined agricultural facilities can supply all the food that may be needed.

For a variety of reasons, no country can or will produce all the raw materials and commodities that its economy consumes. As a result, there exist only a few relatively balanced economies in the world. The United States and the Soviet Union may be considered as so privileged. Although the level of production in quantity and quality is much higher in the United States than in the USSR—though the gap is narrowing in certain industries such as steel production—the USSR unquestionably has potential self-sufficiency. It may be added that Communist China, though far inferior to the economies of the more developed free world countries, is struggling to become self-sufficient. Indeed, Peking has little choice because it lacks hard currency and has few exportable products; it has received little or no aid from Moscow, especially since the Sino-Soviet dispute came into the open in 1959-1960; many free world markets are closed to it and it lacks industrial skills since the Soviet technicians left mainland China without finishing their projects. Nevertheless, for political and ideological reasons, Peking sends support to Albania and promises help to third world countries in one form or another.

Communist China is a dramatic example of a totalitarian state whose economy, by Western standards, should have collapsed some time ago but did not and—it seems fair to say—will not. The Mao regime's "Big Leap Forward" program, combined with the natural disasters that have beset China since its earliest history, brought terrible suffering upon most of the Chinese population. Yet, despite some grumbling, the people did not revolt against the program but generally went along with its leadership, hoping that at least the revolution would eventually provide them with a better life than most of them had known. If Western policy makers had built their plans on the assumption of a Chinese Communist collapse, they would have badly miscalculated, and it is important to remember that under a communist regime the economic doctrines of advanced societies are not applicable.

Most other countries, not excluding some of political and strategic importance, do not have a balanced economy. They may have to import vital raw materials to keep their industrial establishments running. They are compelled to supplement their basic commodities with imports of luxuries that have become necessities. Examples of predominantly industrial economies are Germany and England. Japan has learned to exploit its small agricultural areas so effectively that it has almost achieved a balance, which will depend on its vast industrial establishment's ability to continue producing for export and obtaining the requisite raw materials. In the wake of postwar recovery, both France and Italy have succeeded in making strides toward greater balance as they developed their industries.

Cooperative action has brought new forces to bear on economies both East and West. In the West, the creation of the Common Market has decreased the significance of imbalanced national economies and, through a lowering of customs barriers and a free distribution system, has produced a high level of prosperity. The East, which created a Council for Mutual Economic Assistance (CEMA or COMECON), has been less successful. The USSR conceived of a division of labor within its orbit, allocating to the individual central-eastern European states certain economic areas in which to specialize. It took COMECON several years to reach the point where such allocation was to be determined, but it seems that some of the COMECON members objected to the projected one-sidedness of their economy which inevitably would follow concentration on production of raw materials, industry, or agriculture. Rumania, in particular, appears to have refused to forego industrial development and concentrate on exporting her natural resources and agricultural products (June, 1963); it stands to reason that primarily industrial satellites would object to abandoning whatever agricultural potentials they possess.[7]

Nineteenth-century economists believed the possession of colonies was indispensible to the survival of the mother countries. Events following World War II have shown that this is not necessarily true. Despite losing its rich Indonesian empire, for example, the Netherlands is nonetheless prosperous; on the other hand, Portuguese possessions in Africa have not made Portugal wealthy. The colonial powers, with few exceptions, found out that exploitation was not enough; they had to invest as well. Such investments were very costly and it is doubtful that any of the colonialist countries is worse off for having lost its colonies. (To be sure, there still are economic life lines between the motherland and its former territories overseas; the Sterling area is a case in point.) Moreover, as World War II demonstrated, the military value of overseas possessions is questionable; the defense of transportation routes is costly and the political reliability of most dependent peoples is open to doubt.

Military and political leaders will want to survey the world's natural resources, the deficiencies or surpluses in raw materials, and the ways and means of transportation to and from crucial areas. They know that a nation that lacks food or raw materials must make certain that it can import them and consequently must try to establish the most economical, most easily protected, and fastest routes of communication. A nation will plan its foreign policies accordingly and attempt to conclude agreements with key countries so as to ensure unimpeded continuation of its traffic and provide the safest possible routes should war occur. Such agreements are best negotiated on the basis of mutual self-

---

[7] Rumania has in 1964 engaged in official trade talks with the United States and even sought to obtain entry into the GATT organization, much to the discomfiture of Moscow.

interest and a businesslike give and take. They are essentially political measures to strengthen and balance strategic potentials, and their economic aspects are often secondary. Apart from such politico-economic insurance policies, key nations stockpile raw materials that are unavailable within their borders. This seems wise because agreements are kept only so long as they serve the interests of the contracting parties, and since international law has no provisions for law enforcement, a violation of such treaties would have to be looked upon as nonjusticiable.

Policy officials must be sensitive to their own economic stability and fluctuation in other countries. Prosperity and depression are subject to political interpretation and possible policy revision. Thus it is understandable that the economies of the communist bloc countries are of more than statistical interest to the Western allies just as Western and free world economies are being watched intensely in both Moscow and Peking. For the same reason, the economic status of each member of the two groups of nations is pertinent for the maintenance of their potential. Besides, it has happened that statesmen had to achieve political objectives through economic action. In such cases, political and economic objectives are merged; this was demonstrated by the American plan to help European recovery and thereby accomplish an economic stability which would serve as the most effective answer to political extremism. Since then, economic aid has become a major instrument of policy both in the United States and in the USSR, particularly in relations with the third world. Even Peking, which cannot afford it, spends money and effort to create at least the impression of being helpful to the underdeveloped areas. The important problem of foreign economic aid will be discussed later.

HUMAN GEOGRAPHY

The density and character of the population in the policy maker's own and other countries loom large in his calculations.

He must examine three aspects of demography: first, density of the population; second, the national character and its relation to climate and environment; and third, the question of national and ethnic minorities which are a political problem in almost every country comprising a sizeable territory and population.

Countries become what they are through the people who inhabit them. Thus foreign policy not only considers facts and figures by seeking to ascertain the number of people who live in a given area and the rate of population increase or decrease; it also attempts to determine how people live and what kind of people they are. Human geography, like physical and economic geography, demands comparative study and analysis along psychological, sociological, anthropological, and ethnical lines. Without a reasonably accurate estimate of demographic conditions at home and abroad, policies may be evolved on unsound premises and thus endanger national security and peace itself. Thus, figures on the population density or on the birth-death ratio in one country as compared with another tell only part of the story and are, in themselves, not reliable indicators for policy planning. They must be considered in conjunction with a nation's physical, economic, and political geography, its scientific level and industrial skills, its ethnic composition, and what is vaguely termed the "national character."

The Population Issue

Crowded nations are likely to strive for living space. Nazi Germany was one such country and prewar Japan sought to syphon its surplus population into Korea and China. In these cases, crowded conditions and land hunger were used as a rationale for political expansion. Fascist Italy, using its surplus population, tried to revive the Roman Empire, claiming the Mediterranean as its own sea (*mare nostrum*). These nations, far from trying to limit their population density, stimulated high birth rates with the promise of financial and civic rewards and thereby further aggravated demographic claustrophobia. The political motive is clear: The population surplus was directed or channeled toward the outside or used for, if nothing else, cannon fodder. In the pre-atomic era, overpopulation, especially if fostered deliberately, was bound to lead to clashes. Such policies have since come into disrepute, although ideological, religious, and socio-economic resistance to Malthusian maxims are hampering efforts to master the problem on a large, international scale.

Nature has its way of replenishing what is lost. The enormous World War II losses seemed to have stimulated a trend toward large families; prosperity in the fifties contributed to this situation. Moreover, medical science made great strides in prolonging life and life expectancy rose in many, though not all, parts of the world. A decline in deaths combined with an increase in births has caused a population explosion of such extraordinary dimensions that there is increasing concern among policy officials as well as demographers. If such increase of population occurs in countries where strong ideological convictions are accompanied by technological advances, a potential for revolution is created which must concern those responsible for national security. Communist China, for example, with a population increase of 2 percent per year now claims 650 million people.[8] Consider the revolutionary fanaticism of the Peking leaders and their covetous policies in South and Southeast Asia; consider that the Soviet population of about 225 million is concentrated in or near Europe with the Central Asian areas rather thinly populated, while at the same time ideological and methodological differences have caused severe discord between Moscow and Peking. Or consider Japan's 90 million, squeezed into an area the size of California; and remember the ever-growing density of population in India with its approximately 450 million, many of whom live in abject poverty. Compared with these key areas, the United States is as yet in a favorable situation but the birth-

[8] New China News Agency report from Peking, June 30, 1964.

death rate is such that living space is shrinking more and more.

The political implications of these hard facts differ from the days when an increase or decrease of population threatened to upset the balance of power among individual nations. In contemporary world politics, the population issue is a matter of universal concern. Even the communists know that people without space—and hope—tend to be restless and may upset an uneasy peace. In economic terms, poverty and lack of opportunity in large parts of the world do not foster long-range prosperity elsewhere. In strategic terms, limited numbers of skilled persons are more valuable than endless masses of illiterates—and if the unlettered have become literate, they will not be content with their lot. In human terms, the suffering of the underprivileged, exposed to malnutrition and disease, must weigh on the conscience of those who have a better fate.

It has been asserted that, as population grows, it is paralleled by a growth of science and technological organization. Modern postwar Japan is cited as a country where there are advanced agricultural techniques, a scientific exploration of such natural resources as are available, a parallel development of industry and foreign trade, and a reasonable policy of birth control; these programs, of course, are easier to implement in an advanced and literate country like Japan than in India. It has also been pointed out that with intelligent, cooperative action, including opening the less populated countries to immigration, there should be increasing possibilities for expansion in nonspatial terms because of the advance of science, technology, and social organization, which has unearthed a multitude of opportunities for more people to live better within the boundaries of territories with dense populations. No country's national resources are fixed forever: New discoveries may increase their yield. Thus population pressure, it is said, is a relative factor. Yet it cannot be disregarded that scientific progress alone is no cure-all.

Those responsible for policy and strategy in the West are naturally concerned not only with population explosions in certain parts of the world but also with increases in human resources in the major communist countries. As early as 1944, population statistics indicated that in 1970 the Soviet Union will have more men of military age than its six biggest European rivals combined.[9] Almost twenty years after publication, it is evident that this estimate was too conservative despite the fact that there was, in the fifties, a shortage of manpower due to the number of men away from home during the war and the death of tens of millions. But already in the sixties, this deficiency has been made up and so confident is the Soviet government about its population growth that it has relaxed its ban of birth control measures and is unofficially tolerating a limited policy of abortions.

Measures of the Peking regime to halt further sharp increases of population have been intensified since 1962. This must have been a difficult decision for the Mao regime since it has always opposed Malthusian theories as anti-Marxian. This doctrinal position has prevented birth control measures—except for a short period in the fifties—from being promoted. China cannot develop its economy as quickly as its population increases; it is saturated with human beings. The collapse of the Big Leap Forward and the moderation of the communes probably contributed to the decision to launch another cautious but energetic birth contol campaign in spring 1963. Whether this new attempt will succeed outside the cities remains to be seen. It is not easy to change the ways of the peasants—and China's mainland population consists overwhelmingly of a peasantry which has produced large families for millennia.

According to the *Demographic Yearbook of 1961,* issued by the Department of Social and Economic Affairs of the United Nations, New York, the world population now stands at almost three billion and the annual global increase is 1.8 per cent. Table 1, covering the last four decades, illustrates the world's steady growth, despite wars, revolutions and natural catastrophes.

[9] D. Kirk, "Population Changes and the Post-War World," American Sociological Review, February, 1944.

TABLE 1

POPULATION GROWTH OF WORLD

In millions	1920	1930	1940	1950	1960	Annual rate of increase
Africa	141	157	176	206	254	2.2%
America	208	244	277	329	405	2.1
Asia	966	1.072	1.212	1.386	1.679	1.9
Europe	329	356	381	395	427	0.9
USSR	158	176	192	181	214	1.7
WORLD	1.811	2.015	2.249	2.510	2.995	1.8

Demographic Yearbook of 1961, p. 120.

If one considers that the population of the Communist-ruled countries amounts to approximately one billion against the 400 million of the NATO powers, if there are indications that the population increase in the communist orbit exceeds the Western rate, and if one finally observes that science and economies may not keep pace with the population increase, it is clear that the policy makers are facing an exceedingly grave and complex problem of long-range significance. When we look at a country like India, where the leadership is trying to carry out an enlightened birth control program without much success, despite extreme poverty in parts of that country, then indeed one must wonder whether there will be time enough for the most populous country on earth to take birth control measures before it is too late and apocalyptic events may not only depopulate the earth but destroy life altogether. There seems to be, at present, no way out. The problem is that the more advanced countries, being able to control their population, will shrink in comparison with the giant populations, and, despite all possible precautions, face the possibility of being overrun by them.

The National Character

Whether there is such a thing as a "national mind" has long

been a matter of controversy. Its existence has never been universally accepted. Yet, a nation's history produces not only stereotypes of behavior but also attitudes which common experience sanctifies and which are transmitted from generation to generation. These stereotypes consist of national likes and dislikes, do's and don't's, *ideés fixes* and what the psychologists call favorable and unfavorable "associations." All these are the consequences of the natural and social environment and the political atmosphere which has historically prevailed. They are also the result of the physical and political geography of the country and its role in the concert of neighboring nations; they have brought forth not only national customs but also fairly consistent attitudes toward neighboring countries in particular and the outside world in general. Altogether, this heritage has produced friendships and enmities, often illogical, and has created deeply ingrained predilections and prejudices.[10]

Historic prejudices thus shape a people's national character and also color the views of the men in responsible policy-making positions. Inheritance of atavistic attitudes, positive and negative, cannot easily be neutralized by rational judgment. There are exceedingly few independent thinkers of real maturity who can free themselves, to a significant degree, from such mental ballast. Certainly an entire nation cannot so free itself unless it revolutionizes its traditional concepts and keeps reinvigorating them. This is possible only through unprejudiced education. The United Nations Educational and Scientific Organization (UNESCO) has tried to eliminate international prejudice through education but it is hampered by totalitarian nations whose governments are opposed to such a goal: They *want* to retain prejudices against every system which differs from their own.

A representative statesman is the product of his country's civilization. He more often than not represents its national character. In the age of nation-states, this was considered a requisite

---

[10] See Michael Demiashkevich, *The National Mind, English-French-German*, New York: American Book Company, 1938.

virtue, but it has all too often worked against international understanding. "Grass roots" attitudes, so popular among traditionalists, can be pernicious in an era of multinational collaboration. Indeed, it might be said that Western grass roots attitudes are almost as divisive as Eastern ideologies. In both cases, national character is vitally influenced and, directly or indirectly, driven to national parochialism.

This is the significance of the national mind for the policy maker, who has to contend not only with his own people but also with many others of various attitudes and behavioral patterns. If the scientists are in doubt about the concept of national character, the politicians cannot afford to ignore the realities of its manifestations. They would rightly reason that people who have lived for centuries in approximately the same territory, under identical climatic conditions, using the same language, growing up in the same culture complex, experiencing the same fortunes in good and bad times, must have developed similar traits, views, preferences, and aversions.

This is not to say that such attitudinal patterns cannot be influenced or changed. Indeed, human nature is changing rapidly:[11] Most likely there is an inherent need for adjustment to new conditions and environments. Moreover, it can be made to change into desired directions through the process of brainwashing, which has been clearly described by Lifton in the case of Chinese Communist techniques applied in prisons,[12] although it is uncertain how long the effects of such intensive indoctrination will last or whether similar techniques can be employed on a large scale. Under the guidance of various scientific bodies, the entire educational system in the Soviet Union is geared to create a "new communist man," an extraordinary specimen designed to live in the communist society which the Kremlin plans for the future.

Foreign policy officials have to reckon with existing realities

[11] Gardner Murphy, *Human Potentialities*, New York: Basic Book Publishers, 1958, pp. 5-6.
[12] Cf. Robert J. Lifton, *Thought Reform and the Psychology of Totalism: A Study of "Brainwashing" in China*, London: V. Gollancz, 1961.

for the solution of current problems, but they must also take into account indications of changing national character and consider them in their long-range planning. This is all the more difficult because no one, not even the most independent thinker, can wholly escape his own heritage. The result may be bias, for policy makers are human first and statesmen second. Ideally, their professional experience should have given them more than average breadth of mind and intellect and the mature objectivity to realize their own human shortcomings. If so, they may use this self-recognition to advantage when estimating the course of their foreign colleagues. But they are seldom free to be what they are. Not only do these officials symbolize their nation's traditions and aspirations; they also must stand as spokesmen for their government's ideological position. To the extent to which their people have adapted their national character to the impact of political ideology, they themselves are compelled to deny historic tradition. It would be interesting to find out, for example, how much less of a Russian a Soviet communist is than his forefathers were before the revolution or whether a Chinese Communist is still a Chinese in the traditional sense, as he might have been for millennia prior to Mao's victory.

There is abundant evidence that ideology has, more often than not, deeply affected traditional historic or cultural traits. While the Soviet people continue to have certain specifically Russian—or Ukrainian or Georgian or other minority—characteristics, the theory and practice of Marxism-Leninism is inevitably changing their national mind. This is a slow process but intensive efforts toward educating the New Soviet Man are under way and are given high priority by the Kremlin. These efforts were initiated by various educational reforms, notably the broadening of the boarding school principle, by the growing emphasis on cybernetics as an instrument for developing new training methods, and the Kremlin's insistence on the creation of the New Soviet Man for the "transition to communism" as expressed particularly in Khrushchev's report to the Twenty-second Congress of the CPSU in 1961.

Communist China, always in a hurry, is trying to develop

brainwashing methods designed to take much quicker effect while China is at the same time displaying a national fervor that oddly contradicts the principles of Marxism-Leninism, a phenomenon that may be attributed to the pride of newly won sovereignty after a long period of semicolonial status. Besides, Chinese nationalism is being used tactically for the same reasons that Stalin fanned the flames of Russian nationalism during World War II.

Policy makers who do not understand the metamorphosis of national character under the impact of the secular religions of the East and rely on the traditional estimate of national power and national interests run the risk of misunderstanding the rationale behind communist policies and the methods of their implementation. It is not enough to read the communist classics: It is necessary to acquire a facility for their interpretation and, one may say, "translation" of communist double talk into understandable terms. Distinctions must be made between theory and practice, between strategy and tactics, between the sound and the meaning of words and phrases. Foreign affairs analysts who do not have such facility are a drawback. Analysis of communist policies cannot be successful if strained exclusively through Western thought. To people imbued with Judeo-Christian traditions, or those who grew up under the influence of Mohammedism or any of the schools of Buddhism, the double standard of communist dialectics is hard to recognize and harder to accept.

This is not to say that Western or other types of noncommunist policies are above reproach. There is hypocrisy this side of the Iron Curtain; diplomacy has always used lies as tools of its profession. But it has done so only to a degree; it has not divested itself entirely of all ethical considerations. Under communist rule, deception and dialectical "contradictions" have become a way of life, and the only reliable techniques for finding the needle of truth within the haystack of falsehoods, are knowledge, intuition, and hard analytic labor.

Differences in national character among peoples have always been accepted as natural. While different cultures and languages have produced disparate views of international relations, they could be bridged by serious efforts by far-sighted statesmen. However, the broadening of the schism between peoples and groups of nations caused by divergent socio-political philosophies has made it increasingly difficult to come to an understanding: The West desires understanding but the communist orbit often does not genuinely want it except for temporary accommodation. As a result, "communist ideology has become a tower of Babel in that it not only confuses the issues at stake between nations but also perverts concepts, meanings and terms."[13]

Climate and Topography

The impact of climate on national achievement and potential has long been debated. Have excessively hot or cold climates shaped basic traits of individuals and nations? Under the influence of continuous heat, do the body and mind lose alertness? Does prolonged cold hamper the development of civilization? In considering the question, let us remember that no great nations have ever flourished in the torrid or arctic zones, and that all powerful modern states have developed in more or less temperate zones.

On the other hand, modern science rejects the theory that people from the temperate zones cannot function properly in the arid and arctic zones. Ways and means have been found to help one adjust to a harsher climate not only by such auxiliaries as air conditioning, but also by changed diets and, most important, a different mental approach. Examples may be found in the lives of members of the U.S. Peace Corps. Corps workers undoubtedly are highly motivated, do not have access to modern technological devices, share the lives of the natives and, with few exceptions, succeed in adjusting to adverse conditions. They do not, for the

[13] K. London, *op. cit.*, p. 71.

most part, lose their mental and physical alertness. They prove
that mental effort and motivation can overcome the hazards of
radically changed environment.

Still, this does not explain why extreme climates hinder the
development of civilizations with otherwise reasonable development potential. Investigations by microbiologists, pathologists,
and psychologists have not yet been conclusive. Men like Huntington, Shaw, and Missenard have opened new lines of investigation developed since the beginning of the century—although the
problem of climatology and national character is by no means
new to social scientists. In general, their conclusion is that "the
geographical distribution of health and energy probably depends
on climate and weather more than any other single factor . . .
This arises not only from the direct effect of weather but also
from the effect of climate upon agriculture, diet, disease, occu-
pations, and general progress."[14] If, as has been suggested, an
average temperature of 62.5° Fahrenheit is the healthiest climate,[15] it would follow that, the more prevailing temperatures
and humidity levels exceed this average toward either higher or
lower extremes, the less creative strides toward national or individual greatness can be expected. "Where climate is stimulating
and people's health is good, it is easy to be industrious . . ." Such
people "do not necessarily have more ideas than others, but their
energy enables them to put their ideas into practice."[16]

Even within temperate climatic zones, outbursts of the elements (storms, rains, earthquakes, droughts) or the lack of them
seem to contribute to the physical and mental makeup of a people. Similarly, topographical characteristics—which are climatic
as well—cause distinct national peculiarities. We know that
mountain folk differ in their behavior from people living in the
plains, and it is possible to discern variables in the character of
littoral and inland populations. Human beings exposed repeat-

[14] E. Huntington and E. B. Shaw, *Principles of Human Geography*, New
York: John Wiley & Sons, 1951, p. 399.
[15] A. Missenard, *In Search of Man*, New York: Hawthorn Books, 1957, p. 191.
[16] Huntington-Shaw, *op. cit.* p. 140.

edly to such natural phenomena as the hot winds (sirocco, mistral, fön, monsoon, samum) frequently experience emotional outbursts which are alien to people living under steadier weather conditions. Indeed, the law in some countries recognizes that citizens cannot be held entirely responsible for acts they commit while exposed to prolonged periods of hot winds. People living under southern skies tend to be more outgoing than those whose climatic environment is characterized by northern cloudiness, rain and snow. Concomitantly, the ease with which the soil is tilled under favorable weather conditions cannot help but produce people of higher humor than those who must struggle against an adverse nature to gain the barest necessities of life.

Thus it is possible that climatic variations create human diversities which contribute to the formation of national character. Statesmen, perhaps more than generals, have frequently underestimated climatic influences on national psychology. The character of a nation cannot be analyzed without considering national environment; history tells only part of the story. To cite one example: The character of many national groups in the Soviet Union was forged by the vastness of endless steppes, extreme contrasts of temperature, and long, hard winters. In general, the people living under these conditions are hardy, reticent, but basically stable, with introspective dispositions; their emotions are as full of contrasts as their climates. But other groups, living in the southern regions of the European section of the USSR, for example Ukrainians and, even more, Georgians, show much less of the slow and subdued character of their northern and eastern fellows. They are less steadfast, less reliable, and have given the Soviet government more internal trouble than all of the other groups combined.

Ethnic Minorities

Few nations are completely homogeneous and those that are may not be of world political significance. When the nation-state emerged, it did not result from ethnic exclusivity; generally its frontiers were the result of wars or political agreement. This is not true of Europe alone; national minorities exist in Asia as well. In Africa, the minorities south of the Sahara are white and there are ethnically foreign groups in North Africa, though they are small and weak. The two leading opponents in the East-West struggle, the United States and the Soviet Union, are both melting pots. The United States became what it is today because of the mixture of nationalities and races, although the original core of the nation's founders were Anglo-Saxons who transferred their civilization to the new world. Similarly, the Soviet Union is dominated by the Great Russian group, which happens to be the strongest and the most numerous; however, the many nationalities within its frontiers, from the large Ukrainian minority to the small Central Asian group are pressed into the mold of Soviet concepts, a process that has had increasing success. Nor is Communist China free of minority problems even though the non-Han peoples are numerically small in comparison with the enormous mass of Han Chinese who traditionally absorbed every minority within their reach.

Nevertheless, it is a fact that the assimilation of ethnic minorities has never been easy and, in many instances, has failed over long periods of time to accomplish the desire for homogeneity in a nation. Even before the emergence of the modern nation-state, migration, voluntary or enforced, obstructed this desire. Furthermore, there has always been a continuous intermixture of heteronational elements, especially along the many border regions of Europe. Some such groups, once established in national territories, have occasionally become majorities or even nations in their own right. Other elements, less fortunate, were never absorbed and have kept their culture identifiable by preserving their customs, language, and religion.

Let us note here that homogeneity is no prerequisite for the development or maintenance of a strong nation. The few relatively homogeneous populations in the world today have been geographically isolated or inaccessible for a long time, for example the Scandinavian countries. But even in these areas blood mixtures from other European nationality groups have continually occurred. One could say that the greater the ethnic intermingling, the stronger the strain became; again, the United States and the Soviet Union are good examples. Purity of race or ethnic composition is not a condition for national greatness. On the contrary: Too much inbreeding has in the past reduced the intellectual and physical vigor of national renewal. What makes a nation great are its ideas for progress, its imagination, and vision. It was Hitler's fatal error to ignore this truth in Nazi Germany.

The communists have always paid great attention to the nationality question.[17] Their policy, from the outset, was directed toward the eventual eradication of the minorities' political significance by subordinating nationalism to international communism. The implementation of this policy has been successful, although the problem still exists for the communist administrators.

In contrast to Hitler, the communists are primarily interested in eradicating the *nationalism* of the minorities, not—for the time-being—the nationalities themselves. Such coexistence of nationalities within the political framework of the Soviet Union was called commonwealth or comity (*sodruzhestvo*) by Stalin, and it is interesting to note that, after the establishment of the "socialist camp," the term *sodruzhestvo* was applied to the "commonwealth of socialist countries." In both cases, the concept is of temporary importance: Eventually, all nationalities (and countries) are to be molded into a solid communist world state.[18]

An important aspect of the issues concerning national minorities is religion. The separation of state and church is a relatively

[17] Lenin's interest in the "national question" stimulated Stalin as early as 1913 to write an article, "The National Question and Social Democracy," in the periodical *Provyeshchenye*. Stalin's first governmental position in the newly established Bolshevik regime was Commissar for Nationalities; his best known writing on this issue is *Marksizm i natsional'nyi vopros* (Marxism and the National Question) in January, 1913. See *Sochineniia* (Works), Vol. II, 310, Moscow (1948-51).

[18] See Elliot Goodman, *The Soviet Design for a World State*, New York: Columbia University Press, 1960.

new trend. For thousands of years, the individual living in a certain area had to adopt its religion or become an outcast. Even today, religious differences create friction in European and Asian countries where adherence to religions other than the one ordained by the authorities or predominating among the people has fostered discrimination if not persecution. Protestantism is virtually outlawed in Franco's Catholic Spain, and even in the more liberal Italy, where Catholicism predominates, Protestants have trouble maintaining their churches. At times in history, Islamic minorities in Christian countries or Christians in Islamic areas have found it difficult to practice their rituals. The Jews had to struggle constantly for the preservation of their beliefs since the time of the Diaspora, some two thousand years ago. The great Indian subcontinent had to be divided into Hindu and Moslem areas although Indians and Pakistanis are of the same ethnic stock. Even in the most enlightened countries, religious and ethnic prejudices come to the fore from time to time; we have seen that the equalizing ambitions of the USSR did not eradicate one of Czarism's ugliest legacies, anti-Semitism. Peking, while tolerating its small Moslem minority, is careful to keep it in bounds and politically ineffective, and Christianity, which is ideologically suspect, has been all but annihilated by the Chinese Communists.

Policy makers need to observe these trends closely. Many aspects of the minority problem, whether ethnic or religious, might well provide pertinent clues to the understanding of internal conditions of countries—friends, neutrals, or foes. For we know that internal and external policies are parts of the same polity.

The Level of Education and Know-how

As already noted, human geography goes beyond the counting of noses. A nation's power potential can no longer be measured in terms of population statistics; it must also consider the skills of its citizens. The development of high scientific standards and the parallel progress of technology have become decisive factors in world politics. This, however, is only one of the measures of the educational level of a nation. The other is the general development of knowledge among the people through liberal education and the intellectual and emotional maturity thus achieved. In the long run, a nation remains viable only if its population is motivated, not through indoctrination and incessant propaganda, but by way of free reasoning and acceptance of more individual responsibility.

Technology not only produces devices: It also alters social and international relations, modifies national attitudes and foreign policy and even changes human character. As new inventions become part of our lives, they create or demand new moral and political values and they often destroy old ones. On the whole, science has outrun cultural and ethical standards and all too often is a dangerous toy in the hands of the immature. Consequently, the need continues for appraisals of the effects of scientific triumphs on human life and international relations. In their search for solutions to this problem in foreign affairs, free world statesmen can hardly find precedents in history.

While the impact of these developments on international relations and on human life everywhere was bound to defy the imaginations of political traditionalists, the revolutionary leaders were in a somewhat better position, not because of superior insight into the meaning of the new technology, but because they were preparing to uproot the past anyway. They were less hampered by their connection with tradition. Furthermore, they do not depend, as do the majority of free world leaders, on domestic support; once they control the armed forces and the police, the decision is theirs to make in disregard of whatever public opinion exists. But neither the communists nor the noncommunists can fail to realize that the international scene has changed radically as a result of scientific discoveries and that resultant social changes have altered the lives of individuals and nations. Without modern communications systems, for example, the modern "isms" of the right and the left would have had only local impact and not affected the entire globe. Furthermore, the concept of war and peace has changed: Since war, in the atomic age, has become too risky and no longer offers much advantage to the victor, since genuine peace with "imperialism" is not now acceptable to the Marxist-Leninists—the international confrontation indicates that the class struggle is being transferred to world politics—a twilight zone of cold war has developed and appears to be slated for a long life, despite temporary relaxations of tension.

Aside from the fact that science and technology have revolutionized national economies, the race toward the conquest of space has begun. Ever since the first Soviet Sputnik went into orbit on October 4, 1957, causing the West to suffer a psychological Pearl Harbor, political life has not been quite the same. A re-evaluation of comparative strength caused Peking to claim that, in terms of power: The "East wind now prevails over the West wind."[19] Many uncommitted nations developed a new respect for Soviet might. And the West had to proceed to a truly "agonizing reappraisal" to determine whether indeed its relative power position had weakened and whether it was necessary to correct this situation. The accelerated space program under the Kennedy administration indicated a change in the early U.S. reaction which was expressed by Charles Wilson, Secretary of Defense under President Eisenhower, when he stated that the Soviet sputnik was nothing but a "neat scientific trick" (Oct. 8, 1957).

It is far too early to estimate all the consequences which the post-World War II technological revolution has wrought, but we do know that the traditional premises for national power and foreign policy must be radically revised. It is here that Western and allied statesmen and also those of the nonaligned areas must re-evaluate those factors which have been briefly sketched in previous paragraphs. For example, topographical barriers and distances had lost much of their former significance. Previously unavailable raw materials may either be discovered or even

[19] Mao Tse-tung used this phraseology in a speech to Chinese students in Moscow, Nov. 17, 1957.

synthesized. Transportation will be revolutionized even further. Manpower will no longer be so decisive a factor. But brain power and motivation will. It is essential to realize this. Whatever state has the greatest brainpower at its disposal and can rely on a well motivated populace will be in a favored position.

Motivation and brainpower are the harvest of education and its level is an all-important aspect of human geography. Generally, one could perhaps say that in totalitarian countries the emphasis is on training while education is the prevailing term in Western civilizations. The reason is clear: Youth in the West is brought up in terms of liberal education with vocational or professional training culminating the basic process of "education of the whole man." Under this system, the broad, flexible, democratic philsophy of life is communicated to youth and becomes, hopefully, part of the personality. Thus specialized training, if combined with liberal arts, will leave its mark.

The communist system of education does not foster the liberal arts. It is highly specialized; broader schooling is reserved for a small number of selected students whose record and background make them eligible to become the elite in the universities. Furthermore, it is significant that from his early years a child is subject to planned environmental influences along with indoctrination. This no doubt results in highly successful technical training in fields to which priority is assigned by the Party. At the same time, the program is designed to accomplish one of the most important objectives of Soviet education: the cultivation of the "new Soviet man." The achievement of a communist society has always been the dominant goal of the Kremlin. During the almost half century of their existence, the Soviets have devised and revised several educational reforms. The last two took place in 1958 and in 1960 when Khrushchev sought to combine the goals of his Seven Year Plan with a reinvigorated educational program. Apart from the standing Soviet goal of "organizing the nation for economic and social advancement,"[20] he apparently conceived the new educational theses as another long step toward

[20] George Z. F. Bereday, William W. Brickman and Gerald H. Read, editors, *The Changing Soviet School*, Boston: Houghton Mifflin Co., 1960, p. 6.

the "transition to communism." To reach this objective, to proceed from a socialist to a classless communist society, a "material-technical base" is required, but even more necessary are well motivated citizens who will be satisfied with what they need rather than what they deserve.

To carry out this plan, the powerful scientific academies of the USSR, doubtless directed by the Presidium whose instruments they are, coordinated efforts to develop, with the help of cybernetics,[21] new training systems and methods. The principle of weaning children from parental influence was strengthened by increased isolation of children in nurseries, kindergartens, and boarding schools, where environment is shaped in accordance with Party-dictated rules. All substance, whether it be history, geography, or civics is slanted to the interpretation of the Marxist-Leninist view of the world. Having been exposed during their most impressionable years to the secular religion of their state and having established a record of their attitudes and capabilities, the young people then enter either technical training schools or, in the minority of cases, universities. In both kinds of institution they will be exposed to various aspects of manual labor by way of "polytechnical education"[22] a time-honored Soviet concept that has been re-emphasized since the 1958 educational reforms.

It is idle to speculate whether this program ultimately can be successfully carried out and whether a "new communist man" can indeed be produced. We do know, however, that the effects of communist training, education, and indoctrination are already visible. "Many groups in the West underestimate the people's enthusiasm for their own system"[23] which demonstrates the effectiveness of the Soviet educational system which has been

[21] See A. I. Berg, *Kiberneticu na sluzhbu kommunizmu* (Cybernetics in the Service of Communism), Moscow: Gosenergoizdat, 1961, *passim*. Translated into English by Joint Publications Research Service, U.S. Dept. Commerce, Washington, D.C. JPRS: 14,592, July 25, 1962.

[22] A combination of academic studies with actual production work in industry or agriculture.

[23] Bereday, Brickman, and Read, *op. cit*, p. 13.

copied, with minor national variations, by almost every other state in the socialist camp. This is not encouraging for future East-West understanding, for the new communist generations speak a different language.

Thus the results of their education and training are of crucial importance in the policy maker's realization of the caliber of human resources of both his opponents and allies. In Khrushchev's "peaceful competition," the relative success or failure of the national systems is of major consequence, not only because the West stands to lose the race for more and better scientists, but also because the different values of life taught on both sides of the Iron Curtain more and more reduce the chance of agreements.

2. Factors Contributing to Foreign Policy Making

THE INFLUENCE OF DOMESTIC POLITICS

Indivisibility of Foreign and Domestic Politics

THE CONVENTIONAL DIVISION of politics into foreign and domestic may have practical advantages, but not even the systematic study of political science should, in mid-century, isolate the one from the other. In the operation of politics, such separation is not feasible. "The line between foreign and domestic policy, never clear to begin with, has now almost been erased."[1] Foreign and domestic politics resemble the positive and negative components of electric current: Eliminate one and the other will not function; they produce power only when combined. Although issues of exclusively domestic interest may exist, rarely are there significant ones not vitally affected by world conditions and a country's position vis-à-vis other countries. There are good reasons why foreign and domestic politics have almost merged into one concept: Technology and ideology have changed, even shifted the foundations upon which the nation-states were built.

In order to understand the meaning of and the reasons for this

[1] *Organizing for National Security*, Committee on Government Operations, U.S. Senate, by its Subcommittee on National Policy Machinery, Senator Henry M. Jackson, Chairman, Washington, D.C.: U.S. Government Printing Office, 1960, p. 1.

development, it is necessary to keep in mind that the age of nation-individualism came to an end during the first half of the twentieth century. There were no outward signs of this until after World War II, when groups of countries were driven into cooperative blocs, either because they considered that a union of like-minded countries was the best way to preserve their respective social and political beliefs or because they were forced by stronger neighbors to join their "camp." Many of the newer states which were undergoing a stage of rampant nationalism had no choice but to affiliate with others of similar interests. This situation initiated nation cooperativism in the West or nation collectivism in the East. Even the United States, the greatest adherent of nation individualism, was in no position to maintain its rugged *status quo,* for it was destined to assume leadership of the democratic group of nations and thereby become a member of a nation cooperative.

This phenomenon was accompanied by a slow, persistent lessening of individualism among the persons who make up a nation. This does not mean that—in the democracies—the dignity of the individual or the cultural individuality of nations was sacrificed. It does mean that both individuals and nations had to be more circumspect in their actions lest their activities harm their community or the community of nations. As in the life of individual citizens, so in the life of nations the emphasis of political and economic life was gradually placed upon mutual liability.

In terms of foreign relations this development signifies that, in a shrinking world, those conditions within a given country which might endanger the peace are no longer permissible. Outside pressure may be unavoidable for the greater good of the greater number of states. Such conditions are, for example, genocide or a consistent flouting of the law of nations. There are, however, situations which do not *appear* to affect the community of nations but which, when tolerated or supported, may lead to severe upsets in foreign relations. Such instances are liable to occur chiefly in democracies where both public opinion and the internal political objectives of the administrations may force legislative action (for example, in budgetary matters) resulting in seriously impaired international power ratios.

There are various reasons for such attitudes. In the first place, a country's constitutional law may not permit an easy adjustment to world politics in the bipolar era. Second, the population's realization of dangers may be clouded by selfish, material motives. Third, a people may not bother to acquire an insight into the problems of relations between nations in the age of ideology and nuclear technology.

Yet the security and prosperity of one nation may depend upon the nature of its relations with other nations, and the attempt to shape foreign policy on the basis of domestic exigencies can lead to disaster. Ideally, cooperative nations would not follow isolationist or egocentric impulses, but rather develop a new kind of international self-discipline as it must be practiced by the members of every well-functioning cooperative unit. Since the demise of monolithic and the development of polycentric communism, interbloc discipline has left much to be desired. In fact, while there are clear indications of opposition to Soviet-enforced cooperation even in Eastern Europe (Rumania), there has been relatively much better progress toward the goal of cooperative self-discipline in the free world. However, the change in the character of international relations has not yet brought a corresponding revision of views concerning the impact of domestic politics on international policies. Too often internal problems continue to obscure foreign issues, confusing the mind of the average voter whose understanding of foreign affairs is inadequate.

Domestic Politics and Foreign Policy

In any political system, domestic issues have an important bearing on the management and substance of foreign policy. The extent and nature of this influence varies with a nation's political creed; it may tend to be individualistic or collectivistic, but it is part and parcel of international affairs. There are differences between strictly parliamentary democracies, such as the United States or Great Britain, and types of "guided democracy" such as that of the French Fifth Republic or Indonesia where De Gaulle or Sukarno make decisions with, or against, a weak parliament. There are differences between authoritarian governments such as persist in Spain and Portugal, where "benevolent" dictators make decisions with little interest in the general will without employing all the tools of autocracy, and the totalitarian ideological regimes. Leaders of the totalitarian regimes seek to implement their party's objectives by completely dominating all aspects of life, public and private. In all these instances, internal conditions leave their mark on foreign policy, often demonstrating that internal and external politics are but different branches of the same tree.

Omitting the grey areas of modified democracy or semi-authoritarianism, let us compare the differences between genuine parliamentary democracy and communist dictatorship. In the former, which seeks to embody both political and economic democracy, the government has to contend with political parties, the interests these parties represent, the desire to further improve a generally high standard of living, traditional ethics, religion, and a multitude of pressure groups of both selfish and altruistic character. Most important is the role of the electorate which in the last analysis determines what kind of government is to reflect the objectives of the winning party. This is a truly enormous accumulation of factors, all of which influence the international position of a nation. In democracies, the government rules by the will of simple majority which may be quite precarious; the very nature of democratic multiplicity of interests rarely, if ever, permits unanimous approval of a policy.

Thus to maintain political equilibrium, democratic governments must rule by compromise. They have to trade one principle against the other. Democratic administrations will make internal concessions to gain endorsement for foreign policies or, vice-versa, sacrifice foreign policies in order to carry out domestic measures. Fiscal legislation offers a good example for such give and take: The combination of national security and foreign policies requires heavy outlays, and it is the parliament that holds the purse strings. An administration's monetary requirements are geared to the policies it recommends. Appropriations are needed for the conduct of international relations by various government agencies, for the maintenance of a military establishment, and for keeping a strong and progressive economy. Severe cuts in appropriations demolish planned policies, and the constitutional prerogative of most parliaments to approve money bills every year is a serious handicap to long-range policy making.

Since a democracy depends on the electorate to influence decisions on which may hinge the fate of every citizen, the political education of its people is of utmost importance. We do not expect supermen such as the "new communist man" of Soviet origin, whose dedication to society supposedly has an almost monastic character. But we hope that democratic man will develop a greater sense of civic responsibility, generously sprinkled with self-discipline—realizing that freedom does not mean license. The fulfillment of this hope will take time, for man is basically selfish and self-centered unless forced to the contrary. The liberties of parliamentary democracy have not existed for long, in historical time; there is still too much take and too little give. The more cognizant the electorate is of these facts, the more it tries to isolate its own wishes from the needs of its society, the better will its government be and the less chained to selfish interests its foreign policy.

The democracies have their constitutional provisions for the organization of international affairs. There is some maneuverability within the framework of this law, as we shall see later, but fundamentally, whoever is in power must conform to the constitution. These provisions sometimes render policy formulation and implementation awkward except in emergency when the nation closes ranks behind its leaders. Nonetheless, parliamentary supervision remains active under any circumstances: Not even in wartime can the leader of a parliamentary democracy assume that he is above accounting to the legislative body which holds the summit of power. And yet parliament is rarely agreed on vital measures concerning international security. Its divisions are reflected among the people (or perhaps the differences of opinion among the people are reflected in their representatives). It is well known that most people and many legislators work for immediate and parochial aims, perhaps because they find it infinitely more difficult to understand and appraise long-range developments in world politics.

In communist-ruled countries, the position of those responsible for foreign policy is at once easier and harder. Easier because the monolithic system of the one-party dictatorship permits decision making without the supervision of parliamentary bodies. Such parliaments as Moscow's Supreme Soviet or Peking's National People's Congress are mere sounding boards. Ever since the Russian Constituent Assembly, having out-voted the Bolsheviks, was dispersed by force of arms in 1917, the Russian or Soviet peoples have had not a parliament but a rubber-stamping assembly of props. Thus there is no legislative supervision; if the leaders must justify themselves at all, it is to the Central Committee of the Party. As we shall see later in more detail, the Presidium or Politburo is the decision-making organ and woe to those who dare contest this supreme ruling group.

Constitutions exist in communist countries, but they have little meaning except in terms of propaganda. To read the Soviet Constitution of 1936 is one thing; to live under it quite another. It came to prominence at a time when the great purges began during the rule of Stalinist tyranny. It made scarcely any reference to the Party's significance, an omission which probably will be corrected in the new Soviet constitution that the Kremlin has ordered written and which may be publicized at an advantageous time. In their own constitution, the Chinese Communists are more outspoken about their aims and intentions, more fundamentalist in their political phraseology. Like the Soviets, the Communist Chinese rulers are in a position to formulate their policies without interference from democratic processes. Technically, it is much easier for Moscow and Peking to make decisions.

It is more difficult, however, to weigh theoretical considerations against the practical necessities of the world situation. Since communist foreign policy is international communism first and national second, the communist decision makers must take into account, first, whether their ideology can be applied in the face of anti-communist obstacles; second, whether a policy is in the interest of the international movement *as well as* that of the nation; third, whether a political decision might affect the population adversely by undermining ideological indoctrination; and fourth, whether a foreign policy contains all the elements of propaganda value which must be an integral part of the policy itself. Therefore, one may conclude, the communist policy maker, while technically in a more favorable position than his Western counterpart, is confronted by some serious problems which, though different in nature, are at least as hard to solve as those of non-communist officials.

Public Opinion

This brings us to the much debated question of the role of public opinion in international affairs and foreign policy. The general assumption is that, in the democracies, public opinion exerts considerable influence on policy makers. But how articulate is it? Can it be accurately measured? Is public opinion as decisive as the peoples of the free world like to think? Does it exist at all in the non-democratic states, especially under communism?

Public opinion in the democracies is an important factor, but a relatively negative one. The human tendency is to say no quicker than yes, to give easy answers rather than take the trouble of thinking out the problem. If scientific methods of opinion sampling produce more or less accurate indications of public opinion, the results of the polls, in so far as foreign affairs are concerned, reveal most often a lack of understanding of the cen-

tral problems and reflect emotional rather than objective thinking. Also, it can be said that public opinion offers abundant
criticism but rarely, if ever, has constructive advice. And how can
it offer such advice? Foreign policy formulation is a highly specialized art requiring long training and experience. No way has
yet been discovered to produce a public opinion on specific issues
of foreign policy that could inspire a responsible official.[2] Thus
public opinion may express itself either for or against a policy
(which means for or against the leader who is responsible for it)
without being able to make an intelligent contribution. This is
no reproach: A layman should not be expected to diagnose an
illness as if he were a licensed physician. Similarly, no person
without an adequate education and background in foreign affairs
can fully exercise his critical faculties in this field however he
may excel in hindsight.[3]

There is no constitutional provision in any country, democratic or totalitarian, which would include public opinion as a
co-determinant in policy making. Nevertheless, in the democracies the electorate may cast its vote for leaders or parties which
could aid or jeopardize sound policies. People *are* impressed by
foreign issues or the fear of conflict; the trouble is that they do
not know whether or not to subscribe to their government's policies for coping with these problems. Yet the development of a
well-informed, clear-thinking electorate is of paramount importance. Such development could be stimulated through formal
and informal education; government information services with
outlets to newspapers and broadcasting; and supplementary
activities of private associations specializing in international
affairs. Interest in foreign policy in itself does not suffice; at least
some knowledgeability is required if democratic public opinion
is to exert a healthy influence on questions of international
relations in a divided world.

[2] Cf. Leonard W. Doob, *Public Opinion and Propaganda*, New York: Henry
Holt, 1948, 144 ff.
[3] Cf. T. A. Bailey's excellent study on the impact of public opinion on
foreign policy, *The Man in the Street*, New York: Macmillan, 1948, *passim*.

Is there a "public opinion" in communist-ruled countries? If there is, the difficulties in isolating public opinion trends are great and have not yet been resolved. Some authors have attempted to feel the public pulse in the Soviet Union; defectors have talked on domestic and foreign issues; articles reporting the views of Western visitors have added some background for the more scholarly investigations; but altogether the picture seems far from clear.[4]

The communist "propaganda and agitation" (Agitprop) section of the Party is set up to coordinate the mass mind with the regime's policies and stop at its source popular criticism of actions the government has taken. Unquestionably there are pockets of opposition to certain party and governmental policies. But, most likely, this is a rejection of methods and not of the system as such. The virtually complete isolation of communist mass media from Western news and views, the secretiveness of communist policies, and the brainwashing process of channeling and controlling thought along the party line make it almost impossible for a citizen in communist-ruled societies to acquire an objective or informed view. International relations are seen through Marxist-Leninist eyes and "objectivism" is condemned. The merger of the system with what used to be called nationalism makes it unpatriotic to deviate. The antagonism against all noncommunist states, especially the "imperialist" ones, produces exactly those prejudices which are desirable from the Party leaders' point of view. Indoctrination has permeated the new generations of children growing up under the system.

Thus public opinion has no chance to develop. The Party can do no wrong and even traumatic experiences such as the denigration of Stalin or turnabouts in the political line must not be expected to lead to civic schizophrenia. Yet the communist authorities never cease to strive for the consent of the masses. It

[4] See for example R. Bauer and A. Inkeles, *The Soviet Citizen,* I. R. Levine, *Mainstreet USSR,* J. Novak, *The Future is Ours,* F. C. Barghoorn, *The Soviet Image of the USA.*

is a continuous process, spurred on, from time to time, by new campaigns. It would be a mistake to assume that criticism is non-existent: Communist citizens and even party members are only human. The "new communist man" has not yet materialized. The outside world knows little about isolated nonconformists and cannot measure their quantity and quality.

In any event, foreign affairs are exclusively a matter for the Party to decide and for the government to implement. Thus it might be said that whatever elements of public opinion enter into the discussion are part of the power potential rather than forces active in foreign relations.

ECONOMIC FACTORS

General Considerations

During the nineteenth century, the pound sterling was the center of financial gravity around which world economy fluctuated. In the twentieth century, the dollar has overtaken the pound to become the economic yardstick among both capitalist and socialist nations. But the shift of economic power from the city of London to New York's Wall Street was not altogether a happy development for the United States. In a world still abounding in destitution and poverty, the responsibilities of a rich nation have proved very heavy.

This study is not limited to one particular country but tries to outline the forces, organizations, and sources that create and implement foreign policy in many lands. Yet when it comes to factors of commercial policy, conditions in and decisions by the United States are of such overpowering importance for the world that special emphasis must be given to this country's economic position. However, there has been developing, since the late fifties, another locus of economic power in the free world: the European Common Market. It still has many serious political and economic problems to solve, but its success has been great enough to arouse fear among communist governments lest capitalism, instead of disintegrating as predicted by ideologists, prove much hardier and sounder and create a new anti-communist power center: a united Western Europe. The communist answer is limited to COMECON (Cf. above pp. 31-32), which since its organization in 1949 does not seem to have made much progress. Indeed, the opposition of some Eastern European satellites, particularly Rumania, to the intended unbalancing of national economies through specialization indicates that COMECON may not be the answer to the Common Market.[5]

Against United States commercial policies, which reflect the free enterprise concept of a more or less uncontrolled economy, stand Soviet-communist principles of a strictly planned and controlled economy whose production capacity is geared, not to the consumer, but to political priorities. The United States has always believed with the framers of its Constitution that economic liberalism guarantees the political freedom of its citizens. It has ever wanted to maintain a state of economic individualism with as few governmental controls as possible. The American people have been suspicious of planned economy, although cooperatives find much favor in some regions, and federal projects such as the Tennessee Valley Authority are, on the whole, no longer regarded as government interference in the people's affairs. To be sure, capitalism has been restricted, compared with its status a century ago, but in view of the power of the great corporations, most of these restrictions are regarded as safeguards rather than as obstacles to free enterprise. Another factor, bearing on nongovernmental "checks and balances," are the trade unions which have grown powerful and often wealthy. They are, in a way, a counterpoise to corporate power enabling labor and management to balance each other. Nevertheless, the state must assume certain responsibilities for the sake of the vast majority of citizens who are not in a position to contend with the powerful sources of management or labor.

[5] See also Nicolas Spulber, "Economic Problems of Socialist Cooperation" in Harry G. Shaffer, ed. *The Soviet Economy*, New York: Appleton-Century-Crofts, 1963.

The communist group, in contrast, believes in liquidating private enterprise because, according to Marx and Engels, capitalism cannot avoid exploiting those who have no capital. Therefore, all means of production, all land and natural resources, are the property of the state. Without attempting to equalize incomes or needs during the socialist stage of the transition to communism, the regimes have, from time to time, offered incentives of money or kind but they have eliminated profits on capital investments. Soviet capitalists may buy state bonds or acquire some extra conveniences (if available), but they cannot own producing industries, farms, real estate, or trade establishments employing salaried workers.

Whatever restrictions on United States overseas trade exist—such as the ban on exporting strategic materials to communist countries—are sanctioned by law for reasons of national security. Such measures are dictated by political exigencies and have no bearing on the freedom of trade and transportation. The belief is held that reciprocally granted freedom of the seas and the air is essential for the maintenance of world peace and prosperity. In contrast, communist regimes have set up import and export monopolies that operate in accordance with the requirements of over-all planning which are mapped out and supervised by state planning agencies such as Gosplan in the USSR. Foreign trade is directed by the State Committee of Foreign Economic Relations which is, in effect, an agency of the Ministry of Foreign Trade.

Even if we consider the fact that American economic liberalism no longer subscribes to a laissez-faire philosophy and that Western European economies are traditionally more controlled than those in America, there is a deep chasm between the extremes represented by the United States and the Soviet Union or Communist China, the leading proponents of different worlds. These differences must of necessity influence many aspects of foreign policy. Economic fluctuations in the West, expressed in cyclic recessions, are interpreted by Moscow and Peking as evidence of the disintegration of capitalism; lack of progress in Soviet agriculture and such near-catastrophes of the national economy as those caused by the Peking leaders' Big Leap Forward are interpreted in the West as indications of the failure of communism as a socio-economic system.

These are eminently political considerations which show that politics dominates economics on basic issues. There are many instances, however, where foreign and commercial policies overlap. It might be useful to cite a few particularly pertinent—albeit specialized—situations in which economic objectives have had important political ramifications.

Equal Trade Opportunities

Leading to trade expansion, equal trade opportunities have always been a fundamental principle of U. S. policy. The assumption is that abundance of production and consumption rather than scarcity will contribute to the maintenance of peace. Many free world policy makers have agreed with their American colleagues that the difficult task of overcoming the impediments of low living standards and fettered internal and external economies is of prime importance for the elimination of strife and war.

Trade relations between sovereign states are regulated by treaties, the character of which is determined by the commercial policy of the signatories as well as by their political-economic position. Among the devices through which the United States tries to carry out its commercial policies—and thereby serve its foreign policy—is the application of the most-favored-nation clause to some of its trade treaties. The clause means that the contracting parties undertake to guarantee their citizens the advantages of a more favorable treaty than their governments may conclude with a third state.[6]

A crucial problem is that of *tariffs*. If there are to be equal trade opportunities, import barriers must progressively be removed. There are sometimes valid reasons why such trade barriers have to stand: They may reciprocate foreign discrimination or dumping and they may, in certain cases, protect domestic

[6] Cf. Royal Institute of International Affairs, "The Most-Favored-Nation Clause as an Instrument of Commercial Policy," London, 1963.

industries. However, the application of tariffs must be non-discriminating if the principle of equal trade opportunities is to be realized. In a free enterprise economy, policy makers may find themselves in a predicament. On the one hand, there is clamor by interest groups for high protective tariffs; on the other hand, such tariffs, if applied, would seriously hamper relations with another country whose good will may be of importance. From the general point of view of national interest, protection of international relationships is, in the long run, more important than protection of a single industry or a group of similar enterprises which have lobbied for tariffs. The policy maker in a democratic government may be forced to incur the wrath of vested interest groups and suffer political consequences, but he would betray the duty of his office if he did not, after serious consideration, decide for the nation rather than for private interests.

Protectionist laws did not even begin to cure the great American depression. In 1930, against the protest of 40 foreign countries and at least a thousand American economists, the Smoot-Hawley bill was enacted, considerably raising U. S. tariffs. The effect on world trade was disastrous in that it fell in volume and value. For both economic and political reasons, the Reciprocal Trade Agreements were introduced in 1934, permitting the President to reduce tariffs and prohibiting changes in already free articles. Further reductions were permitted in 1945. In view of the numerous and complex trade treaty negotiations between the United States and many countries, in 1947 a comprehensive General Agreement on Tariffs and Trade (GATT) was created in Geneva, Switzerland. By 1964, 95 countries had become full members of GATT.

In 1934, Congress approved the "establishment of foreign trade zones in U. S. ports of entry to expedite and encourage foreign commerce;" since 1950, exhibiting and manufacturing in foreign trade zones also has been permitted. Between 1936 and 1949, New York City, Mobile, New Orleans, San Francisco, and Seattle were created free trade zones. The first inland zone was established at the Municipal Airport in San Antonio.

Even though these measures have stimulated trade for the benefit of the United States as well as the rest of the free world, every renewal of the reciprocal trade agreements sought from Congress has caused considerable argument. And whenever the President, on the advice of proper authorities, has raised individual tariffs in order to protect domestic industries, such measures have aroused the ill will of the nation whose products were thus prohibitively priced, with the result that international relations suffered. (Switzerland and Japan exemplify these difficulties.)

In the communist bloc, foreign trade tariffs play a smaller role. For example, through its Ministry of Foreign Trade, the USSR controls exports and imports and is in a position to adjust its foreign trade to the fluctuations of free world economy even though this may entail sacrifices for Soviet citizens. Since the state controls imports, it needs no tariff protection. It will export if it needs foreign exchange or barter for desirable foreign goods. Since it is not in business for profit, its exports prices are set to cope with any foreign tariffs.

In view of this freedom of action on the part of the Soviet government, the Kremlin can use exports or imports as political threats or rewards, or as an inducement to neutralists. The ruble has no internationally recognized standing, and the Soviets have never seriously attempted to establish it on capitalist stock exchanges. Thus the party leaders may freely determine to what lengths they will go in sacrificing their cost accounting books for long-range political objectives.[7] For it must be clearly understood that Leninism rather than Marxism calls for a politically directed economy. In other words, it is the political and ideological objective which decides economic policies in Moscow, Peking, and elsewhere in the socialist camp. Obviously, such differentiation between the economic practices of the blocs does not help create international understanding and economic tranquility.

[7] Internally, such objectives may be concerned with priority projects, such as space conquest or agricultural progress; externally with foreign aid, particularly to politically promising countries in the underdeveloped areas.

One may add that equal opportunities for world trade or the expansion of such trade must wait for an international currency stabilization in which communist governments are not particularly interested. The value of money in the orbit is determined to suit internal purposes and those of the state trade monopoly. The official exchange tourists are compelled to pay for the Russian ruble is unlikely to be accepted by international finance in the free world.

Economic Alliances

The communists are increasingly concerned about the success of the European Economic Community (EEC), the Common Market, which has contributed so much to West European prosperity. General de Gaulle's blocking the admission of Great Britain to the EEC has doubtless harmed not only the economic but, even more, the political basis of the Common Market concept. Since the rejection of Britain's membership, communist denunciations of the EEC have been more subdued.

During the summer of 1962, the Soviet bloc somewhat belatedly recognized the increasing strength of the EEC. This was expressed in various ways: "a war of words against the Common Market; Soviet Premier Nikita Khrushchev's proposal for an international trade organization; a trend within the Soviet bloc toward strengthening its own economic ties; and intermittently, apparent overtures toward the Common Market."[8] *Pravda,* on August 26, 1962, accused the EEC of being an "imperialist agency." But Khrushchev, in an article of September, 1962 in *Problems of Peace and Socialism* (Prague edition) suggested no less than the "possibility of economic collaboration and peaceful economic competition not only between individual states with different social systems but between their economic associations."

Communist countermeasures to the Common Market are concentrated in the attempted re-invigoration of COMECON. This Eastern European organization (which in early 1963 elected

[8] See *Bulletin from the European Community*, Washington, D.C., Sept. 1962, p. 8.

Outer Mongolia as a member) consists of the Soviet Union and the Eastern European States (Poland, Czechoslovakia, Hungary, Rumania, Bulgaria, East Germany and Albania, the latter being shunned since its defection from the USSR to Communist China). China is an observer but has rarely sent delegates. Founded in 1949, COMECON lay almost dormant for years and only since the late fifties has shown some signs of life. Since 1962, there have been indications of resistance on the part of some "satellite" states, notably Rumania, against the basic concept, a division of labor. However, following the adjournment of the Sino-Soviet Conference in Moscow and the agreement on a partial nuclear test ban treaty in July 1963 between the USSR, United States, and the United Kingdom, Nikita Khrushchev called for a regional summit meeting and apparently succeeded in finding a compromise formula which would permit COMECON to become more active and strengthen the economy of the East European bloc.

Communist apprehensions almost certainly are not limited to economic issues; there is recognition that the Common Market will help to cement the political unity of Western Europe and perhaps also of free world countries outside Europe. This was demonstrated by eighteen African countries which have sought to associate themselves with the EEC since 1958; the final agreement of the association was signed in July, 1963.[9] Joining of the Common Market by other African states is possible and several have expressed an interest; Morocco, Tunisia, Libya, and Algeria, although not yet associated with EEC, have ambassadors in Brussels. Guinea is entitled to join but has never so opted. The only state opposed to EEC is Ghana, whose government views the Common Market as an "intolerable device" for neocolonialist intentions.

[9] African countries associated with the Common Market are Burundi, Cameroon, Central African Republic, Chad, Congo-Brazzaville, Congo-Leopoldville, Dahomey, Gabon, Ivory Coast, Mali, Mauretania, Nigeria, Rwanda, Senegal, Somalia, Togo, Upper Volta, Malagasy Republic.

Although De Gaulle's refusal to permit Great Britain to become a member has confused the Africans, they have gradually become convinced that they can accept trade agreements with EEC without having to fear political involvement. No major document with political overtones has been signed by EEC and the African associates. In the report of the Economic Commission for Africa of the UN Economic and Social Council it was stated that "increasingly close relations have developed between the secretariat of the Commission and the staff officials of EEC, in view of the growing interest in the effects of the EEC on African development and trade . . ."[10] And under Resolution 31 (III), The Economic Commission for Africa, at its third session, requested the Executive Secretary "to keep under constant review and inform members and associate members of the Commission of the continuous and changing impact of the European economic groupings on African economies."[11]

The partnership agreement between EEC and the eighteen associated African states, negotiated since 1958 and signed in July, 1963, renews in fact a previous convention which lasted from 1958 to 1962. The new agreement also runs for five years. The EEC will provide financial aid for the African countries totaling $800 million, which is $219 million more than under the previous treaty. Of this amount, $730 million will go to the eighteen associated countries and the rest of $70 million to the dependent French and Dutch associated territories. Most of this sum, $620 million, is in the form of non-repayable grants.

It would seem that other African states may in time follow those associated with EEC. As the Common Market increases its strength, especially if the seven countries of the European Free Trade Association (of which Great Britain is a member) become members or associates of the EEC, it can do more for the

[10] UN Economic and Social Council, E/CN.14/229/Rev.1, 36th Session, item 12, para. 160, p. 34 (Annual Report March 4, 1962, to Feb. 3, 1963).
[11] Economic Commission for Africa, UN ECOSOC, E/CN.14/207, Jan. 28, 1963, p. 1.

Africans. Although some of the African leaders have, from time to time, expressed fear of EEC's growing influence, on the whole, the results of its politico-economic unity have impressed them.

In Latin America, consideration of the Common Market began at the Economic Conference of the Organization of American States in Buenos Aires, August-September, 1957. A report on the first year of the EEC operations was circulated in 1960.[12] The Charter of Punta del Este of August 1961, preoccupied with possible harmful effects of EEC trade on OAS trade, dealt with this problem in Title IV, Chapter II concerning joint efforts to end preferential agreements which would work to the detriment of Latin American exports.

Thus, from the Latin American point of view, the developments of the EEC "point to a situation serious enough to warrant immediate consideration by the Latin American governments as a group . . . and the Latin American countries are taking a keen interest in legitimate movements toward formation of common markets in other regions of the world."[13] Indeed, "several of the countries now believe that the formation of the Central American Common Market and the establishment of the Latin American Free Trade Association have paved the way for joint consideration, when expedient, of compensatory measures aimed primarily at the elimination of restrictive trade regulations applied at destination."[14] It is interesting to note that, from the Latin American standpoint, "the competitive position of Latin America's exports in EEC would deteriorate if their counterparts from the Commonwealth were accorded any kind of preferential treatment as the result of the United Kingdom's entry into the EEC."[15]

[12] The Treaty of Rome, which established the EEC, became effective January 1, 1958.

[13] UN Economic and Social Council; Commission for Latin America: "Recent Developments and Trends in Latin American Trade with the European Economic Community," General-E/CN.12/63, 15. September, 1962, pp. 1-2.

[14] UN Economic and Social Council; Commission for Latin America: "Recent Developments and Trends in Latin American Trade with the European Economic Community," General-E/CN.12/63, 15. September, 1962, p. 6.

[15] *Ibid.* p. 30

The Central American countries recognized the significance of the Common Market and took action to match it in their own way and within their means. In March, 1962, a "little common market" was organized and codified in the Treaty of San José, Costa Rica, in the presence of the U. S. President, John F. Kennedy. But, with this exception, one might say that Latin America's policy toward and interest in the EEC has not yet fully crystallized. While there is opposition in some areas of trade, there seems to be acceptance in others. The success of the EEC remains challenging, and it is hard to believe that Latin American governments will not eventually face up to the problems which EEC has created and solved.

THE ROLE OF NATIONAL SECURITY POLICY

At one time, when war was regarded as the continuation of policy by other means, the responsibilities of policy makers and military leaders were strictly divided, as were policy implementation and security operations. The diplomats and the military worked on different planes. There were instances of overlap, of course; both diplomats and military officers usually came from the aristocracy (the United States is perhaps the only country in which this was not the rule) and had many views and aspirations in common. Certainly there were mutual influences at work affecting policy and strategy makers. On the whole, however, the formulation of foreign policy remained separated from military considerations except where crises were expected or fomented.

Modern technology has changed this situation and so has the polarization of the world into antagonistic blocs. Foreign and security policies have merged to the point where statesmen and military strategists must collaborate closely. This does not mean that national security can be ensured only by advanced weapons technology, manpower, and military doctrine. They are indispensible for defense but they are, after all, the last resort. In the past as well as in the present, political constructs have been tried in the hope that they would contribute to security without the use of force. Many have failed; some are being explored and others are being practiced. We must briefly examine these concepts and expose their failures or point out their benefits. They are such devices as isolationism, neutralism, balance of power, collective security or protective alliances.

The attempt to be isolated from political entanglements or foreign influences has been made repeatedly by countries that were reasonably self-contained and, more important, blessed with geographical barriers. These periods rarely lasted as long as the isolation of Japan under the shoguns which was ended in 1853, when Commodore Perry forcibly opened Japan's ports to the occident. Likewise, the isolation of Nepal and Tibet under the Lamas lasted a long time; both countries were of little political significance but their inaccessibility protected their isolation for centuries. England's "splendid isolation" was splendid political propaganda, but it had its uses from the military point of view. Not even Hitler's legions succeeded in invading the British Isles, although air attacks created terrible devastation. The isolationist phase of the United States between the World Wars demonstrated the parochial attitude of legislators who did not understand President Wilson's preoccupation with policies designed to prevent future wars; the Senate, in denying approval of U. S. participation in the League of Nations, stimulated a rapid deterioration of international relations. One might say that United States isolationism, instead of strengthening security, greatly weakened it.

A different type of isolationism may be found in communist countries which try to shut themselves off from the rest of the world by the Iron Curtain. The Soviet Union, in the times of Stalin, showed very strong isolationist tendencies. This was a considered policy, regarded as necessary in order to prevent the people from being exposed to unfriendly influences. Since Stalin's death, however, the tendency has somewhat abated, and the Soviet "peaceful coexistence" strategy at least partially removed isolationist policies from the international arena.

Domestically, however, isolation of the Soviet people persists, though not quite so extreme as in Stalin's time. Communist China, which in its first years showed strong tendencies to isolate itself, at least from the non-communist world, has increasingly tried to break out of this isolation. The principal reasons for this new policy lie in Mao's desire to play a role in world politics and in the conflict with Moscow, which could lead to isolation from the communist orbit. Domestically, however, the Chinese people are as isolated as ever.

Neutralism and Neutrality

In a sense, neutralism is somewhat related to isolation although it does not actually rule out foreign contacts; rather it is isolation from political commitments to either the West or the East. Neutralism, therefore, is quite different from *neutrality*; the two concepts should not be confused.

Neutrality is a legal term, indicating that a state will abstain from participating in war between other states and during the period of this war will deal impartially with the belligerents. This was anticipated by The Hague Convention of 1907, when the rights and duties of neutral states were codified in international law. However, both the League of Nations and the United Nations viewed with disfavor neutrality among their members, perhaps agreeing with President Wilson who in 1917 had declared that neutrality is no longer possible or desirable when the peace of the world is involved. The era of collective security was climaxed by the Pact of Paris in 1928. This created a dilemma, however, because the Pact recognized the concept of *nonbelligerency* wherein states could remain outside the actual combat but were no longer compelled to keep silent about their sympathies in the struggle. Indeed, the International Law Association expressed the view in a meeting at Budapest, Hungary, in 1934, that aggressor states violating the Pact could not expect that other parties of the Pact would observe all traditional obligations arising out of the neutrality laws even though they continued to refrain from participation in the conflict. This concept is called "permissive sanctions." Its recognition by an antagonistic belligerent depended entirely on his strategic position in the war, his resources, and the importance he attributed to the non-belligerent state or the help such non-belligerent could muster for his enemy. It is interesting to recall American neutrality legislation of November 4, 1939, which, in effect, favored the Allied cause. Some of the provisions of the Act were removed on November 17, 1941, even before the attack on Pearl Harbor. Of course, the Act became obsolete after December 7, 1941, when the United States joined the Western Allies. Nevertheless, during World War II, when international law was flouted by the Nazis and Fascists, a number of countries managed to maintain their status as neutrals, for example, Switzerland, Sweden, Turkey, and Spain, although the latter was so sympathetic toward the Nazi cause that it could be called a non-belligerent.

Neutralism, on the other hand, connotes a situation in which a state wishes to remain non-aligned, that is to say unattached to either the Western or Eastern powers. It is a new concept in international relations which is the direct result of the struggle between the communist and non-communist blocs, as it developed after 1945. It is confined mainly to the underdeveloped states of Asia and Africa. Latin America is neutralist only in part; the Organization of American States cannot be called neutralist because its interests coincide with those of the Western world, a fact which was clearly demonstrated in the Cuban crisis when the OAS opposed Soviet penetration of Cuba and in virtual unanimity voted to take measures against Castroism.

Although non-alignment implies a certain opportunism—because it does not preclude a neutralist state's trading and maintaining relations with components of the opposing blocs—one can understand the neutralists' desire not to jeopardize their newly won sovereignty. Also, as long as they remain uncommitted, they obtain assistance from both sides, for East and West are eager to be in their good graces. Foreign policy in the sixties is characterized by the wooing of neutralists; the communists do it to get them on their side; the Western allies will be satisfied to keep the neutralists from joining the socialist camp. Both sides would like to see the other's being denied the strategic resources from non-aligned areas.

A policy of neutralism, however, is no guarantee of national security, as India learned from its experience with China. Indeed, India was a strong exponent of non-alignment, which became its national policy. Yet the Communist Chinese attack on the contested Sino-Indian border areas in the winter of 1962-63 forced the Nehru government to retreat, to some extent, from its neutralism by accepting Western military aid. Communist China remains a serious threat to the neutralism of non-aligned states, which are the fulcrum of its aggressive political strategy. In advocating "wars of liberation", it intends to carry the revolution to these areas, the domination of which Peking believes to be crucial for the achievement of a communist world conquest. The Soviets, supporting this doctrine in principle, are more cautious in its interpretation, lest a local "liberation" war escalate into a conflict with nuclear weapons.

The international communist movement has indicated that it regards as priority targets the non-aligned areas of Asia and Africa as well as Latin America, not merely to liberate them from "neo-colonialism" but eventually to receive them into the socialist commonwealth. This would end Western access to the natural wealth of the areas and would channel it to the communist states, isolating Western Europe and North America both politically and economically. In such circumstances it can be said that neutralism contributes to a country's national security little more than a reprieve from actual involvement in the East-West conflict.

Neutralists strive to remain non-aligned and non-alignment is based upon neutralism. Both non-alignment and neutralism "are international policies inspired largely by domestic concerns. By the same token they are political policies largely motivated by economic needs and interests."[16] Since neutralism is the ideology

[16] George Liska, "The 'Third Party': The Rationale of Nonalignment" in *Neutralism and Nonalignment*, Laurence W. Martin, ed., New York: Frederick A. Praeger, 1962, p. 89.

of underdeveloped countries, the quest for non-alignment is understandable and neutralism is assumed to create something like "automatic protection"[17] from aggression. This automatic protection is a mistaken notion as an analysis of Chinese Communist policies toward the third world clearly demonstrates.

Balance of Power

Does the creation of a balance of power contribute to national security? The answer is no. But so great is the fascination with this concept that even today it has not died although attempts to create a power equilibrium have rarely succeeded in preventing a clash of arms. Perhaps this is so because peace was a marginal issue; the maintenance of power was considered decisive and its increase desirable. Since the balance-of-power concept still is so much in the minds of political analysts, regardless of its failures and obsolescence, it must be examined closely.

The concept was known to ancient statesmen, though perhaps under a different name. The struggles between Rome and Carthage, Athens and Sparta, Egypt and the states of Asia Minor, to mention only a few examples, were attempts to match power and possibly so to increase its weight that the scales were tipped in favor of the state that outstripped its competitor. To be sure, in most cases, there was no group of countries whose statesmen tried to avoid war by creating a secure balance. Rather, it was a wrangle between two states, or empires, for the greater power and, therefore, the greater spoils.

With the consolidation of the Roman Empire, the efforts and needs for balancing power diminished, at least in Europe, around the Mediterranean basin and Asia Minor. When this Empire became the heart of the medieval church, the balance of power concept lay dormant, to awaken only in the sixteenth century. On a small scale, it was then applied in Italy, where city states and small principalities sought the most advantageous position by any means, fair or foul. In the seventeenth century,

[17] *Ibid.* p. 88.

Hugo Grotius incorporated the concept into his philosophy of international law. The Peace of Westphalia in 1648, which ended the Thirty Years' War, is perhaps the first modern example of efforts to establish an equilibrium throughout the war-weary European continent. A further step in that direction was the Peace of Utrecht in 1713, which concluded the War of the Spanish Succession and Louis XIV's abortive attempt to gain hegemony over Europe.

As the nation-state reached its zenith in the eighteenth and nineteenth centuries, the power-balancing doctrine became the leading principle of international relations. Indeed, the Napoleonic Wars, ending in defeat for the Corsican and victory for the European allies, led to the Congress of Vienna in 1815, which canceled out France's predominance in Europe. A variety of new state groupings heavily outbalanced France without actually annexing territory. The statesmen of Vienna proved better diplomats and psychologists than those of Versailles and St. Germain more than a century later.

After Vienna, the balance established and watched over by the Holy Alliance kept the peace until well into the eighteen fifties. Although it succeeded in preventing a general conflagration for the rest of the century, it could not stop a series of local wars such as the Crimean, the Prusso-Danish and the Austro-Prussian conflicts, and the Franco-Prussian war which led to the unification of imperial Germany, thus creating a new and unforeseen disturbance in the European balance of power. When the Russo-Turkish conflict threatened to upset the already precarious balance, the 1878 Congress of Berlin became the last attempt at stabilization.

In 1758, Vattel had demanded that the European powers constitute federations organized to maintain equilibrium and that none of the members be permitted to upset this balance—by punishment of armed retaliation.[18] In a somewhat similar vein, the Congress of Vienna formulated the idea of a "European concert". The Holy Alliance's function was to maintain the har-

[18] E. de Vattel, *Droit des gens*, Neuchâtel, 1758.

mony of this concert. But, towards the end of the century, the dissonances increased with a shift in the power constellation caused by an increase in German strength and aspirations. The result was a new attempt to balance the power. The "Entente Cordiale," linking France, Britain, and Russia, maneuvered for predominance against the triple alliance consisting of the Central Powers, Germany and Austria, with the half-hearted participation of Italy. However, this scheme failed and World War I was not averted.

The alternative set forth by the political idealists was international cooperation leading eventually toward world government. The League of Nations was conceived and established. But it remained a rump organization. The United States Senate rejected American participation, thereby expressing the isolationist mood of the country and breaking President Wilson's spirit. Russia, which had become the Bolshevik-ruled Soviet Union, became a member only much later. Germany, the former enemy of the founders of the League, remained ostracized and chained by the burden of hatred expressed by the Treaty of Versailles. Even when it was permitted to join, much too late, it did not receive the democratic support, psychological or economic, which might have saved the world from Hitlerism. The Austro-Hungarian monarchy was torn asunder under the slogan of national self-determination; but none of the components of this former conglomeration of nationalities could really stand on its own feet. This dissolution not only created a political vacuum, much of which would later be filled by the USSR, but also eliminated a natural balancing force in the most incendiary part of Europe. Those new states which formerly belonged to the Vienna monarchy were neither strong nor mature enough to assist in the creation of a new European equilibrium.

It is idle to speculate whether the League, with all sovereign states of consequence participating, could have achieved the objective for which it was established. But although it failed, we must remember that it constituted the first conscious effort by modern nations not to rely on a precarious balance of power but to develop instead a system of international mediation and cooperation. The urge for peace at any price, the vague hope that the League might yet succeed, the isolationist policies of the United States, the failure to help Germany toward implementation of its Weimar democracy, the dissolution of the self-balancing multinational Austro-Hungarian empire, and the bolshevization of Russia—all these factors prevented international organization from becoming effective. Moreover, the ideological threats of Nazism and Communism, whose gospels were open for world inspection, were ignored and therefore remained largely unknown or misunderstood. Thus, World War II was permitted to break out at a time when a genuine power equilibrium did not exist.

There have been attempts to balance power in other parts of the world, but nowhere does there exist a clearer example of this political strategy than in the Europe of the eighteenth and nineteenth centuries. The existence of several great powers within a comparatively small space compelled each of them to contribute individually to an equilibrium as well as to participate in balancing efforts with other powers whose interests were similar. Alliances concluded between states were not designed primarily to maintain the peace, even though they paid lip service to this ideal. They were, rather, moves in a political chess game, the objective being to checkmate a potential aggressor or, more bluntly expressed, to deprive him of his competitive status, if not peacefully, by force of arms.

With the exception of the few decades following the creation of the Holy Alliance, the balance-of-power concept has been a failure. It has not prevented war; it has sometimes precipitated it. The League, designed to end this state of affairs, failed. The United Nations, a much stronger organization than the League, has thus far been unable to prevent the formation of an essentially polarized power system which contains at least some elements of the power-balancing concept.

In other words, the maintenance of a balance of power requires flexibility in foreign relations which no longer exists.

The only areas where this aim might still be attractive would be the neutralist third world, which seeks to protect itself from the superpowers by a policy of non-alignment. Perhaps some of these new states have established regional associations to gain additional protection among themselves; perhaps this is an attempt to create a balance of power of sorts. But, on the other hand, the more prevalent trends go further than regional groupings. In Africa, the objective of most sub-Saharan leaders is Pan-Africanism. In the Middle East, it is Pan-Arabism. In Latin America, the Organization of American States is trying, not without success, to reach a consensus on political and economic problems. None of these constellations is attempting to balance power.

Nor can one call the East-West confrontation a political-military balancing act in the traditional sense. The decisive difference between the flexibility of political and military alliances in the nineteenth century and the rigidity of the communist blocs is the lack of maneuverability in a polarized world. In the nuclear age, war is no longer a practicable instrument of foreign policy. The availability of thermonuclear weapons and their delivery systems covering every corner of the globe virtually precludes shifting political loyalties. It follows that only the development of a decisive technological advantage could end this petrifaction of the balance of terror—temporarily. New inventions have a way of quickly becoming common knowledge. The scientific race between the United States and the Soviet Union in particular demonstrates this vividly in rocketry and ventures into space.

It has been claimed that "if the respective nuclear capabilities of the United States and the Soviet Union should come to neutralize each other and should continue to do so, they will drop out of the scales as a positive balancing factor."[19] This seems to imply that power must be balanced in terms of conventional forces, economic competition, ideological appeal, and subversive operations. This line of thinking has become fashionable. It fails

[19] Arnold Wolfers, "The Balance of Power," *SAIS Review*, Washington, D.C.: School of Advanced International Studies, Spring 1959, Vol. III, No. 3, p. 15.

to recognize, however, that, when hard pressed by an enemy superior in conventional armament, a nation possessing nuclear weapons may try to equalize its position through their use. In the end, the nuclear potential remains the decisive factor in the matching—and containing—of forces.

We can see now that the scales for balancing power are locked by the ideological rigidity and nuclear arsenal of the chief antagonists. Is there a way out of the deadlock? Could collective security achieve what the balance of power cannot?

Collective Security

Collective security is exactly what it says: an association of nations dedicated to mutual defense. No power balancing is attempted; the partners have identical interests insofar as security is concerned and therefore are pledged to regard an attack on one as an attack on all. The League of Nations Covenant established a modern precedent in sponsoring collective security (articles 10-16); even clearer did the Treaty of Locarno (1925) express this policy by mutual peace guarantees from Germany, Belgium, France, Italy, and the United Kingdom. Note that Germany, the former enemy was a partner in this Pact which was received with considerable enthusiasm throughout the civilized world. In 1936, Hitler marched into the demilitarized Rhineland, breaking the Pact. In retrospect, this was particularly regrettable because, without the rise of Fascism and Nazism, Western Europe might have been able to contain or perhaps block the growth of Soviet Communism. For Hitler and Mussolini dragged the world into a war from which the Soviet Union emerged a world power and, in addition, gained control over large parts of Central-Eastern Europe. Without this war, China's revolution would not necessarily have ended in communism.

After World War II, the combined impact of ideology and technology changed the character of collective security by limiting it to regional or ideological groups. NATO, of course, is the best example of a Western collective security arrangement.

SEATO and CENTO are in this category, although much less potent.

Whether the Warsaw Pact, designed as a counterpart to NATO, can be looked upon as an organization of collective security is highly questionable. The member states are under Moscow's sway and the observers have little to say. Indeed, communist governments oppose the Western concept of collective security which, they fear, may block their attempts to undermine the strength of the "imperialists."

The West finds it useful and necessary to close ranks against a potential enemy; however, if the nuclear stalemate continues to make world war improbable and only the cold war is to be fought, collective security must be extended to the social and economic fields of the allied nations. For example, the Common Market is a splendid organization to strengthen Europe and thereby the West. Eventually all of Western Europe will, hopefully, be united: politically, economically, and culturally. In this way, and in association with the United States and other non-European states, collective security, without losing sight of military needs, could cope with the Soviet "peaceful competition" and come to grips with the difficult problems of conducting a cold war.

Can international organizations such as the United Nations achieve collective security? The League of Nations, as we know, failed. The United Nations is a stronger organization; it has learned from the League's mistakes. But it is still inadequate to enforce genuine worldwide security cooperation. There are several reasons for this.

First, the United Nations consists of nation-states which often have contradictory interests. Action to be taken against a rebellious power usually is not considered from the point of view of the UN but rather from that of each voting government which considers the consequences to its own position vis-a-vis the aggressive nation or a third nation which happens to be friendly with the offending one. The UN position toward Communist China in the Korean war illustrates the caution adopted by many member states which hedged in recognizing Peking as an aggressor.

Enforcement action is possible wherever local conditions permit the UN members to take a genuinely impartial position or feel that a commitment would harm neither their interests, their political goals nor their propaganda objectives.

Second, the communist members of the United Nations, whether or not they proclaim the principle of peaceful coexistence, have only a limited interest in world stability. The degree of this interest varies among the members of the socialist camp. Global war is not an objective of either Moscow or Peking, but both would probably agree that communism has little chance of taking hold in stable areas. The doctrine of class struggle which, according to Lenin, must be transferred to the international scene, has not been abandoned. How to accomplish this best and quickest in view of the nuclear deterrent has not been resolved and has become one of the areas of contention between the USSR and Red China. Both, however, remain committed to destroying capitalism or imperialism, preferably by means short of war. This commitment is not conducive to national security for non-communist powers nor does it help to establish unified action in the United Nations. Clearly, the interests of the communist states do not coincide with those of the non-communist world, whether they belong to the Western alliance or to the third world.

Third, the United Nations does not comprise all nations. One of the potential great powers, Communist China, is not a member. It has expressed acceptance of peaceful coexistence but it has done so with serious reservations. The Mao regime has faced the dilemma of combining the recognition of its own military weakness and the nuclear balance of terror with Leninist fundamentalism, which preaches that only warlike action can dislodge imperialism from its position and that no compromise is permissible. In other words, Communist China is cautious in wishing to avoid world war, but it insists upon the possibility of limited war and has elevated "national liberation war" (predominately a type of guerilla war) to one of its foremost policies. It is improbable that this dangerous stance would be abandoned were Communist China accepted as a member of the United Nations.

Finally, the many new states, mostly African, which now constitute a high percentage of the UN membership, are further complicating unity of action for security. The Charter gives even the smallest of these states a vote equal to that of the great powers; tiny Mauritania, for example, with approximately 650,000 inhabitants has the same vote as the United States (190 million) or the Soviet Union (220 million). But, like Mauritania, quite a few of the new states seek security primarily for the promotion of their own political influence and economic development. This is reasonable provided it does not interfere with the collective security concept of the United Nations. Since the new states are the target of communist infiltration, their reaction to security problems is highly significant: Their response to these problems can contribute to or reduce international security.

These factors are not conducive to collective security and have left the United Nations in a state of uncertainty. The division of the world into inimical ideological camps and the resurgence of national self-interest as represented by Gaullist France or the newly independent nations have created formidable obstacles on the road to international unity. There have been isolated actions where United Nations peace-keeping units have prevented bloodshed and local wars such as in the Arab-Israel conflict; but on the other hand, events in the Congo and in Cyprus have exposed weaknesses in the United Nations' peace-enforcement powers.

Unquestionably, the United Nations is useful in the areas of economic, social and cultural development and in the work of its Specialized Agencies. But it is far from fulfilling the ideals of its Charter in that it has not succeeded in contributing essentially to the security of its member nations. We cannot expect this to be otherwise unless the United Nations becomes an effective world government, with an international police force ready to deal with any potential threat to peace quickly and thoroughly, regardless of the national interests of individual nations.

The UN Charter permits regional alignments outside the framework of the international organizations. Several such associated groups now exist; not all of them are effective but all have as their objective an increase of security through mutual defense treaties and economic agreements which have strong political undertones. This type of alignment, referred to as regional security, exists in Western Europe, the Middle East, Africa, Asia, and Latin America. Unless the interests of these groups of nations clash with those of others, regional security pacts are important foundation stones for worldwide security organization.

Protective Alliances

Protective alliances proliferated soon after World War II. Stalin had chosen to initiate a series of aggressive actions in Turkey, Iran, Greece, and Berlin; he had seized the Eastern European countries and driven the Communist parties in France and Italy into seditious action against the prevailing social order. This produced a chain reaction of mutual assistance treaties in the West. Great Britain and France signed a fifty-year Treaty of Alliance and Mutual Assistance in March, 1947; in September of the same year, the Treaty of Rio de Janeiro was concluded among all the American states except Canada, Nicaragua, and Ecuador.

In March, 1948, a development began which ended in the creation of the Western European Union (WEU) in October, 1954, when a Treaty of Economic, Social, and Cultural Collaboration and Collective Self-Defense was signed in Brussels. In April, 1948, the Marshall Plan was announced, one of the most brilliant political and economic policies the United States and, for that matter, any state in the world, has ever pursued. It has since become a global institution, much disliked by some American taxpayers and legislators, but nevertheless an effective force for the security of the United States and the Western world.

The "Vandenberg Resolution" of June, 1948, passed by the U.S. Senate, pronounced American foreign policy to be in favor of the "right of individual or collective self-defense in accordance with Article 51 of the UN Charter." This policy statement made possible American participation in the North Atlantic Treaty Organization (NATO) which was signed by Belgium, Canada,

Denmark, France, Iceland, Italy, Luxemburg, the Netherlands, Norway, Portugal, the United Kingdom and the United States. In 1952, Greece and Turkey joined and the new Federal Republic of Germany became a member in 1955.

In the Far East, the United States and the Philippines signed a Mutual Defense Pact in August, 1951, and in the same month the ANZUS Pact, a Mutual Defense Treaty between New Zealand, Australia and the United States was sealed. Owing to the communist danger in the Pacific, the Southeast Asia Treaty Organization (SEATO) came into being in September, 1954, by the conclusion of the Manila Treaty. Finally, in the Middle East, the Baghdad Pact was concluded in February, 1954, between Turkey, Iraq, Iran, and Pakistan. After the 1958 revolution in Iraq, when that country seceded from the Pact, it became the Central Treaty Organization (CENTO). Britain joined the Pact in 1955; the United States did not join, but in a statement of 1956 made clear that it would regard any attack against a CENTO power with the utmost gravity.

Of particularly great importance was the Act of Chapultepec, in 1948 (a follow-up of the 1947 Inter-American Treaty of Reciprocal Assistance, signed in Rio de Janeiro), which led to the establishment of the Organization of American States. The OAS has since proved one of the most durable and productive of all treaties.

In addition, several bilateral mutual assistance treaties have been concluded since World War II, all of which more or less fit into the pattern of protective alliances as a result of the communist threat. The economic arrangements in Western Europe[20] have sought not only to restore and strengthen the West European economic potential but also to achieve eventual political

[20] Organization for European Economic Cooperation (OEEC); European Coal and Steel Community (ECSC); European Atomic Energy Community (EURATOM); European Economic Community (EEC), usually called Common Market; European Free Trade Association (EFTA), sometimes called the "Outer Seven."

unity and, though not expressly stated, to provide a solid foundation for mutual protection against predators.

Undoubtedly enormous efforts have been made in the free world to foster both collective security and the concept of protective alliances. Not all these efforts have been ineffective. In the economic sphere they have been quite successful. Militarily, they have made some progress although not nearly as much as would be required in case of aggression. Thus for purposes of national security, these are unreliable peace keepers so long as there is no real unity of politico-economic purpose and action. The deterrence of nuclear weapons remains the major protective factor— but even in this dangerous area there is no unity: In the West, General de Gaulle insists upon his own nuclear *force de frappe* and is unwilling to coordinate his efforts with those of the Allies; in the East, Peking, after having exploded its first atomic bomb, will hardly be persuaded by the Kremlin to submit to Soviet nuclear planning.

It will be noted that all these alliances and agreements are part of the allied defense system. No similar arrangements can be noted in the East. To be sure, there is a host of mutual defense treaties between the Soviet Union and its Eastern European satellites which, however, have merely perfunctory meaning because these states, being contiguous to the USSR, are under direct or indirect Soviet influence in matters concerning bloc security and foreign policy. The Sino-Soviet Mutual Defense Treaty of 1950 meant little after the dispute between Moscow and Peking broke into the open in 1959 and came to a climax in 1963; it remains to be seen whether Khrushchev's ouster will save the Treaty from eventual disintegration. The Warsaw Pact, supposedly countering NATO, is a Soviet creature and merely puts the individual mutual assistance treaties into a coordinated military framework. But even though disagreements within the Western and Eastern camps threaten disagreements or splits, still, the *basic* ideological polarization remains. It has become more complex and more challenging to policy makers and those responsible for national security.

There is, then, a situation which requires new security concepts since "the traditional balance of power . . . has been modified by its contact with collective security."[21] One may add that the concept of international organization has also contributed to such modification, indicating worldwide security concerns as contrasted with the parochial concept of power balance prior to 1914. Above all, there is the nuclear stalemate which intensifies attitudes of political rigidity.

In sum, the security problem for the decision makers is one of extreme complexity. It is no longer simple for the Kremlin since the tendency toward more freedom of movement in Eastern European spheres of interest, at least in domestic affairs, has been growing consistently since 1956; it has become more complicated through the Sino-Soviet dispute which has created turmoil among the Communist parties throughout the world and ended the monolithic unity which distinguished the communist world under the rule of Stalin. The problem is equally, if not more, complex in the West where statesmen have to work with the slowness and individualism of democratic processes, a variance of beliefs and approaches, and the insistence of France upon playing the role of a world power, which it has not been for a century.

A combination of collective security efforts, combining regional arrangements, international cooperation, and nuclear power may constitute a reasonably well balanced security system of the West vis-à-vis the East. But the term "balance" does not connote maneuverability. Communist flexibility is tactical only; the basic principles of Marxism-Leninism and its major strategy remain. The methods have changed, modifications of methodology have been introduced, but the fundamentals have not been touched, nor have ultimate objectives changed.

[21] George Liska, *International Equilibrium, A Theoretical Essay on the Politics and Organization of Security*, Cambridge, Mass.: Harvard University Press, 1957, 23 ff.

WAR AND PEACE IN FOREIGN POLICY

"The history of the world is primarily a history of wars."[22] It is a sad reflection on the human spirit that only in the past three centuries have men come to study seriously the possibilities of *organized* efforts for preventing war. Men like Erasmus, Grotius, Penn, Bentham, and Kant, educators, philosophers, and jurists, concentrated primarily on concepts of international law, its ethics, legal implications, and organization. To be sure, there have always been thinkers and rulers who detested war and praised peace but not before the nineteenth century did world peace become a matter of political action, and not before the twentieth century were international organizations to preserve peace established.

Prior to World War I, peace was sought on the chess board of the balance-of-power game. This was a bitter experience; all too often policy (diplomacy) was continued "by other means" (war). Nations grew tired of carnage, and war became a hated word. This was quite evident in the joyful reaction of the peoples when the Pact of Paris (the Kellogg-Briand Pact) was signed by the most powerful nations of the time (1928) and ratified by the isolationist United States in 1929. It was not destined to last long. After Japan attacked Manchuria in 1931, aggression followed aggression until the Pact became a fading memory. Its only tangible result was the innovation of undeclared wars, called "incidents" by the Japanese war lords and "police actions" by Hitler and Mussolini. In this way, aggressor nations could claim they had not violated the letter of international law even though they clearly negated its spirit and brazenly so boasted. They successfully circumvented Article II of the Pact of Paris, which stipulates that settlement of disputes "should never be sought except by pacific means" and thus maintained a legal fiction by avoiding formal declarations of war.

The conditions which permitted such violations no longer exist. A new era began the day the first atomic bomb was exploded in 1945. This set in motion a development which eventu-

---

[22] London, *op. cit.* p. 173.

ally ended the flexibility of power relationships among nation-states and led to a polarization of world politics. Furthermore, the yardsticks by which national power was measured no longer were accurate. For centuries, certain facts of national and political life were taken for granted by policy makers. Their relative estimate of power made sense, and the errors seldom were crucial. But after 1945, the appearance of nuclear weapons and the means to deliver them any place in the world through supersonic jets and rockets nullified the former valuation of power ingredients, whether geographic, topographic, demographic, or climatic. What mattered now was scientific and technological expertness, industrial skill, and certain raw materials necessary to manufacture the superbomb. The indescribably destructive force of nuclear weapons raised the hazards of war to such a level that major warfare was to become self-defeating. Policy now had to accomplish either peace or compromise or face the prospect of having no country left for which to make policy.

The irony is that the nuclear stalemate did not force the powers to accept the situation and stop arming. Indeed, without continuation of armament, the stalemate might be ended and the disarmed or underarmed country become the target of superior technological weapons. Thus the stalemate became an armed truce in which the armament race went on. Lacking international trust and confidence, the contestants of the East-West struggle could only muse with Harold Laswell: "If we do not expect war, we invite aggression."[23] The ancient Romans had similar thoughts more than two thousand years ago when they proclaimed: *si vis pacem, para bellum* ("if you want peace, prepare for war").

Could it be otherwise in a world shaken by ideological contests? Could the Western powers contemplate an end of the armament race when they considered the communist doctrines on war and peace, when Marxism-Leninism still remained the rationale of the two giant states which claimed to adhere to this

[23] Harold D. Laswell, *World Politics Faces Economics*, New York: McGraw-Hill Book Company, Inc., 1945, p. 8.

body of beliefs? Could the communist regimes be expected to step out of the armament race if their doctrine proclaimed that imperialism (the highest stage of capitalism) would remain an acute danger to peace and that extreme vigilance was required to cope with this danger? Hardly. Yet, as the Sino-Soviet conflict intensified, as the economic conditions of the Soviet Union worsened, as the continuing nuclear armament program produced what is called an "overkill" capability, Khrushchev's coexistence policy went beyond the ideological frontiers of this concept and strove to relax international tensions. International organizations supported the move and Presidents Kennedy and Johnson, while maintaining vigilance, responded. High-level statements from Moscow, Washington, and London assured the world of peaceful intentions.

All these measures and protestations, however, are not reliable safeguards for national security. They were possible because of the Soviet initiated *détente*. Such periods of relaxation have occurred before but they ceased when their purpose had been fulfilled.

For these reasons, even governments traditionally against delegating too much power to the military are compelled, for security's sake, to require close collaboration between their policy makers and those responsible for national defense. Foreign policy and security have become intertwined.

The nuclear test ban, the establishment of the "hot line" between Washington and Moscow, the ban on orbiting nuclear weapons, the 18-nation disarmament conference, the limitations of production of fissionable materials, and many statements of goodwill are hopeful signs of understanding on nuclear issues but do not constitute a real safeguard against surprise attack. These measures are the result of an easing of tensions which was required by the USSR for its own purposes. It is impossible to estimate how genuine are the Soviet peace efforts and how long the *détente* will last. Marxist-Leninist scholasticism sets up a distinction between peaceful coexistence and genuine peace. The former is a temporary accommodation during which the ideological struggle continues and competitive endeavors seek to outclass "bourgeois" society in order to convince it that "socialism" is better; genuine peace is possible only after capitalism and imperialism have been liquidated and the world has united in a "classless" society. The concept of war is as complex as that of peace in Marxist-Leninist terms.

The cause of a war determines whether it is "just" or "unjust." It is immaterial who starts hostilities and where they take place; the question is what class directs the conduct of war and what policy objectives are to be reached. In other words, whether a war is just or unjust depends, first, on its class rationale. Therefore, just wars are conducted by an oppressed class against its oppressor; war for national liberation is just as are wars of the proletariat against imperialism. Unjust wars, on the other hand, are fought to conquer territory and peoples. It is possible for the character of war to change in the course of events; for example, while the French revolutionary wars were just, they became unjust when, under Napoleon, they turned into imperialist struggles for conquest. In reverse, World War II began as an imperialist war but, according to the new version of the History of the Soviet Communist Party of 1959, became a just war of liberation once the USSR entered the conflict.

Marx and Engels prophetically recognized that with technical developments future wars might become so great a risk that nobody would be willing to start them. Lenin, however, believed that the danger of war had increased to such an extent that wars had become inevitable. He foresaw wars between individual imperialist powers, between colonial powers and liberation movements in the colonies, and civil war inside imperialist states. Only in the last years of his life did Lenin become uncertain and agreed with Marx and Engels that wars might become impossible through new inventions. However, he kept these views "in the family" although they were recorded by his wife, Nadezhda Konstantinova Krupskaya. Decades later, the Soviets did not hesitate to publish these views at a time when Khrushchev's peaceful coexistence policy and the modification of Lenin's "inevitability" line had become official Soviet policy.[24]

For almost half a century, Communist congresses proclaimed the inevitability of war. Only in February, 1956, at the Twentieth Congress of the CPSU did Khrushchev modify Lenin's doctrine. It is very likely that Lenin, had he been alive, would have done the same, for he was both a realist and an opportunist. Khrushchev's official reasons for the reversal of the inevitability thesis ("war is no longer fatally inevitable") were first, that the "socialist camp" had developed into a world socialist system, controlling a billion people; second, that there existed a neutral zone of peace in the new states of Asia and Africa; and third, that workers and peace movements had gained enough strength to prevent governments from conducting war. In his report to the Twentieth Party Congress, Khrushchev made it clear that the danger of aggression by "reactionary forces" still existed since the economic bases of war in imperialist countries had been unchanged. Nevertheless, the thesis that wars could and should be avoided became mandatory for the party line of all communist parties throughout the world. At the Twenty-First and Twenty-Second Congresses in 1959 and 1961, this thesis was further strengthened and has since become the basis of Soviet political thought without, however, essentially changing the military establishment of the USSR or its adherence to Marxism-Leninism.

This does not mean that Moscow is now benign in its attitude toward war. Rather, it is the recognition that, as Khrushchev liked to put it, "life itself" has forced this policy upon the communists. Indeed, if nuclear parity should ever be lost by default of the West, there should be no doubt in the minds of Western policy makers that the Kremlin would reverse itself—as it has done so often in the past.[25] Moreover, there is the problem of

[24] Quoted by Wolfgang Leonhard, *Sowjetideologie Heute* (Soviet Ideology Today) Frankfurt/Main: Fischer Buecherei, 1962, p. 95. Krupskaya's book *On Lenin* was published in Moscow, 1960.
[25] This undoubtedly applies to agreements such as the limited nuclear test ban, referred to below, p. 99-100.

Communist China, whose fundamentalist leaders pay lip service to peaceful coexistence but do not share the Kremlin's view on its implementation. No documents have set forth this disagreement more forcefully than has the exchange of letters between the Soviet and Chinese Communist Parties. On June 14, 1963, the Chinese party made it clear that peaceful coexistence cannot supplant the revolutionary struggle.

It said: "There can be no peaceful transition to international communism; there is no historical precedent for such a peaceful transition from capitalism to socialism. . . . As Marxist-Leninists see it, war is the continuation of policy by other means, and every war is inseparable from the political system and the political struggles which give rise to it." It is not necessarily true that revolution must be carried out through world war, but national liberation wars cannot be opposed unless one is against revolution itself. World war can be avoided, not by concessions to the imperialists but by the "struggles of the people in all countries." The Chinese Communists do not believe that national liberation wars will lead to a global conflagration. In any event, wars are inevitable so long as capitalism exists and it is a mistake to be paralyzed by fear of nuclear weapons. Peking claims that nuclear weapons have neither changed world politics nor have they modified communist views about the course of world history. Disarmament cannot be expected so long as capitalism continues; basically, disarmament is a propaganda device without actual meaning. Thus, peaceful coexistence does limit actions of communist foreign policy, especially in the realm of the "oppressed peoples", i.e. the countries of Africa, Asia, and Latin America.

In its reply of July 15, 1963, the Central Committee of the Soviet Communist Party said it "realistically appraises the balance of forces in the world and from this draws the conclusions that though the nature of imperialism has not changed, and the danger of the outbreak of war has not been averted, in modern conditions the forces of peace . . . can, by their joint efforts, avert a new world war." The CPSU also "soberly appraises" the "radical, quantitative change in the means of waging war, and, consequently, its possible aftermaths. The nuclear rocket weapons that were created in the middle of our century changed the old notions about war. These weapons possess an unheard-of devastating force."

The letter then explains that one powerful thermonuclear weapon "surpasses the explosive force of all ammunition used during all previous wars, including World Wars I and II" and that many thousands of such weapons have been accumulated. Communists, the CPSU states, have no right to ignore this danger; telling the people about the consequences of nuclear war cannot have, as the Chinese party claims, a "paralyzing" effect on the masses but on the contrary "will mobilize the will and the energy of the masses to the struggle for peace, against imperialism." When the Chinese say that "on the ruins of destroyed capitalism"—in other words, as a result of unleashing of war—"a bright future will be built", the Soviets, refuting the concept of imperialist "paper tigers," would "like to ask the Chinese comrades—who suggest building a bright future on the ruins of the old world destroyed by a thermonuclear war—if they have consulted the working class of the countries where imperialism dominates . . . If both the exploiters and the exploited are buried under the ruins of the old world, who will build the bright future?"

Differing from Peking, Moscow fears that limited, local wars are dangerous in that they can escalate into general war. In 1960, a general officer of the Soviet army wrote: "It has been proven that under present-day conditions local or limited wars would be nothing but the prelude to a general missile-nuclear war, and one of the forms of unleashing such a war."[26] In the past, he explained, "limited wars were possible under totally different economic, political and strategic conditions."[27] And another

[26] Major General N. Talenskii, "Modern War, Its Character and Consequences," *Mezhdunarodnaia Zhizn'* (International Affairs) No. 10, October, 1960, p. 36.

[27] *Ibid.* Cf. V. D. Sokolovskii, Marshal of the Soviet Union, Soviet Military Strategy, analyzed and annotated by Herbert S. Dinerstein, Leon Gouré and Thomas W. Wolfe, Prentice-Hall, New York, 1963, 290 ff.

officer wrote that "the possibility of an expansion of a small war into a large-scale war is as old as war itself. It has always existed. But in our time this possibility is particularly great . . ."[28] It is for this reason that the Kremlin, while in doctrinal agreement with Peking on the nature of national liberation wars, does not in practice follow the Chinese arguments in favor of such wars, realizing not only the danger of escalation but also the fact that conditions and "correlation of class forces" differ in the various countries to be "liberated" so that a specific, not a general, approach to these problems and timing is needed.

While Soviet statements such as these should be taken with a grain of salt, Moscow's position has indeed undergone considerable doctrinal change since *Pravda,* on March 5, 1955, asserted that nuclear war would lead not to the end of the world but only to the end of capitalism. Only a year later, this illogical thesis was dropped. From then on, the Soviet peace campaign increasingly emphasized the devastating consequences of a nuclear war. The Kremlin, however, did not hesitate to break a gentleman's agreement on a test ban at just about the time Tito's meeting of non-aligned nations took place in Belgrade in 1962. The United States, of course, resumed testing also. Test ban negotiations in Geneva failed until, to the surprise of the world, Khrushchev initiated new negotiations on a partial test ban (permitting only underground testing to continue) which led to the conclusion of such a treaty between the United States, Great Britain and the USSR on August 5, 1963, in Moscow. This treaty was subsequently adhered to by some hundred states but not by Communist China or France.[29]

The treaty may be said to be the first tangible result of a ten-

[28] Colonel I. S. Baz', "Soviet Military Science on the Character of Contemporary War," as quoted by Sokolovskii, *op. cit.* p. 291.

[29] Communist China harshly denounced the agreement and subsequently circulated a proposal for universal disarmament and destruction of all nuclear weapons. North Korea and North Vietnam sided with the Chinese Communists. France did not object to the treaty but continued to pursue President de Gaulle's aim to develop his own *force de frappe,* or nuclear striking force.

year effort to obtain a disarmament agreement. President Eisenhower, in his inaugural address of January 20, 1953, stated this objective for the first time. On June 11, 1954, the United Kingdom and France introduced to the Disarmament Subcommittee of the United Nations a joint memorandum, supported by the United States and Canada, pulling together and refining the several proposals of the Western states and the Soviet Union concerning the prohibition of atomic and hydrogen weapons except in defense against aggression. (The Subcommittee had been established on April 19, 1954; members were the United States, Canada, United Kingdom, France and the USSR.) From then until August, 1963, an almost incessant round of conferences concerning disarmament in general and nuclear disarmament in particular, debated the problem of premises and inspection.[30]

The zigzag of communist strategy and tactics presents a serious dilemma to Western policy officials. On the one hand, communist ideology remains basically militant, especially in Communist China; the doctrinal concept of imperialism as a breeder of wars has not been eliminated from the Marxist-Leninist gospel, not even by Moscow. On the other hand, the nuclear arsenal is a fact of life which makes limited or national liberation wars hazardous ventures. While the partial test ban agreement of August, 1963, might presage further developments of efforts at disarmament, it is too much to expect a meaningful disarmament treaty between the two camps, particularly in the face of Communist Chinese opposition. Following its rejection of the US-UK-USSR agreement, Peking's recommendation of a "complete, total and resolute prohibition and destruction of nuclear weapons," contained in a statement of the Chinese Government of July 31, 1963, and proposing a conference of government heads of all countries of the world (reiterated on October 16, 1964, after the first explosion of a Chinese nuclear device) must be regarded as a move countering the gradualist approach of the Kremlin in the

---

[30] See *A Chronology of the Development of United States Disarmament Policy 1953/62*, Historical Office, Bureau of Public Affairs, Department of State, Washington, D.C.

partial nuclear test ban agreement. Owing to Peking's doctrinal position, it cannot be taken at face value.[31]

In view of the unlikelihood of major hostilities in which the use of nuclear weapons would be a certainty, an entirely unprecedented situation has emerged: Tests of weapons have been replaced by tests of the cold war devices of economic competition, social appeals by the communists to underdeveloped societies, vast political propaganda, and subversive infiltration, especially in the neutralist third world. For this kind of conflict the democracies are ill prepared; democratic processes are awkwardly slow and governmental decisions must be approved by parliaments whose members more often than not are concerned with their constituencies rather than national issues. In the democracies it is only in times of war that establishment of quasi-authoritarian rule is permitted. In dictatorships, quick and flexible concentration on specific targets permits frequent changes of course by a few men at the center of power. While the West has learned—though all too slowly—to cope more efficiently with cold war exigencies, it is still engaged in the race of the turtle against the hare—with the possibility that the proverbial hare will not always make the mistakes that throw the race to the turtle.

Thus, the Western policy maker, in dealing with the problem of war and peace, is compelled to think along both military and non-military lines. He will have to determine—if he can—how much influence the military may be permitted to exert on foreign policy decisions and whether the generals and admirals should be permitted to state conflicting views in public. It is interesting to note that the influence of the military leadership is stronger in the democracies than in communist-ruled states. In various high councils of the United States and its allies, there is joint military and civilian membership. In the Soviet Union (and certainly also in Communist China), the Party Presidium (or Politburo)

---

[31] For the text of this proposal see *Peking Review*, Peking, August 2, 1963, Vol. VI, No. 31, 7 ff.

is the sole dispenser of high policy and the armed forces serve as an arm of the party.[32]

That military leaders are needed for expert advice goes without saying, and it is possible that their considered opinion can strongly influence policy decisions. This is also the case under communism which, after all, is a militant movement and has always endeavored to maintain a very strong military establishment. But, as the decline of Marshal Zhukov of the USSR has shown, political ambitions of military men are not tolerated if they become too pronounced. In the West, cooperation between civilian and military leaders has become increasingly close although it is true that constitutionally civilians supersede the military. Since they serve together in the high councils of most Western states, it is difficult to assess the actual political influence of the military but it cannot be closed off or blocked as easily as in Moscow or Peking. On grounds of national security, cooperation between all branches of defense, including intelligence, propaganda, and the sciences is vital.

After most wars in the United States and Britain as well as in other countries, there has been a tendency to hold the influence of the armed forces to a minimum, although military heroes have frequently risen to postwar political power—notably in recent times, Generals de Gaulle and Eisenhower. Physical and psychological fatigue, accumulated during the strenuous years of emergency, has tended to express itself in opposition to everything military. The popular "bring-the-boys-back-home" sentiment in the United States after V-E Day clearly demonstrated the reaction against the military. But the Stalinist policy of anti-Western aggression in the aftermath of World War II prevented the traditional swing away from military influence, at least so far as governments were concerned. Political tensions between East and West did not subside; on the contrary, they were brought

---

[32]See "Soviet Strengths and Weaknesses" by the writer in *National Security: Political, Military and Economic Strategies in the Decade Ahead*, D. M. Abshire and R. V. Allen, editors, New York: Frederick A. Praeger, 1963, 50 ff.

out into the open. Ideological warfare did not cease but, rather, became virulent. The end of the shooting did not establish a sense of security; indeed, the world has never felt secure since 1945. Consequently, the influence of military leaders upon the formulation of foreign policy remained strong, and the reorganization of governments all over the world, taking account of existing conditions, provided for continuous and close cooperation between foreign policy makers and military strategists.

It is perhaps this fact which led to the use of armed forces to implement certain announced policies by means of armed demonstrations. History is full of examples of this "gunboat diplomacy." However, it has been employed with greater caution since the advent of nuclear weapons. To "show the flag" has at times been helpful to make it clear that a government "means business." Recall the display of U. S. naval might in early 1947 near the Greek port of Piraeos or the display of American ships in the Mediterranean during the Trieste negotiations in the same year. The show of force in the Lebanon in 1958 successfully helped to re-establish that country's political equilibrium, and the naval quarantine around Cuba in 1962, which approached the brink of war with the USSR, led to a withdrawal of Soviet missiles from that island.

Finally, military policy cannot help but be of signal importance in all disarmament negotiations. Vice versa, such treaties as that of Rio de Janeiro in 1947 between the United States and all the nations south of the Rio Grande relative to Western Hemisphere defense and exchange of weapons obviously had diplomatic as well as military significance. More recently, the counsel of scientists has become indispensable as nuclear weapons and rocketry play a decisive part in policy concepts of both East and West.

Whether the influence of military leaders can be kept within bounds by a civilian government will always be crucial to a nation's position in international affairs and to its own internal politics. "A strong statesman . . ." commented one writer as early as 1935, "can probably control a General Staff and keep its offensive spirit within what he decides to be its due bounds. Even the strongest statesman, however, may be overborne by the arguments of the military experts, which naturally he cannot refute on technical grounds. Less strong witted and less assured statesmen . . . are always liable, in times of crisis, to yield, against their better judgment, before the arguments of the General Staff, and to subordinate political to military aims."[33]

In post-nuclear times, one may add, the military must bow to the judgment of the scientists who, as a rule, are civilians and thus inclined to defend the civilian rather than the military point of view. In a sense, this new situation relieves the statesmen of some responsibility and diminishes the influence of the military leaders. Unquestionably, this is a fact not only in the West but also in the East where the scientific academies, like the armed forces, are arms of the party; their judgments on the technological developments which today dominate weaponry and strategy, almost certainly are taken very seriously.

The question of war and peace, as we have seen, involves a number of extremely complex problems on both sides of the Iron Curtain. Neither side trusts the other: They believe they cannot because of inimical positions in their political and social philosophies. There is, at the same time, a realization that war can no longer resolve foreign policy issues. Although it is true that Communist China is in a different category, the probability is that its belligerent attitude cannot be implemented at least until the middle seventies: it simply is not powerful enough, and in modern war manpower alone cannot decide the conflict. By the middle seventies, Peking's leadership probably will have changed and, as its economy slowly improves, its aggressive stance may relax.

Thus, security demands strength on three fronts—the military establishment, national economy, and rapid development of science and technology. These factors must underlie the thinking

[33] R. B. Mowat: *Diplomacy and Peace*, London: Williams & Norgate Ltd., 1935, p. 125.

of foreign policy officials. In all such efforts, the West must compete with the East and it undoubtedly can. There is but one field where the East is stronger and more clever—propaganda.

ADMINISTRATIVE INFLUENCES

Among the factors contributing to foreign policy decisions there are, at least in the non-communist countries, certain intra-governmental influences brought to bear upon the administrators of foreign affairs. The proliferation of departments and agencies which may exert such influence is particularly evident in the United States, although one may presume that in the other Western democracies a similar process has developed as a result of the increasing tendency toward achieving a consensus among responsible government leaders on matters of national security. At least twenty-eight departments, agencies, and bureaus of the U. S. Government have actual responsibilities in foreign affairs.

It is interesting to note that all these bureaus contribute to the training of foreign service officers as do the Bureau of the Census, Civil Service Commission, Federal Reserve Board, General Accounting Office, the Military Assistance Program and the Subversion Activities Control Board. Clearly, there are very few government offices which do not contribute to foreign policy making in one form or another.

A few examples may indicate the scope and type of interest in foreign affairs of various agencies and their cooperation with policy makers. The closeness of military establishments with foreign offices is self-evident. We shall discuss their influence on security policy later on. Similarly, scientific, intelligence, and propaganda agencies are, by the very nature of their responsibilities, integral parts of the policy machine. This is so in the West and in the East.

Less well known, or perhaps less recognized, are the functions of the treasury departments which play a decisive role in com-

U. S. FOREIGN AFFAIRS COMPONENTS

Departments

Department of State
Department of Defense
Department of the Army
Department of the Navy
Department of the Air Force
Bureau of the Budget
The Treasury Department
Department of Agriculture

Department of Justice
Department of the Interior
Department of Commerce
Department of Labor
Department of Health, Education and Welfare
Post Office Department

Agencies

Central Intelligence Agency
Atomic Energy Commission
National Aeronautics and
  Space Administration
Agency for International
  Development
U. S. Information Agency
U.S. Arms Control and Disarmament Agency
Federal Communications
  Commission

National Academy of
  Sciences
National Science Foundation
Peace Corps
Securities and Exchange
  Commission
Export-Import Bank
  of Washington
Federal Aviation Agency
Civil Aeronautics Board

mercial policies, at least in the United States and Great Britain. In the United States the Treasury Department actively participates in international commercial relations. For example, in 1942-43 it devised the program of the International Bank and Monetary Fund which was later accepted as a basis for the establishment of these agencies. It finances wars, controls enemy assets, and administers tariffs, for which reason it is in control of the Coast Guard in peacetime. Its officials sit in a number of specialized United States agencies concerned with foreign affairs wherever financial problems are involved. The Bureau of the Budget, an autonomous agency, must approve all money bills drafted by the departments for presentation to Congress.

In Great Britain, the Exchequer plays an even greater role in the country's over-all policies. Whereas in the United States approval for funds to be allocated comes from the Congress, while the Treasury is merely an executive agency, the British Exchequer must approve all funds to be spent—a condition that makes this ministry one of the most important in the United Kingdom. Also, top-level Exchequer officials exercise control over government business that is not strictly financial, such as the civil service. The nominal head of the Exchequer, the First Lord, is the Prime Minister himself; the actual head, the Second Lord, generally called the Chancellor of the Exchequer, is the finance minister of the nation. Under parliamentary orders, the Exchequer has an imposing list of duties and, because of its semi-independence and because its chancellor is the ranking cabinet member of the United Kingdom, it has often influenced foreign policies pertaining to financial, political and defense matters. For example, the Exchequer, concerned about Britain's post-war economic crisis, was an important factor in the cabinet decision that British occupation forces in Europe and elsewhere be reduced or withdrawn.

Such extraordinary influence on the part of the treasury in international affairs is unusual. A similar influence will not be found, for instance, in the Ministry of Finance or the Ministry of Budget of the French Republic. Even before Charles de Gaulle's administration, the personal initiative of leading men rather than the constitutional position granted to finance officials made them as influential as circumstances permitted. In the Fifth Republic, the standing of these ministries has been further diminished since the President, under the constitution, has virtually an authoritarian power of decision.

In prewar Germany, financial departments were strictly subordinated to political agencies; in the postwar Federal Republic of

Germany, the first years of reconstruction were dominated by decisions of the economic agencies, especially since, during the occupation, political decisions in foreign affairs were made by the occupying powers. Later, when the "economic miracle" of West Germany had made it a prosperous nation, the political power of Konrad Adenauer outweighed that of Ludwig Ehrhard who had contributed much to the speedy recovery of West Germany. Adenauer's retirement in October, 1963, and the succession of Ehrhard may well bring about another increase in the influence of the financial and economic agencies of the Federal Republic.

In the Soviet Union as well as in Communist China and the other countries of the socialist camp, the role of money differs considerably from the non-Marxist economies. Not often does the Marxian maxim that economics determines policy prevail; the opposite is the case. The policies formulated and ordained by the Party Presidium are made on the basis of ideological, political, military, social, and economic factors, with the latter rarely being given priority. Moreover, Soviet domestic currency is not on the international money market and its course of exchange is arbitrary. If the Soviet government wants to purchase abroad, it pays in foreign exchange or, in the case of buying larger quantities such as Canadian wheat, it sells gold to finance the purchase. It is questionable whether Soviet foreign policy is affected by monetary considerations; priorities are established to serve the purposes of policy, and capital investment is then channeled into those sectors of the economy which have been assigned such priorities.

How little the Peking regime's policies are influenced by economic necessities, even though Chinese economy is in serious trouble and will continue to be for a long time to come, is a matter of record. The ideological fanaticism released by Mao Tsetung and his lieutenants is directed not only against the hated imperialists but even against the Soviets who could do much to alleviate China's economic difficulties.

The commerce departments, to mention another example,

play a different, although important, role in the formulation of foreign policy. Some of their functions have in fact been taken over by the foreign offices, all of which have economic bureaus concerned with commercial policies. This is the case in the U. S. Department of State; the importance attached to commercial policy is demonstrated by the fact that the third highest officer in the State Department's hierarchy is the Under Secretary for Economic Affairs. On the other hand, the role of the U. S. Department of Commerce is mainly advisory. Its commercial agents or attachés are under the wing of the State Department and its offices concerned with international trade are responsible for research and analysis rather than for policy.

In the United Kingdom, since the abolition of the Department of Overseas Trade in the course of the 1944 reforms, overseas commercial officers (in countries other than colonies and the Commonwealth, where they come under the Board of Trade) are members of the Foreign Service. Commercial policy abroad is formulated by the Cabinet Committee system, the main departments being the Foreign Office, the Board of Trade and the Treasury. The Ministry of Power and the Ministry of Agriculture, Fisheries and Food also make important contributions to foreign policy.

The position of the Ministries of Commerce in France and Germany resembles that of the U. S. Department of Commerce. In the USSR, however, the situation is quite different. The Soviet Ministry of Foreign Affairs is less concerned with foreign economic relations than any other such agency. The Ministry of Foreign Trade is in charge. This ministry supervises the state trading monopolies and is an executive organ of the policies laid down by the CPSU. The principles of Soviet administration prevent the ministry from formulating commercial policy; it merely recommends methods. But in Soviet eyes, the existence of this Ministry is but a temporary expedient. Trade between state monopolies and private enterprise is awkward for both parties, at best; the Kremlin would prefer to deal only with other state monopolies and then develop barter trade, which it is now developing with neighboring countries in central and southeastern Europe. Commercial as well as political policies are decided by the Presidium, and the Ministry of Foreign Trade plays the role of an executive organ as does the Foreign Ministry. The most important organ in the sphere of economy is the Supreme Council of National Economy in which the State Planning Commission (Gosplan) is situated. Its so-called State Committees, formerly ministries, are responsible for the major economic tasks of industry. There is little doubt that this Council's concerns are influenced by world conditions.

The contributions of the ministries of the interior differ with the respective governmental organizations. In the United States, the Department of the Interior happens to be in the business of oil administration. Oil is an explosive issue in international politics. The State Department, trying to cope with the stubborn problems of oil, has set up a specialized bureau to deal with this matter. Oil, wherever it is found, has universal implications and thus the Secretary of the Interior, who controls the Petroleum Administrator's Office, cannot help invading the scene of foreign affairs. Although the particular tasks of the Department of the Interior pertain to the improvement of internal productivity rather than to political matters, it contributes, in this respect, at least indirectly to America's position in the world. For example, its reclamation and conservation projects may considerably affect the thinking of policy makers and strategists.

In contrast, the British Home Office's duties are much narrower. It is exclusively concerned with domestic administrative matters such as internal safety, supervision of elections, or processing petitions to the Crown by British subjects and naturalizing aliens. In the United States many of these tasks are carried out by the Department of Justice. In a number of other countries, the departments of the interior are in charge of the police and we know from history that the use of police for political purposes created conditions which had strong repercussions in foreign relations. In the USSR, there is no longer an All-Union Interior Ministry as such but rather security agencies which have no influence on or connection with foreign policy making. Ministries of home affairs, however, have been established in the constituent union republics, which, as we recall, have their own "state" governments. These agencies have no connection with foreign policy issues.

In the democratic states, the Labor Departments have played an increasingly important role in policy making. Being concerned with Labor's position in a changing world, union representatives participate in international attempts to improve Labor's condition and influence wherever trade unions have not been perverted into mere state organizations by ruling communist regimes; they have no genuine standing and rights for bargaining or strike. The U. S. Department of Labor selects the United States delegates to the International Labor Organization (ILO) and presumably most other non-totalitarian labor ministries select their own delegates in a similar fashion. In the Soviet Union and Communist China there are no labor departments in the Western sense, since there is no problem of management-labor relations in these countries. The trade union organizations handle whatever questions arise regarding working and living conditions; they also function as indoctrination agencies promoting the party line.

Labor is, of course, a vital element of national strength in any country. Its position toward the government, its morale, its standard of living, and its view toward the prevailing philosophy, democratic or otherwise, is a matter of prime concern to policy makers; the Labor Departments or trade unions for that reason perform essential work for the men concerned with international affairs.

Similarly, the ministries of agriculture play their roll in foreign policy. Being responsible for their countries' food situation, their counsel is indispensable for policy and strategy. Agricultural attachés, especially those assigned to lesser developed countries, have become an institution since World War II. Under the supervision of the embassies, American agricultural attachés collect information on the world's agriculture, exchange new inventions, counsel where counsel is sought and, in the United States, protect agriculture from foreign animal and plant diseases. The British Ministry of Agriculture, Fisheries and Food and the French Ministry of Agriculture perform about the same duties for their countries, as their counterparts in other states.

In addition, two specifically British departments still exert some influence on the Foreign policy makers—the Colonial Office and the Office of Commonwealth Relations.

The Colonial Office, which is in charge of the Crown colonies, probably has had to abdicate what little influence it had on foreign policies as more and more territories became independent. There are some critical areas, such as Hong Kong, where international complications will have to be handled by both the Foreign Office and the Ministry of Defence. Moreover, the Colonial Office faces increasingly important problems in Africa, where national independence movements have made considerable headway. As a result, British colonial administrators will have to face unrest for some time to come. There is some degree of collaboration between the Colonial Office and the Office of Commonwealth and the Office of Commonwealth Relations.[34]

Of far more importance is the Office of Commonwealth Relations, which is "in constant touch with the dominion governments, usually through their ministers of external affairs."[35] But the Commonwealth is not a tightly forged bloc of dominions; each of the members has its own foreign policy although some degree of consultation is maintained between the dominion capitals and London. The Prime Ministers of the dominions participate in full-dress conferences in London. Yet "there is no such thing as a Commonwealth foreign policy."[36] However, a constant exchange of views with the Foreign Office, in conjuction with the Commonwealth Relations Office, keeps the dominion governments informed of the British position in international relations. In matters of Commonwealth defense and strategy, a

---

[34] Stout, *op. cit.* p. 406.
[35] *Ibid.* p. 375.
[36] *Ibid.* p. 392.

considerable degree of close cooperation with London presumably takes place and the dominions may contribute—as they have in the past—men, money and material to the common cause. Nevertheless, stresses and strains within the Commonwealth remain, and its future development will depend chiefly upon the fortunes of the motherland, the British Isles.

The departments of justice contribute their part to foreign affairs if they are empowered, as in the United States, to fight international cartels or to work on such cases of international law as the legal advisers of the foreign offices may not handle. In the United States, the Federal Bureau of Investigation, a component of the Department of Justice, is deeply involved in foreign affairs by fighting attempts at subversion, sabotage or espionage by foreign agents in U. S. territory. Indeed, such issues can create delicate situations which must be handled in cooperation between the Department of Justice and State. The USSR has no all-Union Ministry of Justice, seemingly leaving it to the republics to supervise their legal organization. However, the law is laid down by the Presidium, i.e. it must be approved by this supreme body. Questions of international law are dealt with by the Soviet Foreign Office (Minindel) so long as they do not raise important political questions which, again, must be decided by the Presidium.

Among the many other agencies which, in one way or another, may have influence on or contribute to the formulation of foreign policy are the technical, transportation, and communication ministries, as well as the mails. Their contributions are mainly technical. However, the impact on foreign policy of the work of those organs which are charged with policy formulation concerning atomic energy or space technology is obviously very great. These new developments have changed the entire picture of international relations and while, strictly speaking, such information is scientific by nature, the implications of nuclear development and the conquest of space (emphasizing rocketry) are vital international issues.

There are also instances of indirect contribution, such as educational agencies, which help shape the minds of new generations, condition them to certain attitudes and established tradition or break them away from tradition and prepare them ideologically and technologically for an age of revolution. There is a sharp contrast between Western principles of liberal education and communist training which seeks to create a new communist man.

3. Intelligence, the Crux of Foreign Policy Making

CONCEPT AND CONTENTS

WE HAVE DISCUSSED THE BASIC, universal factors which characterize international relations and lead to certain *prima facie* concepts of foreign policy. Without these underlying factors, policy is like a building without foundation. But once the foundation is laid and is strengthened enough to support a policy, it must be broadened and deepened by current information and the long-range forecasts which we call intelligence. The late Gen. William J. Donovan, Chief of America's wartime intelligence organization, the Office of Strategic Services, once wrote that "no foreign policy can ever be stronger than the information on which it is based."[1] Information is the fuel for the machinery of foreign affairs. Without it, the machinery will slow down or idle.

Intelligence provides fuel for the policy machine. But it must not be confused with policy. Necessarily linked together, intelligence and policy nevertheless differ in form and content. Undeniably, intelligence may strongly influence policy evolution, formulation, and decision, if the men charged with the conduct of foreign affairs read and digest intelligence reports. Such influence would seem to be normal since policy is the result not only of known quantities but of information on new developments, collected and analyzed by intelligence agents and analysts. Intel-

[1] "Intelligence: Key to Defense," *Life*, September 30, 1946, 108 ff.

ligence, obviously, must have some influence on foreign policy makers or it would have little reason for existing.

To be sure, it has happened and may happen again that intelligence personnel force the hands of policy makers at home and diplomats abroad. Intelligence operations could interfere in the affairs of a foreign country, causing a shift of political forces that would necessitate a change of policy. Such events do not often occur, however. They need never occur if sufficient coordination between intelligence and policy work prevails. If intelligence were permitted statutorily to invade the policy field, the result would be confusion and a struggle for dominant influence. For these reasons the laws of most non-totalitarian countries provide for strict organizational separation between intelligence and policy. Under communism, such distinction may exist on paper but not in fact: Both agencies are subject to strict party discipline and are therefore virtually interchangeable.

Intelligence is all-encompassing. It covers manifestations and endeavors of every nation regardless of whether it is friendly or hostile. Since the vital statistics of nations are insufficient for the creation of correct policies, they must be made productive through constant renewal of information which indicates the character and direction of their development. Such information is of infinite variety, covering all possible emanations of national and international life. It may pertain to events, attitudes, conditions, factual matters and intangibles. It has practically no limitation, either quantitatively or qualitatively. The more intelligence is available, the better for the education of intelligence officers, the clarity of perception of policy makers and, thus, for the determination of crucial policies.

In general, intelligence work has three major aspects:
1. to collect all intelligence pertinent to international relations, foreign policy, and national security, wherever it may be found;
2. to analyze, evaluate and relate the available material to policy problems, objectively and impartially;
3. to disseminate the processed information quickly to the responsible officials.

The process of dissemination is a purely technical one; we need not concern ourselves with it in the context of these observations.

The edifice of intelligence is constructed with inescapable logic. The foundation, basic intelligence, is concerned with a study of those fundamentals which have been called contributing factors to policy making. It aims at producing textbook-like documentation and surveys concerning the political, economic, social and cultural history of a target area. Basic intelligence sets the scene of a country, provides the intelligence analyst with the prerequisite for his task, and gives him a comparative framework. It must be accurate and factual; it must contain facts and figures untainted by sympathy or antipathy. Since it comprises the contemporary scene, it must constantly be revised and updated. Repeated study of these intelligence texts is necessary even for those well acquainted with the country of the specialization.

The middle layers are concerned with the bread-and-butter work of intelligence: factual reporting, mainly current, and an interpretation of the facts in the political, social, scientific and cultural fields. It is the analyst who derives information from the unfinished, "raw" intelligence and who, on the basis of his knowledge and experience, interprets the meaning of reports from overt and covert sources. It is the analyst and his colleagues who solve the jigsaw puzzle by carefully fitting together the fragments of information to form a clear picture.

The "roof" of the intelligence edifice is its crowning achievement: high-level synthesis and deduction, leading to estimates called strategic intelligence. These refined products of the information machinery are the particular concern of the policy makers and next to espionage have become the primary object of interest to foreign policy professionals and amateurs.[2] What makes strategic intelligence so particularly important is the coordination process between the departments in charge of intel-

[2] Among the recent publications on this problem are, aside from many articles, the following books: Sherman Kent, *Strategic Intelligence*, Princeton, 1951; W. Platt, *Strategic Intelligence Production*, New York, 1957; R. Hilsman, *Strategic Intelligence and National Decisions*, Glencoe, Ill., 1956; H. H. Ransom, *Central Intelligence and National Security*, Cambridge, Mass., 1958; and A. W. Dulles, *The Craft of Intelligence*, Harper & Row, New York, 1963.

ligence, foreign affairs and defense, as well as other agencies whose responsibilities are pertinent.

The raw material of intelligence is obtained from overt and covert sources. It is important to realize that the overwhelming percentage of information is derived from overt sources. Intelligence professionals estimate that only about 10 per cent of the entire take comes from clandestine activities and agree that even this limitation does not guarantee its value. In other words, intelligence is both a science and an art—a science because investigation and analysis is as painstaking as research in chemistry or physics; an art because intelligence analysts and estimators need intuition and vision to interpret or forecast events.

First among sources of overt intelligence are the diplomatic staffs of the embassies, legations, and other missions. Assigned to these missions are attachés in specialized fields such as agriculture, commerce, labor, science, culture, and military affairs (Army, Navy and Air Force). In some of these fields, a give-and-take is intended, that is, the attachés give out and receive information. As for the military attachés, it is a well known and accepted international custom to permit them a certain degree of observation. This is reciprocal and the statement that "military, naval and air attachés are simply official spies" is putting the matter crudely because these "spies" have come to be universally recognized and are protected by international law.[3] Every government knows well that other governments wish to gather as much intelligence as possible. The only question is to what lengths their agents may go to obtain foreign state secrets, and the eternal problem remains of when a diplomat transgresses the bounds of hospitality, taking undue advantage of his immunity.[4]

[3] R. Boucard, *The Secret Service of Europe*, London: Stanley Paul & Co. Ltd., 1940, p. 14.

[4] A similar description of the intelligence collection process was distorted by a Soviet writer in the following way: "Kurt London declares in his book *How Foreign Policy is Made* that the apparatus for foreign political intelligence is the most important part of the whole government machine; it formulates the foreign policy of the USA and the diplomat-spy is a customary phenomenon." E. P. Dimitriev in *Sovietskoe Gosudarstvo i Pravo* (Soviet State and Law), No. 4, Moscow, 1951.

Since much of the factual information on a target area can be obtained through radio broadcast monitoring, newspapers, periodicals, books and other printed publications, the task of diplomats and specialized attachés is one of reporting first-hand impressions, experiences, incidents and, most of all, interpretation. Indeed, almost all reporting from the missions to their headquarters may be called intelligence; an ambassador talking to the foreign minister of his host country and sending a dispatch containing the details and interpretative data of the discussion is as much grist for the intelligence mill as the cable of a military attaché concerning new weapons sighted during a parade. Exchanges of ideas with foreign officials or interviews with private individuals frequently offer significant keys to the understanding of the opponent's point of view.

Overt information of prime importance is gained from the study of mass communications media. Radio, television and picture material (moving and still), book publishing, and the press are controlled or semi-controlled in large parts of the world. Yet, although censorship is active even in less controlled countries, enough material can be found in these media to indicate trends or point to specific attitudes and actions. Nowhere else can so much official material be detected than in broadcasts and "inspired" editorials or articles from behind the Iron and Bamboo Curtains. Periodicals close to party or governmental circles publish papers that may provide striking insight and elucidate policies or forecast measures of international significance. Photographic materials, including the high-altitude reconnaissance photos taken by U-2 planes of the United States, may offer clues not to be found in printed or broadcast statements. Communications media also transmit the speeches of leaders or high party and government officials which must be studied closely for indications of intentions. Altogether, the flood of obtainable overt intelligence is so great that to keep up with it is an increasing challenge.

The much smaller volume of covert intelligence is still considerable. Such material is much more difficult to evaluate than overt information. It is also more risky and expensive to obtain. "Clandestine intelligence collection is chiefly a matter of circumventing obstacles in order to reach an objective."[5] This is an elegant though correct description of what is generally called espionage—an aspect of intelligence that has caught the fancy of fiction writers for many years. Yet adventure, sex, high and low living, or scientific exploits, are extremely rare in the life of spies and, in this age of electronics, on their way out. In general, the life of spies is humdrum existence, led in constant fear of discovery and paid with penurious salaries.[6]

Nevertheless, clandestine services are here to stay. In some respects, the political divisions of the twentieth century have spurred efforts for information as well as for subversion. The lengths to which the Soviet Union goes to infiltrate the West, particularly the United States, is shown in reports about schools for spies in the USSR where highly selected and trained men and women are isolated from the rest of the country and live under the simulated conditions of the country in which they specialize. Foreign characterizations are practiced for several years, after a careful pre-training in the Marx-Engels and Lenin Technical Schools. Only candidates who pass rigorous examinations in these institutions are admitted to the area spy schools where they learn all the details of the daily lives and customs of the countries to which they will be assigned. Altogether this course lasts about eleven years. Among the graduates were such accomplished agents as "Lonsdale" in England and Colonel "Abel" in the United States. [7]

Clandestine activities require a large investment without guarantee of return. All too often the information obtained from agents is of minor importance; it may even be nothing but con-

---

[5] Allen Dulles, *The Craft of Intelligence,* New York: Harper & Row, 1963, p. 58.

[6] One of the best and most authentic examples of a secret agent's work and life is A. Foote's *Handbook for Spies,* Garden City, New York: Doubleday and Co., 1949.

[7] J. Bernard Hutton, *School for Spies: The ABC of How Russia's Secret Service Operates,* New York: Coward-McCann, 1962.

jecture, personal ax-grinding or so-called "paper mill" reports in which already known facts are dressed up as original information. Most trained intelligence analysts should detect such meaningless or confusing agent reports in time to prevent their dissemination. There is no doubt that espionage history can single out extraordinary achievements. The penetration of the Nazi general staff by the agent "Lucy" undoubtedly helped the Soviet leaders make the right decisions. Klaus Fuchs was one of the master spies who succeeded in stealing secrets of nuclear energy for Moscow, thereby curtailing the American monopoly of the atom bomb. However, such achievements are rare indeed. The bulk of agent reporting is routine; its importance lies in chance discoveries and the corroboration of analyses derived from overt intelligence.

Although public fascination with espionage and secret services is focused on clandestine intelligence, it must be emphasized that, in general, information derived from overt sources is far more important than is usually conceded. The value of this information, of course, depends greatly on concise and clear-headed analysis. Intelligence, whether obtained overtly, or *sub rosa*, remains "raw" until it is processed into a readily understandable piece of prose carefully analyzed and wisely interpreted. This is called "finished intelligence" and must be disseminated to those who "need to know." If the recipients do not study such documents or refuse to accept their findings (without good reason), or if they receive them too late, the entire laborious and costly process is wasted.

The processing of raw information into finished intelligence is as important as the information itself. It is done both at home and abroad by several agencies, which leads to some duplication. This, however, must not be regarded as waste. Duplication of intelligence production makes corroborative sense, provided it is finally computed into one single product. Processing falls into two subsequent stages. The first seeks to strip informational material of unnecessary or beclouding verbiage, leaving the essentials in clear and concise language. The second is an analysis of the information and, possibly, an evaluation of its source. "Processing raw intelligence takes the form of condensation, analysis, evaluation, interpretation and attempts to put the findings in their proper context—that is to say, relating them to pertinent past and present events within the framework of existing conditions. Condensation serves for quick preliminary messages, often followed by more extensive reports. Analysis dissects the facts and aspects contained in the information and investigates their relative significance. Interpretation explains and clarifies them in terms of prevailing policy. Evaluation deduces rather than explains; it searches for the reason behind the facts and events and judges them in the context of over-all conditions, including an appraisal of the source from which the raw intelligence has been secured."[8]

An intelligence paper prepared by an analyst does not differ greatly from an embassy dispatch, insofar as its general organization is concerned. But, since it is written in headquarters from a bird's eye view, the analyst's paper usually has a less localized, more detached approach, taking into account conditions beyond an embassy's responsibility. It thus presents a more consolidated form of narrative and analysis, horizontal rather than vertical. It is, at least partially, based upon not one but many dispatches, originating in various countries. Also, the availability of experts and specialists at home makes for a better coordinated paper, benefiting as it does from advice impossible to obtain abroad. It is a more thoroughly processed document. Similar considerations apply to the reports of the specialized attachés. They cover only certain delineated elements of intelligence and must be related to other available information. The drafters of strategic intelligence in particular must put the entire crop of material in a context which permits them to sum it up for estimation—provided they are given time to read and digest.

What makes strategic intelligence so difficult to produce is, first of all, that it should be written by men who possess scholarly

[8] London, *op. cit.*, p. 241.

knowledge, political acumen, experience in world affairs, and a good deal of unbiased wisdom; second, that the process of coordination and integration of views prevalent in the various government agencies involved in strategic intelligence must not result in watered-down compromises. To complete the process this supposedly finest derivative of the intelligence process must be studied in earnest by the policy makers for whom it is created.

CENTRAL INTELLIGENCE

Strategic or security intelligence is a relatively new development and the direct result of experiences in World War II. It must be remembered that intelligence, such as existed before 1939, was departmental. In most countries, foreign offices and the armed services had their own informational services which were primarily related to the needs and objectives peculiar to individual agencies. There was, however, neither continuity of personnel nor the genuine expertise which can be expected only from professionals who for years have specialized in the various aspects of intelligence collection and production. The personnel in military intelligence offices were—and are—rotated constantly; in the foreign offices, continuity was broken wherever intelligence officers were integrated into the career diplomatic staff. Foreign service officers apparently felt, like military officers, that intelligence work hindered rather than helped their careers and were eager to transfer to new, more promising posts. Furthermore, funds for intelligence offices were sometimes difficult to obtain. In the United States, the establishment of the Central Intelligence Agency (CIA) in 1947 under the National Security Act guaranteed a continuity which formerly did not exist. If this were not so, if CIA's role were limited only to coordinating strategic intelligence, the philosophy which prompted President Truman and his advisers to present the National Security Act to Congress would be lost: Strategic intelligence cannot be created in an ivory tower. The men who produce it must have all available information and receive it promptly; they must be in a position to request interpretive staff work in the strategic vein. Since it is an accepted axiom in American government that no agency can give orders to another, and since departmental intelligence is deliberately not strategic, it is up to CIA to produce what it needs and cannot obtain from other departments. The differences between departmental and national security (strategic) intelligence are clearly defined: The former deals with specialized aspects of intelligence; the latter encompasses and coordinates the broad over-all aspects of world politics based upon the sum total of specialized information.

It is salutary to remember President Truman's account of the status of American intelligence since the beginning of World War II. As the highest ranking policy maker in need of strategic intelligence, he eloquently explained the intolerable situation that faced the chief executive prior to 1946 when information had to be gathered from various bureaus:

> The scattered method of getting information for the various departments of the government first struck me as being badly organized when I was in the Senate. . . I have often thought that if there had been something like coordination of information in the government, it would have been more difficult, if not impossible, for the Japanese to succeed in the sneak attack at Pearl Harbor . . . In other words, there had never been much attention paid to any centralized intelligence organization in our government . . . The war taught us this lesson—that we had to collect intelligence in a manner that would make the information available where it was needed and when it was wanted, in an intelligent and understandable form. . . On becoming President, I found that the needed intelligence information was not coordinated at any one place. . . [9]

In the National Security Act of 1947 which the Congress passed with two subsequent amendments (1949 and 1956) four measures were codified: the unification of the armed forces, the creation of a National Security Resources Board (which in 1953 became the Office of Defense Mobilization), the National Secur-

---

[9] Harry S. Truman, *Memoirs,* Vol. II, Garden City, N.Y.: Doubleday and Co., 1956, p. 56.

ity Council (NSC) and the Central Intelligence Agency (CIA).[10] Section 102, (2) (d) of the law states that for the purpose of coordinating the intelligence activities in the several Government departments and agencies in the interest of national security, it shall be the duty of the Agency, under the direction of the National Security Council:

(1) to advise the National Security Council in matters concerning such intelligence activities of the Government departments and agencies as relate to national security;

(2) to make recommendations to the National Security Council for the coordination of such intelligence activities of the departments and agencies as relate to national security;

(3) to correlate and evaluate intelligence relating to national security, and provide for the appropriate dissemination of such intelligence within the Government using where appropriate, existing agency facilities: *Provided,* That the Agency shall have no police, subpoena, law-enforcement powers, or internal security functions; *Provided further,* That the departments and other agencies of the Government shall continue to collect, evaluate, correlate, and disseminate departmental intelligence: *And provided further,* That the Director of Central Intelligence shall be responsible for protecting intelligence sources and methods from unauthorized disclosure;

(4) to perform, for the benefit of the existing intelligence agencies, such additional services of common concern as the National Security Council determines can be more efficiently accomplished centrally;

(5) to perform such other functions and duties related to intelligence affecting national security as the National Security Council may from time to time direct.

What has happened since the end of the Eisenhower era is the relative eclipse of the NSC which has lost its former luster and does not seem to be used by the President as a major advisory body. Consequently, the CIA advises the President directly since he and the men responsible for national policy and military strategy meet outside the NSC's organization. Furthermore, the

[10] *The National Security Act of 1947,* as amended in 1949 and 1956, Washington, D.C.: U.S. Government Printing Office, 1957.

departmental intelligence organizations (Army, Navy, Air Force) have been combined since 1961 into a Defense Intelligence Agency (DIA), thereby shrinking the number of intelligence bureaus which are supposed to continue under paragraph (3) of the law (see above). But CIA has not otherwise lessened the importance of the intelligence bureaus of the State Department, the United States Information Agency or DIA. Departmental intelligence primarily serves the specific interests of its own agency. However, all these agencies are impeded by insufficient funds and the lack of professional continuity. There is constant rotation in DIA; assignment of career foreign service officers to State and USIA functions prevents the development of long-range professional experience, a fact that is even more evident in the military. In that respect, CIA is much better off. It realized from the outset that the development of expertise over the years demands the establishment of a dedicated career service. For intelligence, whether analytical or operational, is a science which must be studied and practiced for many years before its principles and methods of work can be fully absorbed. Moreover, a special professional attitude develops which distinguishes intelligence officers from any other government service.

From the point of view of the policy maker, the first sentence of paragraph (3) of the law (as quoted above) is of crucial importance. It is concerned with the correlation and evaluation of security intelligence. Although CIA has never become as "central" as the drafters of the National Security Act perhaps desired, it fulfills the vital function of drawing together, from all other sources of information, intelligence which, when correlated and analyzed, creates a pool of facts from which the policy makers can obtain the information they need. However, in order to eliminate all that is not pertinent, two different types of actions are taken: First, daily reports of the most essential items are edited for time-saving perusal by the top government officials, including the President himself; second, on the basis of existing material, intelligence estimates are written which seek to evaluate specific situations and present deductive forecasts of possible development. These estimates constitute strategic intelligence and although they are written in CIA's Office of National Estimates, their final shape is strongly affected by the process of coordination through which the paper has to go. The State Department, the armed forces and other interested departments and agencies have the right to suggest corrections or to dissent.

In theory, this is an ingenious device for cooperative action. In practice, the results are often disappointing. It is true that any important intelligence document should be written by a team of experts. Even the ablest analyst is bound to forget or disregard some aspects of a problem to be considered. The complexities of twentieth-century world politics are too many and too deep for one man to pronounce judgment. Committee work, therefore, is imperative. So long as a committee consists of members belonging to one agency, it is likely to produce a document of consensus without too many difficulties. There is a certain similarity in approach so that disagreement can be ironed out in most instances. Once other agencies become participants, the situation changes since the objectives of different agencies are often at variance. This places many obstacles in the way of a coordinated strategic intelligence estimate. As a result, two developments are possible: The original version of the document is watered down or exceptions are taken in footnotes. This automatically diminishes the value for policy makers who want their briefing "straight." When they find generalizations and vagueness, couched in professional terminology, or when they are confronted with footnotes objecting to the text, they must become confused or annoyed; they will put the paper aside and proceed without strategic intelligence, which may have serious consequences.

It is hard to see how these problems can be avoided in a domestic organization. But a solution has not yet been found and may not be possible at all. Meanwhile the coordination process must proceed as must work on strategic intelligence which is essential for national security. The National Security Act sought centralization of the armed forces as well as that of security information. Therefore CIA has been made the guardian of national intelligence production and must be expected to provide facilities which do not exist elsewhere. It would seem that, owing to its legal responsibilities, CIA should hear the advice of the coordinating agencies but present strategic intelligence as its own product.

DEPARTMENTAL INTELLIGENCE

The State Department's Bureau of Intelligence and Research (INR) is a good example of a departmental intelligence unit. It is relatively new, having been established, not without the misgivings of old-fashioned diplomats, after the demise of the wartime Office of Strategic Services (OSS). As the Office of Intelligence Research (OIR), comprising five geographic divisions, it was first connected with the Office of Intelligence Collection and Dissemination, which has four functional divisions. Renamed INR in 1959, it now consists of eight divisions, six geographic and two functional. The former are the Offices of Research and Analysis for Africa, the American Republics, the Far East, Western Europe, the Near East and South Asia, and the Soviet Bloc. (It is interesting to note that the first attempt to coordinate work on the entire Sino-Soviet orbit was abandoned, presumably when the Sino-Soviet dispute became so acrimonious as to render obsolete the word "bloc," which now refers only to the USSR and the Eastern European socialist states.) Of the functional offices, one deals with the very important problems of intelligence indications (for example, indications of intended communist aggression), the other with economic, scientific, and geographic questions.

The Congress has never allocated sufficient funds for this organization which, consequently, has remained somewhat undernourished. Also, despite the bureau's name, research in depth is rarely possible—primarily because the continuity of personnel is all too often interrupted and second, because the bureaus are kept too busy with current affairs to undertake prolonged research. Furthermore, the exigencies of civil service rules about "production" make it difficult for the personnel of INR to do any long and hard thinking. By "production" is meant the tangible evidence of work accomplished, measured in terms of written papers. Indeed, one of the former heads of INR insisted upon grading the efficiency of his staff by measuring the volume per day of written pages. This kind of paper mill seriously weakens an intelligence research organization, which cannot be conducted as though it were a commercial enterprise based on volume of production.

In line with the frankness with which American publications, official and otherwise, have described U.S. intelligence activities, the State Department has published an unclassified chart of its organization. The armed forces, in contrast, are more reluctant and there is no such chart on DIA. However, wherever Western military officers established intelligence bureaus, the question must arise as to what extent these offices are permitted to take up political, economic and social issues instead of confining themselves to such purely military matters as the "order of battle" of potentially hostile states. It is a question whether military intelligence can be strictly separated from politico-economic considerations. Probably not entirely. Since the communist countries constitute the major threat to U.S. and Western national security, not only military hardware is a target for information but also, in the estimation of further developments, the political and economic potentials must be taken into account. This means political and economic intelligence work for such organizations as DIA and, therefore, duplication of many functions. For once non-military analyses are undertaken, there is no opportunity to develop a dividing line. Thus we see why duplication is hard to avoid.

Is this as bad as some taxpayers claim? The answer is no. Intelligence is one of the costliest of governmental undertakings; it cannot be otherwise if incontestable results are to be forthcoming. Duplication has its merits; it really means teamwork of organizations. To find the truth, fact-finding is one process and corroboration another. If an analyst or estimator wants to verify his interpretations, the different viewpoints of duplicating departments may well give him as valuable a clue as the best information that clandestine intelligence has to offer.

WEST EUROPEAN INTELLIGENCE ORGANIZATION

Outside the United States, where public curiosity is far stronger than the "need to know," information on intelligence is much rarer. These European countries were involved in such work long before the United States launched it seriously. Although intelligence agents were used by George Washington during the Revolutionary War with great success, the concept of organizing intelligence in all its ramifications did not mature until World War II.

One distinctly different aspect of these European bureaus is that they do not have to beg for money from their parliaments. Therefore they have been able to maintain continuity in the development of their work. In Great Britain, the counterpart of the State Department's INR was formerly the Library, which processed political intelligence. In 1953, two of the most important British intelligence units, the Political Intelligence Department of the Foreign Office and the Press Section of the Royal Institute of International Affairs, were amalgamated and became the Research Department of the Foreign Office. Once organized, this Department coordinated its work with the Library, functionally and physically. Set up along geographical lines, its foremost task is the study of historical backgrounds of current foreign policy problems for the use of the political departments.

In addition to this Department and the various specialized intelligence bureaus, including the military, Britain also has a small intelligence coordination organization, centralized intelligence, so-to-speak, called the Joint Intelligence Committee (JIC) which, however, is attached to the Ministry of Defense.[11] Roughly, its functions approximate those of the United States Intelligence Board (USIB), but its staff is much smaller than that of the USIB and must cull its information from all available intelligence sources of the British government. Coordinated strategic intelligence originates primarily with the JIC, which is charged with providing the policy-making bureaus and the Cabinet with intelligence estimates.

In postwar West Germany, similar efforts at coordinated intelligence have been under way for some time. The German publication *Der Spiegel*, not known for discretion, published a frank, but slanted account of what is purported to be the present German intelligence service.[12] The article was primarily dedicated to clandestine operations of General Gehlen's organization but also noted that the "broad picture of the economic, military, and political situation of the USSR and its changes are of the greatest importance. Detailed news is of interest only when it contributes to the clarification of larger issues." This broad picture "generally is easier to see through intensive comparison of publications, statistics, geographic and archivistic material, diplomatic reports, and official sourcebooks than through individual agent communications." This is why "an estimated 400 specialists . . . are working on scientific analyses" and why the original hard core of officers constituting the Gehlen organization as it was taken over by U.S. forces has been joined by specialists in the political, economic, technological fields and the natural sciences.[13] It is significant to note that in the course of the development of the Gehlen organization occasional hints in press and radio seem to indicate that the government of the Federal Republic of Ger-

[11] E. J. Kingston McCloughry, *Global Strategy*, New York: Frederick A. Praeger, 1957, p. 106.

Cf. also L. Farago, *War of Wits*, New York: Funk & Wagnalls, 1954, p. 43 and London, *op. cit.* 246, ff.

[12] "Des Kanzler's Lieber General" (The Chancellor's Dear General), Hamburg: *Der Spiegel*, September 22, 1954.

[13] *Ibid.* p. 22. Translation by the writer.

many has taken the experience of the American strategic intelligence to heart and probably has developed similar procedures in its own central intelligence organization. (Similar intentions have been broadcast by the Japanese Government.)

France does not seem to have followed the concept of centralized intelligence, although matters of national defense now are coordinated in the Defense Committee (see below, p. 182). It may be assumed that its intelligence services are scattered throughout the Ministry of Foreign Affairs, probably attached to the geographic divisions. We do know that such outside institutions as the *Ecole Libre des Sciences Politiques,* the *Ecole Prâtique des Hautes Etudes* and the University of Paris (Sorbonne) are being utilized. However, these institutions suffer from either lack of funds or an antiquated system of inquiry. The University, especially, is far more interested in times long past by than in contemporary affairs; as a result, France lacks experts in fields of such crucial impact as the Soviet and Chinese areas.

One might add that the popular fame of both the British and French intelligence services has little to do with their research and analysis aspects but derives from their activities in espionage and counter-espionage. In Britain, Military Intelligence (MI) is responsible for this work and its various bureaus, especially MI 5 and MI 6, guide it with the help of civilian experts. In France, the famed Deuxième Bureau was the protagonist of many a spy thriller which has made it almost as famous as Scotland Yard.

The question may be asked whether the NATO organization might not be a center for coordinating intra-national intelligence. If such provisions exist, they have not been made public. One may speculate that the governments participating in NATO necessarily contribute the gist of their findings to its leading military and political officers, but that this intelligence does not include matters which they justifiably wish to keep to themselves. NATO as a defense organization obtains the information essential to performing its task, but no further obligation requires the partners to share their archives. Specialized reports from member nations are submitted to the commander of the

NATO forces and his civilian opposite numbers. One may assume that vital decisions continue to be made on the political level in the Western capitals.

INTELLIGENCE UNDER COMMUNISM

Secretiveness in Communist-ruled countries is a way of life. The observation of the Marquis de Custine in 1839 is still singularly applicable:

> In Russia, secrecy presides over everything: secrecy—adminstrative, political, social . . . the Russians are disguised Chinese; they do not wish to acknowledge their observers from distant places. If they dared, like the real Chinese, to brave the accusation of barbarism, they would refuse us entry to Petersburg as the Chinese have excluded us from Peking . . .[14]

The Czarist heritage has well prepared the rulers of the Kremlin, who have developed intelligence into a high art which deeply affects their calculations. More than information, Soviet intelligence has become "a powerful weapon of the cold and hot war against the non-Soviet world. It is aggressive, ever-watchful and untrammelled by any moral scruples or economic limitations . . . The inherent aggressiveness of the totalitarian system forces the Soviet police to go much farther than the mere collection of information. The Soviet intelligence agencies are not satisfied with merely knowing facts. They aspire to influence the policies of the free countries in a way favorable to the Kremlin by using all their freedoms and institutions."[15] This, however, has not prevented Soviet leaders from constantly denouncing Western espionage and staging show trials whenever they succeeded in capturing Western agents. They go farther: They denounce all

---

[14] *The Journals of the Marquis de Custine, Journey for Our Time,* edited and translated by Phyllis Penn Kohler, New York: Pellegrini & Cudahy, 1951, p. 190.

[15] S. Wolin and R. M. Slusser, *The Soviet Secret Police,* New York: Frederick A. Praeger, 1957, p. 138.

efforts at intelligence analysis or mission and attaché reports although such activities are internationally recognized.

In view of tightly enforced secrecy, information on Communist intelligence organizations is naturally difficult to obtain. What we know, we have learned from defectors who, in general, are not the most trustworthy sources. But there are some reports from both the USSR and the East European states, which have added significant knowledge of the "bewildering array of multiple, intertwined organizations" which are "concentrated mainly on espionage and subversive activities" and manned by "professional secret service, police and military agents."[16]

We know that Soviet intelligence makes no basic distinction between internal and external activities although the Ministry of Internal Affairs (MVD), which was formerly in charge of intelligence, was downgraded from an all-Union to a Union Republic agency in 1960, at which time the State Security Committee (KGB) was made responsible for foreign intelligence. There is a clear distinction between military and non-military intelligence. The former is handled by the Main Intelligence Directorate of the Army (GRU) and is therefore specialized and probably not permitted to enter into political work.

Peter Deriabin, a former officer of the KGB who defected to the West, has given us one of the clearest descriptions of Soviet intelligence organization; the KGB table of organization can be found in his book.[17] Since the Kremlin dominates the intelligence bureaus of the East European countries through Soviet "advisers," one may assume that a similar organization exists in the satellite countries, adapted to conditions prevalent in the individual states.[18]

The KGB is a creature of the Presidium. It is unlikely to regain the power it had during the Stalin era when the dictator alone determined its mode of operations and permitted the KGB's

[16] London, *op. cit.* p. 249.

[17] P. Deriabin and F. Gibney, *The Secret World*, New York: Doubleday & Co., 1959.

[18] According to Allen Dulles, *op. cit.*, p. 93.

predecessor, ruled by Beria, to become a state within the state. KGB personnel enjoys privileges unavailable to other services; its officers are thoroughly trained in the unconventional methods of obtaining intelligence. It is "an active, aggressive political arm of the regime. Its purpose is not only to acquire information but to manufacture information and to prevent others from acquiring information, destroy sources of foreign information, terrorize, assassinate, and proselytize, as occasion demands. In short, Soviet intelligence sets out to subvert the political and social life of a country, while at the same time taking utmost pains to see that no foreigners succeed in penetrating the international curtain which the KGB throws around Soviet citizens inside and outside their country."[19] No clearer impression can be given of the vast difference between the Western and Eastern intelligence systems.

Similar to non-communist intelligence organization, the KGB is divided into geographical and functional divisions. But unlike the systems outside the Iron Curtain are the "special" sections, of which three stand out: The Advisory Section watches conditions in the East European satellite countries; the Illegal Section, engaged in espionage and counter-espionage, supports illegal residents abroad;[20] and the Special Operations Section (Spets-bureau), the most sinister part of KGB, is responsible for terrorism, assassination, and large-scale violence and subversion.[21] "KGB is also responsible for training terrorists, saboteurs, wreckers and diversionists. It directs organizations that penetrate the penetrators, i.e. supervise the activities and loyalty of Soviet citizens abroad, from ambassadors to chauffeurs."[22]

One of the great assets of Communist governments is the use they can make of organizations outside their own countries. These consist of the Communist parties, fellow-traveling sympathizers and the various front organizations, among which the

[19] Deriabin and Gibney, *op. cit.*, p. 183.
[20] Cf. "The Story of the Soviet Agent Col. Abel," *Life*, Nov. 11, 1957.
[21] Deriabin, *Ibid.*
[22] Cf. London, *op. cit.*, p. 250.

most important are the World Federation of Trade Unions, the World Peace Council, and the International Student Union. These latter work for communist purposes without Communist Party identification. Communist Trojan horses have provided Moscow and Peking with useful information and have carried out operations implementing tactical or even strategic decisions. "The network of Soviet intelligence agencies abroad constitutes an arm of foreign and military policy, and as such is comparable to analogous agencies of other powers. It is, however, also part and parcel of the international Communist movement, and in this it is a unique intelligence system . . . As a component part of the Communist movement, Soviet intelligence is built on the belief in Russia's unique and supreme role in the struggle to abolish capitalism and build a new and better social system throughout the world."[23] Since the demise of the Comintern and the Cominform, one may assume that intelligence collection and operations abroad are directed primarily by Soviet embassies and missions. As a number of discoveries of communist clandestine operations have demonstrated, this is entirely feasible. This is not to say that non-Communist powers do not make use of foreign groups or individuals to further their own ends. But they cannot rely on a disciplined party apparatus that spans the world.

One may add here that Communist China probably has a problem in penetrating the West because of ethnic differences. This is particularly true in Europe. Although there are numbers of Chinese in the United States, most of them are certainly loyal citizens, but penetration would be somewhat easier than in Europe. The West, on the other hand, has far more difficulty in collecting intelligence in Asia, where Caucasians can be immediately identified and can be traced more easily than Chinese in the United States.

The Soviet and communist intelligence organizations are enormous. They fairly dwarf the West's and spend many times more

[23] D. J. Dallin, *Soviet Espionage*, New Haven: Yale University Press, 1955. pp. 14-15.

for their upkeep. Given all these collection facilities, how do Moscow and Peking process and interpret intelligence?

Two facts are immediately evident: First, intelligence interpretation is not objective but is influenced by doctrinal elements; second, since the party leadership makes the important decisions, it is questionable whether the executive agencies, such as the Ministry of Foreign Affairs (Minindel), are seriously consulted. There is evidence that, in Stalin's time, reports were slanted to please the dictator. It was dangerous to present one's own views; they might differ with those of Stalin, which could have serious consequences for the analyst. While in Khrushchev's era a more realistic information service most likely has been instituted, ideological aspects will nevertheless continue to color interpretation. Historical materialism has its place in intelligence as well as in foreign policy.

We do not know whether the KGB's function includes intelligence analysis. The Presidium will doubtless hear experts from all professions whose judgment may be of importance. It may consult with such bodies as the Collegium of the Minindel (see below, p. 188), the Academy of Science and the Academy of Social Sciences, or with well known individuals. However, there is no evidence that information and interpretation are coordinated by appropriate agencies, and one may assume that the Presidium will render its opinion on pre-selected facts and write its own strategic estimates. The decision as to whether and how such estimates should be carried out is ultimately up to the party leader. Although he must rely on the support of the majority of the Presidium and the party's Central Committee, he remains the supreme arbiter of both intelligence analysis and foreign policy.

The communist world view has an utterly different concept of the course of history. The Westerner views historic developments almost with fatalism unless he relies on the old cliché that "history repeats itself." The communist uses history as his tool because he believes the "forces of life" compel it to move along the road of his choice. His picture of the world is not one-dimensional but stereoscopic. He professes to see it in greater depth because the future is an open book. The picture, moreover, is one of his own composition. Philosophically expressed, his world view is fully systematized, at least in broad terms; details may change as do tactics, but not the fundamentals. Since the system is a materialistic one, unexpected oscillations such as occur under the influence of emotional idealism or of transcendental spirituality will not upset its construct.

The communist *Weltanschauung* thus produces vastly different conclusions from observed conditions and molds opinions concerning possible future developments. The visible world is measured against the system and adjudged accordingly. Having deliberately cut itself off from Western tradition, the East uses its ideologies first as a "guide to action" and then as an intellectual framework for a future world, peopled by men and women whose thinking and reasoning is totally different from either occidental or oriental civilizations. It follows that a strategic intelligence estimate, in Soviet terms, would speculate primarily on timing; for if the course of history is predetermined, what matters is when certain events may be expected to occur.

Furthermore, considering that strategic intelligence, in Western terms, must be the product of coordination, i.e. of democratic "negotiation" between departments and experts, it is hard to conceive that in Moscow matters of high security would be permitted to become subject to negotiation at all. Rather, one may expect that the top-level Party leaders, briefed by specialists within the Party or the pertinent government departments, determine policy without the benefit of coordinated strategic intelligence. Only in exceptional cases would the members of the Party Presidium, the most powerful Soviet policy making body, allow the experts to participate in their meetings. So far as the Presidium is concerned, the experts are technicians; they present the facts and submit their views, but the Presidium determines the course of action. There is no recourse, the assent of the

Supreme Soviet, nominally the highest authority in the land, is an *ex post facto* formality, providing the rulers with a platform from which to proclaim their decisions.

Thus, the conceptual difference between communist and non-communist views of the world cannot but lead us to conclude that the approaches to intelligence reflect such a difference. Although there is no conclusive evidence for the above assumption concerning strategic intelligence in the Soviet Union, in the light of other experience it does not seem to be too speculative. It may fortify the argument to add that the term "strategic" also has somewhat different connotations in communist usage. Strategy is subordinated to the inflexible grand goal, communist conquest of the world. To achieve this over-all objective, various strategies—or stratagems—are devised. They are flexible as far as timing, function, and areas are concerned. In turn, strategies are implemented by tactics which are even more flexible. It is frequently difficult to fix the border line between strategy and tactics; all too often, Westerners confuse the two terms. In any event, doctrinally, communist strategic intelligence differs basically in connotation from that of non-communist countries, thus obviously creating another important divergency in Eastern and Western approaches to forms and contents of intelligence.

A final observation: Intelligence is worthless unless it is used. If the men responsible for political or military strategy believe themselves infallible and do not deign to study their experts' analyses, or if they remain inaccessible to intellectual argumentation, a tremendous investment in work and money is wasted. At the same time, intelligence organizations have a responsibility to provide information and analyses that are adapted to the policy-making function not only in matters of substance but also with respect to timing, format, and language. It goes without saying that total frankness is essential. If intelligence gaps are glossed over or if the personal predilections and politics of high level leaders cause re-touchings of the intelligence reports, such placebos must result in disastrous waste of effort and the jeopardy of national security.

4. Organs Originating Foreign Policy

INTRODUCTORY

THE CONDUCT OF FOREIGN affairs is divided into the formulation, decision, and execution of policies. Since the emergence of the nation-state, this division has been institutionalized by all sovereign nations. The organization of these services and their functions are almost identical everywhere—except in the communist countries.

Foreign policy originates in the seat of government and is administered by foreign offices, usually called ministries of foreign affairs or, as in the United States, the Department of State. These organizations are charged with conducting relations with foreign offices abroad. With exceptions defined by constitutional law, they formulate policies on the basis of considerations previously outlined. They do not make, but recommend, decisions which must be made by the head of the government. They also control their "eyes and ears abroad," the diplomatic staffs that are charged with carrying out their countries' policies in the field. In addition to their diplomatic duties, these staffs must report on conditions abroad and look after the interests of fellow nationals who are residing in the country to which they are accredited.

Such organizational differences as exist among the free world's foreign offices are more constitutional than administrative. They also may be motivated by specific political interests. All foreign offices have political, economic, functional, and administrative divisions. Despite different emphases in their organization charts, they are brothers under the skin. However, particularly since World War II, foreign offices have not always remained decisive in directing foreign policy. This is true not only in dictatorships where the leaders of the ruling party utilize their foreign offices primarily to obtain technical advice and to administer their policies, but may apply also in democracies and quite constitutionally. For example, the history of United States foreign relations has frequently demonstrated such legally unassailable actions as the President's bypassing the Department of State, or the Congress' not wanting the Department to assume responsibility for particular aspects of foreign policy. Such was the case in the early days of the European Recovery Program when the agency administering this program, the Economic Cooperation Administration, was independent. However, in all these instances, it is understood that the predetermined broad outlines of policy are followed and that the men responsible are accountable for their decisions. In the democracies, they are accountable to the people and the chief of state; under totalitarianism, to the party in power.

What really distinguishes the foreign offices is, first, the character and magnitude of foreign policy control that they are allowed to exercise and, second, the type and nature of constitutionally determined relations with other branches of the government (or parties) under which they operate.

Clearly, the nature of policy control is determined by the political philosophy of a nation and the tangible outcome of this philosophy, the constitutional law. Under a dictatorship, be it fascist or communist, the foreign office plays a minor role, limited to administrative and advisory functions and coping with diplomatic procedures of the outside world. The foreign offices in Moscow and Peking are therefore technical auxiliaries, designed to implement the decisions of the ruling bodies which, in turn, are dominated by the dictator himself. The members of these bodies may or may not be members of the government; important only is their standing in the party hierarchy. Public opinion can be managed and recent history has demonstrated how policy reversals can be made palatable by skillful human engineering.

In the non-totalitarian countries, most of all in the democracies, the standing of the executive departments charged with foreign affairs is much higher and their influence on policy formulation stronger. The foreign minister is looked upon as the authorized representative of the nation in matters of foreign affairs. He has a difficult position: His ministry is at the same time a national and an international agency, subject to both constitutional and international law. He must try to adjust national aspirations to international realities. But his powers are limited: He is subject to the orders or pressures of the chief of state, his parliament, his party and, to some degree, public opinion. Indeed, as communications have improved and direct contacts between heads of state have downgraded the positions of both foreign ministers and diplomats, the status of foreign ministers has steadily declined. It is notable that in this respect the foreign ministers of both the West and the East are similarly affected, their influence in communist-ruled countries having deteriorated even more than that of their Western colleagues. Unless they have important positions in the party, they are elevated technicians or glorified messengers.

A brief comparative survey of constitutional and other controls of foreign affairs and a short outline of several foreign office organizations will demonstrate the points raised above and possibly contribute to the clarification of the role of policy-making leaders and organs in world politics. For Western examples, we shall focus on the United States, Great Britain, and France; of the communist countries, the Soviet Union and Communist China will be surveyed.

THE WEST

The United States

The President and Congress in Foreign Affairs. Since the time of James Madison, the power of final policy decision has been invested in the President. The particular issue which brought about the historic strengthening of the President's responsibility for foreign policy was his power to remove the Secretary of State. The Senate at first insisted that it should share this power with the President. However, Madison, pointing to the danger of combining executive and legislative power, finally prevailed. Thus, the President's foreign policy making power was safeguarded and the Secretaty of State became his representative. Still, the President has certain obligations vis-à-vis Congress which prevent his ever becoming an autocrat in matters concerning foreign policy. He must report on the State of the Union, of which foreign affairs are an essential part. He may conclude treaties "by and with the advice of the Senate . . . provided that two-thirds of the Senators present concur." It has become customary for the President to turn to Congress even before a treaty is submitted to the Senate so that possible arguments may be resolved prior to the senatorial ballot. But, on the other hand, the Senate does not ratify treaties; only the President can do that, thereby making it the law of the land. He will, particularly, confer with the Foreign Relations Committee of the Senate and the Foreign Affairs Committee of the House of Representatives. Although the Senate is historically in a much stronger position than the House when treaties or major policy decisions are under discussion, the House controls the nation's purse strings, may withhold appropriations, and trim or deny requests for funds. Indeed, the "rule by appropriation" has been attacked as being against the spirit of the Constitution which insists on separation of the legislative and executive branches of the Government. One of the more recent examples of congressional attempts to determine foreign policy concerned foreign aid and trade relations with countries such as Yugoslavia, Egypt, and Indonesia. In a news conference on November 8, 1963, Secretary of State Rusk called congressional interference with the foreign policies laid down by the executive branch of the Government "a tendency in Congress to legislate foreign policy."

Furthermore, both houses of Congress may pass, modify, or

reject legislation that has a bearing on foreign policy (for example tariffs, subsidies, and price support). Congressional resolutions can have a powerful effect both inside and outside the country. Thus the President, for all his power, is limited by the Congress and public opinion which he must assuage if he wants to be re-elected. (However, Congress may not question the President officially as it does the Secretary of State.)

Declarations of war must be passed by Congress, usually at presidential instigation. However, in practice the President, as chief executive with power to conduct foreign relations, and as Commander in Chief of the Armed Forces, can order military action before or without declaration of war by Congress. In such cases, the constitutional authority of Congress to declare war amounts to official and legal recognition of already existing conditions. This is particularly significant in an era in which missiles threaten to make obsolete even the fastest airplanes. The Constitution is silent about ending a state of war: In practice war may be ended by treaty to be ratified by the Senate or by a joint resolution of both houses of Congress.

Despite his limitations under the Constitution, the President can postpone or circumvent congressional participation in treaty actions. He can negotiate "executive agreements." They have been used by many Presidents of the United States, including George Washington. The vast majority of these agreements were approved retroactively by the Senate, but some were amended, turned down, or never acted upon at all, without necessarily losing their international validity. It should be added that executive agreements may concern not only the initiation of treaties but also the termination of existing treaties. Famous among executive agreements was Jefferson's Louisiana Purchase, which, of course, was later ratified by the Senate. Similar agreements also initiated the United States' acquisition of the territories of Texas, Hawaii, Samoa, and the Panama Canal Zone, as well as a number of Far Eastern and Latin American developments.[1]

[1] See W. M. McClure, *International Executive Agreements*, New York: Columbia University Press, 1941, Part I.

The famous "destroyer deal" in which President Franklin Roosevelt transferred fifty American destroyers, discarded as obsolete by the Navy, to the British prior to the United States' entry into World War II, was an executive agreement never acted upon by the Senate. During the war, executive agreements were also concluded between the United States and the Soviet Union.

As the significance of international relations continues to increase, it overshadows and profoundly affects domestic issues. Presidents might well be elected primarily on the strength of their foreign policy platform rather than for their domestic program alone. As a consequence, the Congress is more anxious than ever to maintain an adequate control over the nation's foreign affairs. Yet, although the Constitution determines the nature of the influence that the Congress is entitled to exert upon the President and his policy agencies, the usage of executive agreements—not mentioned by the Constitution—has become firmly entrenched in the practices of American conduct of foreign affairs. Indeed, there have been important executive agreements, never ratified as treaties, which established such matters as the incorporation of Texas into the Union and United States cooperation with the International Labor Organization.

The Secretary of State. The Secretary of State is a political appointee, chosen by the President. His name must be submitted for confirmation by the Senate. Once he is confirmed, Congress has no right to remove him; only the President can do that. The Secretary requires no vote of confidence of the Congress, as does the British Foreign Secretary. He is the ranking member of the cabinet; however, since 1947 he no longer is second in line of succession. It was reasoned that the Secretary is an *appointed* and not an *elected* official. Hence the Speaker of the House is now second in line.

The Secretary of State has two functions: He is official spokesman for the President in matters of foreign policy and head of the Department of State. His position in the government is somewhat ambiguous. He must carry out the President's policy; should he disagree, he has three alternatives: He can attempt to persuade the President; he can carry out a policy that has been imposed upon him even though he may not like it, or he can resign. There have been few cases in American history in which a President has delegated power to the Secretary; the only recent example was John Foster Dulles, whose influence on President Eisenhower was great and who was his own master most of the time. In the majority of cases, Presidents reserve for themselves the power to make policy and decisions. Thus the U.S. Secretary of State is and is not responsible for the conduct of foreign affairs. His accountability is limited to the business of the State Department.[2]

Yet in the eyes of the world, the Secretary represents the United States. He is regarded not so much as a politician but as a statesman, second only to the President. He is, in popular belief, a man of great influence and one whose decisions affect not only his own nation but the nations of the world at large.[3] Whether such an estimate is accurate depends entirely on his relationship with the President.

As the administrator of the State Department, the Secretary must cope with the problems of a large organization with thousands of employees. Yet it is questionable whether any of the great secretaries were good administrators or did indeed contribute to the smooth functioning of the Department and the Foreign Service. The majority of Secretaries have relied upon their senior staffs for counsel. These are headed by the Under Secretaries and consist of three different layers: the Assistant Secretaries for political and economic affairs, the Assistant Secretaries and Special Assistants dealing with functional matters, the Assistant Secretaries and Bureau Directors for administration, plus the Counselor and the Legal Adviser. Thus in effect, the Secretary has a little cabinet of his own. It, in turn, receives advice from a Policy Planning Staff,[4] a group of high-level

---

[2] Cf. Alexander DeConde, *The American Secretary of State*, New York: Frederick A. Praeger, 1962, Chapter 5.

[3] *Ibid.*, 132 ff.

[4] Now called Policy Planning Council.

ORGANIZATION OF THE DEPARTMENT OF STATE

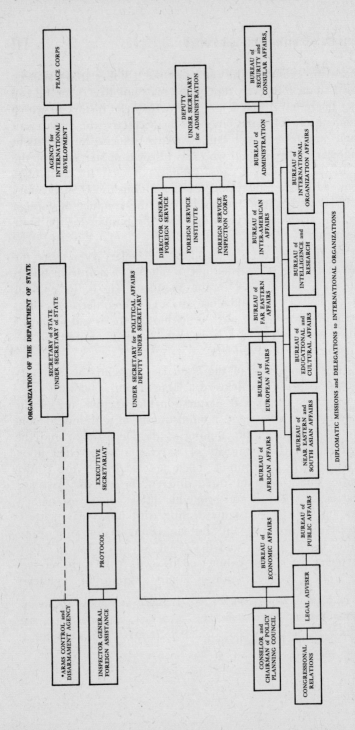

1962

* A separate agency with the director reporting directly to the secretary and serving as principal adviser to the secretary and the President on arms control and disarmament.

experts which was set up in 1947, charged with the task of solving difficult policy problems and recommending new avenues of approach. The value of this Staff depends upon its use by the Secretary.

The establishment of this body of political thinkers presumably resulted from the realization of General George C. Marshall —then Secretary of State—that constant pressure of day-to-day business leaves the top-level policy makers too little time to think problems through and that provisions were needed to permit a more careful consideration of the main issues of world politics by a group of men with both local and global experience. Removed from the exigencies of administrative duties, the group could become a foremost source of policy initiative and a tremendous help to the Secretary and his deputies. Unfortunately, the Staff is persistently called upon to deal with pressing current problems, which hampers its long-range policy planning.

On a lower level, there are within the Department a number of "country committees" and committees charged with solving functional problems. They draw their members from the political, economic, and functional divisions. Their task is to clarify specific problems, such as might arise from treaty negotiations, and to advise higher officials accordingly.

In the office of the Secretary converge all foreign and domestic information relative to international affairs. While theoretically he is a coordinator-administrator rather than a policy formulator, in practice he contributes significantly to the nation's world outlook and, subject to the President's concurrence, he accepts or rejects policy recommendations, or suggests modifications. In certain cases, he initiates new policies; he may be instrumental in changing political methodology and can order reorganizations of the Department. That there is nothing sacrosanct in the Department's organization chart has been demonstrated by its frequent changes. Most new Secretaries bring in their own staffs, which in itself is bound to lead to changes in policy, attitudes, and organization.

Next to the Secretary, the Under Secretary is the most influ-

ential man in the Department. Like the Secretary and his Assistant Secretaries, he is an appointee, but his nomination is
prompted by administrative talent as well as knowledge of world
affairs. His predominant concerns are political and administrative. But perhaps his most important task is to act for the Secretary during the latter's frequent absences on errands of
personal diplomacy or representation of the United States in
international conferences. Owing to the magnitude of these
duties, and in order to reduce the work load of the Secretary and
the Under Secretary, the posts of Under Secretary for Political
Affairs and Under Secretary for Administration were created.
The Under Secretary for Political Affairs has the special task of
coordinating policies with the Departments of Defense and
Justice, the Central Intelligence Agency and the Federal Bureau of Investigation on matters of foreign policy which affect
more than one of the operating bureaus.

The number of Assistant Secretaries who actually head geographical, functional, or administrative bureaus has increased.
Five Assistant Secretaries head the geographic Bureaus of African, Inter-American (Latin-American), European, Far Eastern,
and Near Eastern-South Asian Affairs. Another deals with International Organization Affairs; three are in charge of Economic
Affairs, Public Affairs and Congressional Relations. The Director of the Bureau of Intelligence and Research, although not
titled Assistant Secretary, nonetheless has the level of such a
rank. Further, there are two Special Assistants for Atomic Energy
and Cultural Relations. Science Advisers are a new feature of
the atomic and missile age.

The Counselor, ranking equally with Assistant Secretaries and
not to be confused with the Legal Adviser, has considerable
importance. The Counselor's task is to advise the Secretary on
over-all policy problems. He is also the Chairman of the Policy
Planning Council. His job is peculiar to the Department; no
other foreign office has exactly the same type of position though
all of them use the services of policy consultants. The function of
the Legal Adviser, who also ranks with the Assistant Secretaries,

is to clarify the legal aspects of foreign relations for the benefit of the policy makers and the diplomatic representatives abroad.

Except for the Counselor and the Legal Adviser, all Under Secretaries and Assistant Secretaries are subject to Senate approval—but not Bureau Directors, Administrators, and Special Assistants, whose appointments may be determined by the Secretary regardless of Congressional opinion. The Secretary, dependent as he is on Congressional money appropriations, will try not to antagonize members of either party, but there have been instances where Special Assistant appointments have been made over the protests of influential Senators. A case in point was the 1959 recall of Ambassador Charles E. Bohlen from his post in Manila to become Secretary Christian Herter's adviser on Soviet Affairs.

The Department of State. Foreign offices are subject to constant organizational changes either in response to shifting political emphasis because of world conditions or to improve efficiency. The U. S. Department of State is no exception. Indeed, since its creation in 1789, it has undergone innumerable reorganizations, growing from a staff of half a dozen clerks into an agency employing thousands.

The Department's staff formerly comprised two entities: the departmental and the foreign service components. The former were civil servants, the latter subject to their own statutes and a kind of elite corps of diplomats and consular officers, representing American interests abroad. The relations between these two groups were not the best. Ever since the end of World War II, the U. S. government has concerned itself with making the Foreign Service more efficient and improving working relations between it and the civil service personnel. Several committees studied the problem. Finally, in 1954, the report of the Wriston Committee was accepted and measures were taken to implement it. The report requested complete integration of departmental and Foreign Service personnel which would establish a uniform Department-wide Foreign Service with but few exceptions.

The implementation of the plan resulted in great hardships

for many officers who, because of age or other reasons, could not be integrated. There were also many who had personal reasons for not wishing to go abroad. They were permitted to retain their jobs, but without hope of further opportunities for advancement. Other problems arose as a result of too sweeping an application of the Wriston proposals which tended to endanger the continuity of certain specialized bureaus. This was recognized by the Senate Committee on Foreign Relations during the course of its deliberations concerning amendments to the Foreign Service Act in which it proposed to "make numerous changes."[5] In discussing the main proposals of the bill, the Committee pointed to "evidence which has been accumulating for some time that the Department of State has gone too far in carrying out the recommendations of the Wriston report calling for additional positions in the Department of State to be designated as Foreign Service Officer positions." Singling out the work of the International Educational Exchange Service, the Bureau of Intelligence and Research, and the Policy Planning Staff, the Committee emphasized the specialized work of these three bureaus. It mentioned that "the work of the Bureau of Intelligence and Research is scholarly, specialized, and requires long familiarity with narrowly defined masses of material . . . The work of the Policy Planning Staff requires senior specialists, for instance officers skilled in military planning who must work closely with their opposite numbers in the Department of Defense. The characteristic of much of this work of these . . . bureaus in the Department of State is that long continuity of service is highly desirable. Typical assignments of Foreign Service officers to these bureaus are for 2-year periods. These periods are long enough perhaps for the Foriegn Service Officer to become familiar with the work but not long enough for him to make an effective contribution. Moreover, the nature of the work is frequently so different from that which a Foreign Service officer is accustomed to doing overseas that many officers dis-

[5] Foreign Service Act Amendment of 1959, Senate Report No. 880, Calender No. 907 of September 2, 1959.

like such assignments and fail to put forth their best effort."[6]

These observations are acute and well justified. Indeed, since the Kennedy and Johnson administrations, the "Wristonization,"[7] while not officially abandoned, has been slowed down considerably and may well be on its way out. It had impaired departmental efficiency and lowered the morale of many officers who for a variety of reasons did not want to be part of the foreign service. On the satisfactory solution of this problem will depend the effectiveness of departmental work in the specialized fields under its jurisdiction.

Like other foreign offices, the Department of State is organized around a core of several types of bureaus, most of which are subdivided into Offices which comprise geographic or functional units. The Offices, except for certain functional units, are composed of Officers in Charge and their assistants, usually called desk officers, who perform the basic political and economic work of the Department.

The political nucleus of the Department is in the geographic bureaus, to which may be added the Bureau of International Organization Affairs and the Bureau of Economic Affairs. These bureaus are spearheaded by the Policy Planning Council and supported by the Bureau of Intelligence and Research, both of which have been discussed above. The greatest reservoir of information and the best reasoned policy proposals probably originate in these offices.

The Bureau for International Organization Affairs' five Offices are concerned with Dependent Areas, International Economic and Social Affairs, U. N. Political and Security Affairs, International Administration and International Conference. Cultural aspects of international organizations are the responsibility of the Bureau of International Cultural Relations, which deals with UNESCO and cultural exchanges.

[6] Foreign Service Act Amendment of 1959, Senate Report No. 880. Calender No. 907 of September 2, 1959.

[7] Named for the chairman of the committee, Henry Wriston, who promoted complete integration of departmental and foreign service personnel.

Geographic Bureaus of the U.S. Department of State

Assistant Secretary for African Affairs
1. Northern Africa
2. Eastern and Southern Africa
3. Central Africa and West Africa
4. Malagasy

Assistant Secretary of Inter-American Affairs
1. East Coast
2. West Coast
3. Brazil
4. Central America and Panama
5. Caribbean Area and Mexico
6. Regional political and economic affairs

Assistant Secretary of European Affairs*
1. British Commonwealth and Northern Europe
2. Germany
3. Western Europe
4. USSR

Assistant Secretary of Far Eastern Affairs
1. East Asia
2. Southeast Asia
3. Southwest Pacific affairs

Assistant Secretary of Near East and South Asian Affairs
1. Near East
2. Greece
3. Turkey and Iran
4. South Asia
5. Regional affairs

* Also has functional offices for Atlantic Political and Military and Atlantic Political-Economic Affairs.

The geographic offices, in addition to the political desks, have an economic staff, a Public Affairs Adviser, and in some areas, a Labor Adviser. For example, the Office of Western European Affairs consists of an Officer in Charge for French-Iberian Affairs, another for Italy and Austria, and a third, responsible for Switzerland and the Benelux countries; there are also economic affairs officers as well as a Public Affairs Adviser in charge of all media of communications for the area. Major countries may be subdivided into such functional sections as external, domestic, and economic affairs.

The Officers in Charge and their desk officers must be familiar with all departmental activities concerning their area and also keep fully informed of the domestic conditions and international position of the countries for which they are responsible. They maintain close and continuous contact with United States diplomatic representatives abroad and try to promote American interests and objectives. They must read correspondence, both official and private, concerning these countries, instruct the field offices when necessary, and be prepared to brief their superiors at any time. They also have to be in constant touch with the commercial, technical, and cultural developments in their areas so as to possess complete knowledge of the countries of their responsibility. Their recommendations for policy and procedure are referred to their Office Director, who coordinates them, and—provided he agrees—forwards them to the office of the Assistant Secretary in charge of the entire region. For example, if the Officer in Charge of French-Iberian Affairs receives a policy recommendation from his French Desk with which he agrees in principle, he forwards it to the Director of the Office of Western European Affairs who, if he considers it important, brings it to the attention of the Assistant Secretary for European Affairs.

The Bureau of Economic Affairs is not concerned with individual countries. As we have seen, the geographic offices have economic staffs to handle those problems. Rather, the Bureau deals with economic questions of an international scope. It has Offices for International Resources, International Finance and

Economic Analysis, Transport and Communications, and International Trade. Among its Staffs are those for Mutual Defense Control, Economic Policy Reporting, and Foreign Economic Advisory activities. It should be kept in mind that economic aspects of foreign aid are handled by the International Cooperation Administration which, although located in the State Department and under its political guidance, is semi-independent. Nor does the Bureau of Economic Affairs cut across the Bureau of International Organization Affairs; instead, it concerns itself with over-all economics rather than with organizational tasks.

In addition, there are administrative bureaus which, owing to the Department's multi-faceted functions, are extensive. The Foreign Service, for example, requires not only routine headquarters housekeeping, but also inspection abroad and such training facilities as the Foreign Service Institute. The Bureau of Security and Consular Affairs has combined investigative activities with passport, visa, and refugee affairs. The Bureau of Administration, responsible for all departmental housekeeping, comprises offices and divisions ranging from budget matters to the all-important communications, reproduction, translating services, cryptography and the management of foreign buildings.

Foreign offices, to be efficient, require a great deal of organizational flexibility. Most of them initiate frequent reorganizations in order to cope with new tasks and problems. Looking through the organization charts of the Department of State and other foreign offices, the reader should keep this in mind. Reorganizations rarely alter the fundamental principles of foreign office activities which pertain to policy formulation and administration. In fact foreign offices the world over have a great deal in common; the differences are constitutional posture of decision making and the extent to which a foreign office is, or is not, free to exercise its function.

National Security Policy. This is a new concept which developed after World War II. It means that issues pertaining to national security which are vital to the continued existence of the nation must be reviewed by representatives not only of the State Department but also of those agencies whose responsibilities are vital factors in security policies such as, for example, the armed services. It was found that the policy machinery of the United States can no longer be limited to the President, the Department of State and the "advice and consent" of the Senate but that a process of policy coordination was to be established by statute so as to provide as much support as possible for presidential decisions. This was accomplished by the National Security Act of 1947. In Section 2 of this Act, the Congress expresses its intent "to provide a comprehensive program for the future security of the United States; to provide for the establishment of integrated policies and procedures for the departments, agencies, and functions of the Government relating to the national security; . . ." In other words, above the traditional machinery of international relations, there was superimposed the dominating concept of national security policy, requiring collaboration and coordination of practically all government departments.

As a result of these considerations, the law set up the National Security Council (NSC), composed of the President, the Vice President, the Secretaries of State and Defense, and the Director of the Office of Defense Mobilization.[8] In addition to these permanent members, other participants, though not statutory members, attend the NSC meetings more or less regularly by request. They are the Secretary of the Treasury, the Chairman of the Atomic Energy Commission, and the President's Special Assistant for Disarmament. Other *ad hoc* participants may be the Attorney General, the Director of the United States Information Agency and the Chairman of the Council of Economic Advisers. NSC's advisers are the Chairman of the Joint Chiefs of Staff, the Director of Central Intelligence, the Secretary of Commerce and the Secretaries of the three military services.[9]

In addition to being responsible for policy coordination, the

---

[8] Later the Office of Emergency Management.
[9] Cf. T. V. Stanley with H. H. Ransom, *The National Security Council*, Harvard University Defense Policy Seminar, January 12, 1957.

NSC "advise (s) the President with respect to the integration of domestic, foreign, and military policies relating to the national security so as to enable the military services and the other departments and agencies of the Government to cooperate more effectively in matters involving national security."[10] This seems to indicate that the American policy makers have at last come to the inevitable conclusion that security policy must not be formulated without an integrated consensus of the nation's entire administrative leadership. But what appears to be a maze of legitimate interests in these vital issues is really an interdisciplinary approach to problems of enormous complexity. It is also a sign of democratic organization which permits all interested parties concerned with specific issues to express their views and submit their recommendations. Unquestionably, a number of good ideas will be lost in this vast machinery. This is unavoidable, even in the most efficiently run organizations, for the business is conducted by human beings and not by computers. One cannot expect absolute perfection; one can only strive to obtain the best possible opinions and then rely on the sense, experience, and sound judgment of those on whose shoulders rests the heavy duty of decision making.

An integral danger requires integral counter measures, and the establishment of the NSC as well as other provisions of the National Security Act of 1947 demonstrated that serious attempts were made to cope with a dangerous situation. It cannot be said that these security measures have yet been completely successful, but neither can they be condemned as incapable of effective action. When we consider that, in the end, decisions of real importance must be made by the President, and that to be fully informed the President must have the benefit of the best possible advice, the existing machinery should be equipped to produce such information. Obviously, no single individual can be expected to possess a sovereign knowledge of all issues, nor can he have a clear view of possible future developments. He

[10] The National Security Act of 1947, as amended through August 1956, Title I, Sect. 1 (a).

must base his decisions on mature counsel. Very much depends on the nature of this counsel.

Advice on current issues and estimates on future events are the result of inter-departmental coordination. At present, no alternative is feasible in a democracy. Nevertheless, the method has its dangers. Coordination is likely to result in compromise; its products may be so broad that acting on them would create new problems. This is the price of democracy, a price that probably is not too great, since in the event of emergency, near-unanimity is almost certain.

In comparison with other nations, western and eastern, the United States' foreign policy and national security machinery is large and the decision-making process correspondingly cumbersome. Since it is also relatively new, with growing maturity it will no doubt outgrow some of its shortcomings. In the present circumstances, it is the best that can be devised and certainly has made many provisions for meeting the needs of a polarized world. There is some substance to the criticism that "government by committee" is no way to arrive at concise policies, much less clear-cut decisions. But the case is perhaps overstated. The very complexity and infinite variety of foreign policy problems facing governments today require the study of many experts in numerous fields. As in medicine the general practitioner is becoming a vanishing relic and specialists have emerged as a result of expanding knowledge, so in matters of international relations the larger issues can no longer be solved by one or a few persons. Committees are necessary because they represent an accumulation of experience and knowledge whereby individual opinions can be checked and corroborated with the opinions of others, and thereby possibly modified or corrected. A pooling of brain power has been the answer to many problems, whether political, social, economic, scientific, or cultural. A decision maker needs the consensus of all these fields; he can no longer rely on a haphazard search for solutions but must organize his sources of information into groups or committees. The top-level "committee," the NSC, having received interdepartmental and interdisciplinary distilled information, attempts a further refinement in order to arrive at conclusions and recommendations for the man who has the last word, the President.

Under Presidents Truman and Eisenhower, the NSC was the focal point of such integration. President Kennedy seemed to regard it rather as a flexible organization which would or would not be used as a forum for decision making. Weekly NSC meetings were scheduled but the President's advisers who appeared to have replaced the old NSC Planning Board may well have persuaded him to use specialized groups of the NSC for deliberation on specific problems. The Standing Group, probably the most important of these groups, consisted of individuals who did not represent government agencies. The White House Staff also may be regarded as such a group. Its influence was a heavy one since its members were responsible for selecting the issues to be submitted to the President.

Flexibility was the key word for the Kennedy administration's system of national security policy making. Groups and committees were set up *ad hoc* and dissolved or permitted to lapse if no longer needed. This concept of deliberate improvisation differed greatly from the strict confines of Eisenhower's staff organization which the Kennedy advisers probably disliked so intensely that they turned to the other extreme. Chances are that the NSC concept is basically sound, and it is significant to recall the days of the Cuban crisis when the NSC was summoned for decisions which could have confronted the United States and the world with nuclear war.

It is possible that President Kennedy shared the doubts of Senator Henry M. Jackson, who in 1959 investigated the U. S. policy machinery and called the NSC unrealistic and inefficient: "The proper role of the NSC is to criticize and evaluate departmental planning and proposals in the light of the knowledge, interests, and possibly conflicting policies of other departments. In this way what we would call a coordinated view may be developed, and such a view may be very helpful to the President in making a clear determination of the executive will."[11]

[11] Senator H. M. Jackson, "To Forge a Strategy for Survival," *Public Administration Review,* Summer, 1959, Vol. XIX, No. 3.

Several political scientists seem to have shared the Senator's opinion, and certainly vast coordinating processes do not inevitably ensure wise and lucid estimates. But coordination there must be; in creating national security as in strategic intelligence, there must be a meeting of the minds. It is true that the President remains the sole determiner of policy and strategy but, even though the coordination process may produce weak compromises, the presentation of different points of view and alternative policies will unquestionably provide sufficient background to enable him to reach a final decision.

Great Britain

The Crown, the Cabinet, and Parliament in Foreign Affairs. Although Britain is a parliamentary democracy like the United States, legal control of its foreign policy lies in the hands of the Crown which delegates it to the Cabinet rather than to Parliament. The people have relatively little influence upon their country's foreign affairs beyond their vote for a particular political party's program. The Crown, as a matter of explanation, has been referred to as a "monarchical office" which "embraces those elements of the British governmental organization wielding executive and administrative power."[12] But "the powers of the Crown are wielded by the Government of the day."[13]

Constitutionally, the Crown possesses the sole power for the conduct of foreign affairs. The Sovereign delegates this power to the Prime Minister, who appoints the Secretary of State for Foreign Affairs (Foreign Secretary) to be the Crown's and his own adviser as well as the head of the Foreign Office. With the growth of parliamentary government and popular power, the kings and queens of England have been increasingly careful not to make personal use of their constitutional prerogatives concerning foreign relations. Queen Victoria may have insisted on being informed about the developments in relations with other nations and made it very clear in a letter to Lord Palmerston

[12] H. M. Stout, *British Government*, New York: Oxford University Press, 1955, p. 52.
[13] *Ibid.*, 54.

that she wished to be privy to policy formulation. King Edward, who anticipated war with Germany and loathed his cousin, German Emperor William II, is credited with masterminding the Entente Cordiale to counter German expansionism and competition. However, ultimate responsibility has long been vested in the cabinet or, more specifically, in the Prime Minister, who is the most powerful official in the United Kingdom. He selects the members of his cabinet as does the U. S. President. He may dismiss or reshuffle cabinet ministers as did former Prime Minister Harold Macmillan after the Profumo scandal. So long as his party retains the majority in the House of Commons and continues to support his policies, he occupies a position of power and influence equaled only by the U. S. President. Yet, on the other hand, he "is the leader but not the master of the group, and he is bound to observe the right of those who jointly share responsibility with him."[14]

Parliament has no way of forcing the Foreign Secretary to divulge information should he insist that release of such information is detrimental to the nation's interests. Neither he nor the Prime Minister can be legally compelled or put under pressure to outline their policies or submit the minutes of treaty negotiations.[15] (Compare this with the power of the U.S. Congress to "invite" members of the Cabinet to hearings. The law does not compel these officials to answer unless so requested by the President, but in practice it is considered poor politics to antagonize important Congressional committees, and the Secretary of State would hardly provoke the foreign relations committees by refusing to answer whether in open or closed sessions.)

The British Foreign Office is more powerful than the U. S. Department of State. In the United States, as we have seen, the treaty-making power is in the hands of the President, who is advised by the Secretary of State, but it is controlled by the Sen-

---

[14] Stout, *op. cit.*, p. 57.
[15] Theoretically, the House of Commons can force the cabinet to resign or submit to dissolution and reelection, if it insists upon withholding desired information. In practice, this never happens.

ate directly and by the House indirectly. In Britain, this power is nominally in the hands of the sovereign but actually wielded by the Prime Minister and the Foreign Secretary and, in important questions by the Cabinet. This constellation does not change even in the event of a declaration of war. If the Cabinet finds that it must exercise the sovereign's war-making power, it needs only his assent. There is no legal necessity for parliamentary ratification, and Commons may object only by a vote of non-confidence or a refusal to pass money appropriations. In practice, the Cabinet refrains from using its war-making power without advance Parliamentary agreement: "No British Government would consider a declaration of war against a great power without the support of the people."[16]

The Prime Minister selects as Foreign Secretary a man whom he regards as one of the most capable and experienced members of his party, who commands a prominent position in it, and, if possible, has experience in handling foreign affairs. No Parliamentary approval of his selection is necessary; only the monarch is required to give his consent, which is usually but a formality. The Prime Minister may be assumed to be familiar with his Foreign Secretary's political views, and, at least in fundamentals, to agree with him.

The Foreign Secretary. The office of the Foreign Secretary has a long history in England. It was first established about seven hundred years ago by Henry III. A political appointee, the Secretary is officially responsible to the Crown and to Parliament for the conduct of foreign affairs, but the cabinet as a whole is responsible, too. Lack of confidence in the Foreign Secretary may mean lack of confidence in the entire cabinet except when the Prime Minister replaces him of his own volition. If the Prime Minister supports the Foreign Secretary's policies, he may appear before Commons and call for a test vote. Parliament may decide to give way to the cabinet, particularly if the government has, in domestic matters, acted according to Parliament's

[16] W. I. Jennings, *The British Constitution*, London: Cambridge University Press, 1941, p. 189.

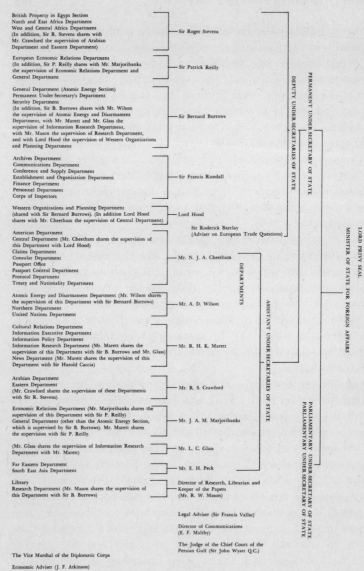

British Property in Egypt Section
North and East Africa Department
West and Central Africa Department
(In addition, Sir R. Stevens shares with
Mr. Crawford the supervision of Arabian
Department and Eastern Department) — Sir Roger Stevens

European Economic Relations Department
(In addition, Sir P. Reilly shares with Mr. Marjoribanks
the supervision of Economic Relations Department and
General Department) — Sir Patrick Reilly

General Department (Atomic Energy Section)
Permanent Under Secretary's Department
Security Department
(In addition, Sir B. Burrows shares with Mr. Wilson
the supervision of Atomic Energy and Disarmament
Department, with Mr. Marett and Mr. Glass the
supervision of Information Research Department,
with Mr. Mason the supervision of Research Department,
and with Lord Hood the supervision of Western Organizations
and Planning Department) — Sir Bernard Burrows

Archives Department
Communications Department
Conference and Supply Department
Establishment and Organization Department
Finance Department
Personnel Department
Corps of Inspectors — Sir Francis Rundall

Western Organizations and Planning Department
(shared with Sir Bernard Burrows). (In addition Lord Hood
shares with Mr. Cheetham the supervision of Central Department) — Lord Hood

Sir Roderick Barclay
(Adviser on European Trade Questions)

American Department
Central Department (Mr. Cheetham shares the supervision of
this Department with Lord Hood)
Claims Department
Consular Department
Passport Office
Passport Control Department
Protocol Department
Treaty and Nationality Department — Mr. N. J. A. Cheetham

Atomic Energy and Disarmament Department (Mr. Wilson shares
the supervision of this Department with Sir Bernard Burrows)
Northern Department
United Nations Department — Mr. A. D. Wilson

Cultural Relations Department
Information Executive Department
Information Policy Department
Information Research Department (Mr. Marett shares the
supervision of this Department with Sir B. Burrows and Mr. Glass)
News Department (Mr. Marett shares the supervision of this
Department with Sir Harold Caccia) — Mr. R. H. K. Marett

Arabian Department
Eastern Department
(Mr. Crawford shares the supervision of these Departments
with Sir R. Stevens) — Mr. R. S. Crawford

Economic Relations Department (Mr. Marjoribanks shares the
supervision of this Department with Sir P. Reilly)
General Department (other than the Atomic Energy Section,
which is supervised by Sir B. Burrows). Mr. Marett shares
the supervision with Sir P. Reilly. — Mr. J. A. M. Marjoribanks

(Mr. Glass shares the supervision of Information Research
Department with Mr. Marett) — Mr. L. C. Glass

Far Eastern Department
South East Asia Department — Mr. E. H. Peck

Library
Research Department (Mr. Mason shares the supervision of
this Department with Sir B. Burrows) — Director of Research, Librarian and
Keeper of the Papers
(Mr. R. W. Mason)

Legal Adviser (Sir Francis Vallat)

Director of Communications
(E. F. Maltby)

The Judge of the Chief Court of the
Persian Gulf (Sir John Wyatt Q.C.)

The Vice Marshal of the Diplomatic Corps

Economic Adviser (J. F. Atkinson)

Labour Adviser on International Questions (W. A. Treganowan)

PERMANENT UNDER SECRETARY OF STATE

DEPUTY UNDER SECRETARIES OF STATE

DEPARTMENTS

ASSISTANT UNDER SECRETARIES OF STATE

ORGANIZATION OF THE BRITISH FOREIGN OFFICE, MARCH 1963.

SECRETARY OF STATE FOR FOREIGN AFFAIRS

LORD PRIVY SEAL.

MINISTER OF STATE FOR FOREIGN AFFAIRS

PARLIAMENTARY UNDER SECRETARY OF STATE
PARLIAMENTARY UNDER SECRETARY OF STATE

desires. If not, the cabinet will resign *in toto*. This is in conformity with the British Parliamentary practice (contrary to the American) of general cabinet responsibility.

The British Foreign Secretary used to have somewhat more latitude in making decisions than the U.S. Secretary of State. But he, too, has suffered loss of power since the advent of the summit conference era in which the chiefs of state or government have direct contact with each other. Still, the Foreign Secretary may decide important issues and only in matters of major importance would confer with the Prime Minister or, indeed, with the entire cabinet. (Cabinet committees, recently set up to deal with special problems, now meet frequently.) He has the advantage of obtaining the services of permanent civil servants whose experience has had a chance to develop during many years of uninterrupted service. These Foreign Office experts, a highly select group, are better protected from budget cuts and attacks by Parliament and the public than are their American colleagues.

Like most ministers of foreign affairs, the Foreign Secretary is a coordinator rather than a creator. His burdens of work and responsibility are so heavy that he frequently must delegate his powers to subordinates. Contrary to his American colleague's duties, his are not exclusively confined to the administration of Britain's international affairs. As an important member of a highly integrated and mutually responsible cabinet, he must give his attention to national as well as international politics; if he is a prominent member of the majority party, he must be ready to appear before Commons and defend Her Majesty's Government policies.[17] He has formal duties toward the Crown. He will have to convince the members of the Commonwealth of his policies' justification, for British foreign policy vitally affects Dominion foreign policy and the Crown colonies. He must see to it that the

[17] The Foreign Secretary need not be a member of Parliament nor must he be a commoner. Lord Home became Foreign Secretary although he was a peer of the realm; nor was he a member of Parliament. However, when he was to become Prime Minister, he had to forego his title and campaign for Parliamentary membership.

policies of his party, and particularly his party's ideas of world politics, are presented in a form acceptable to the voting public.

One might say that the Foreign Secretary's associates consist of assistants and advisers. His assistants are two Ministers of State and two Parliamentary Under Secretaries, all of them political appointees. They assist him in the Foreign Office, but their more important functions are to act as his deputies in the House of Lords and Commons respectively. They may represent him in international conferences which do not require his personal appearance or, if he is present, help direct his staff and share some of his burdens. Each Minister and Under Secretary who represents the Foreign Secretary in Commons has one Parliamentary Private Secretary.

The highest and most important of the Foreign Secretary's advisers is the Permanent Under Secretary who, in contrast to the Foreign Secretary and his assistants, is not a political appointee but a civil servant. He not only heads the Foreign Service, but also controls the Foreign Office's accounting with particular respect to expenditures incurred by the diplomatic missions.[18] His senior assistants are the Deputy- and Assistant-Under Secretaries, whose number depends on the prevailing organization of the Foreign Office. They "occupy a key position in the hierarchy of the Foreign Office . . ." and "in consultation with their department head . . . evolve and formulate recommended courses of action and lines of major policy on the basis of general directions from the Secretary of State . . ."[19] In matters of general policy, the Permanent Under Secretary always has immediate access to the Foreign Secretary. Not even the Foreign Secretary's Principal Private Secretary, an important cushion between the Secretary and the Foreign Office, can prevent this close collaboration. The Permanent Under Secretary usually is a man with vast experience and knowledge of world affairs. His social and professional standing sometimes surpasses

[18] Lord Strang, *The Foreign Office*, New York: Oxford University Press, 1955, Chapter IX.
[19] *Ibid.*, p. 154.

even that of the Secretary himself. No Foreign Secretary can ignore his recommendations; he is a weighty factor in British foreign policy.

The Permanent Under Secretary outranks the Parliamentary Under Secretaries whose primary responsibility is the maintenance of smooth relations with Parliament. Thus the extent of their influence depends upon their personalities and their connections in Parliament. Though not necessarily experts in foreign affairs, they may well be instrumental in initiating policies if their parliamentary standing is high and they have easy access to the Foreign Secretary. On the other hand, they may be little more than the Secretary's mouthpieces before Parliament, sent to answer questions in his name.

Mention should be made of the "private secretaries" of the leading Foreign Office officials. The Principal Private Secretary to the Foreign Secretary is a very important officer who, together with four Assistant Secretaries, is charged not only with keeping the Secretary well briefed on the business of the Foreign Office but also with maintaining harmonious relations among the Secretary, his advisers, and his assistants. These secretaries must ensure proper liaison between the Foreign Office and other government agencies as well as with the royal household and the cabinet secretariat. They are comparable to the "Cabinet" of the French Foreign Minister rather than to the Executive Secretariat of the United States Secretary of State which is a secretariat proper.

The Foreign Office. Like the U. S. Department of State, the British Foreign Office has had to expand since World War II. It used to be a comparatively small organization noted for its efficiency. With many new tasks to be performed, there has been a democratization of its staff. Moreover, the fact that its civil servants are not exposed, as are their colleagues in the United States, to budgetry troubles, insufficient pay, or eternal abuse by Congress and the public has contributed much to its expert working organization.

The Foreign Office does not publish an organization chart but rather a list of officials and their responsibilities in certain areas or functions. However, in order to provide better understanding for this singular type of organization, such a chart has been devised. (Opposite p. 163) From it can be seen that supervision of several bureaus is shared by two chiefs whose job is a matter of dual responsibility which cannot clearly be shown on a chart but appears to be working well in practice. This type of organization also causes a grouping of departments which seem to have little to do with each other. For example, the American Department is grouped with the Passport, Consular and Protocol Departments.[20]

The Economic Relations Department deals with questions pertaining to the International Monetary Fund, the International Trade Organization, the International Food and Agriculture Organization, tariff agreements, and oil. This Department also works on problems of commercial policy.

Cultural relations and news dissemination are handled by two departments. The Library has always had a far more important function in the Foreign Office than its name would indicate. It is a library, an archive, a publications and distribution agency, an internal information bureau, an international conference management and a historical research office all combined. Frequent reorganizations have left the Library's significance untouched; the attachment in the forties of a Research Department and its later separation from the Library to become a Department in its own right has not detracted from the Library's high standing.

The Research Department probably is a counterpart of the U.S. Department of State's Office of Intelligence Research. According to Lord Strang, the task of the Department is "to collect from unofficial as well as from official sources, and verify, digest and present facts, over the whole field of foreign affairs . . . The principal form in which this material is presented are minutes and memoranda produced *ad hoc* in response to particular requests or inquiries."[21]

---

[20] Lord Strang, *op. cit.*, pp. 206-213.
[21] *Ibid.*, p. 210.

KEY BRITISH FOREIGN OFFICE DEPARTMENTS

Northern

Bulgaria
Czechoslovakia
Denmark
Estonia
Finland
Hungary
Iceland

Latvia
Lithuania
Norway
Poland
USSR
Sweden

Southern

Albania
Austria
Greece
Italy
Portugal

Spain
Turkey
The Vatican
Yugoslavia

Western

Belgium
France
Germany
Irish Republic

Luxembourg
The Netherlands
Switzerland

Eastern

Iran
Persian Gulf

Saudi Arabia
The Yemen

African

Egypt
Anglo-Egyptian Sudan
Ethiopia
Eritrea
Libya
Africa-general
French possessions in Africa

Belgian possessions in Africa
Portuguese possessions in
   Africa
Spanish possessions in Africa
Tangier
Liberia

KEY BRITISH FOREIGN OFFICE DEPARTMENTS (*Continued*)

The Levant

Iraq	Lebanon
Israel	Syria
Jordan	

Southeast Asia

Thailand	Tibet
Vietnam	Afghanistan
Laos	Burma
Indonesia	Philippines
Cambodia	French, Portuguese posses-
Nepal	sions in India

Far East

Japan	Korea
China	Tibet

American

Western Hemisphere,	Dominican Republic
including Canada	Haiti
Cuba	Panama Canal Zone

In order to better understand the Foreign Office's inner workings, we must remember that an organization chart cannot show the complexity and flexibility of the relations between the officials and the Ministers. For example, the Permanent Under Secretary comes below the Ministers of State and above the Parliamentary Under Secretaries, but the latter are not so removed as the chart implies. On the contrary, although the line of command does not necessarily pass through their offices, the volume of paper that is submitted to them is very large. They have to be consulted on everything that might affect the government's relations with Parliament—a most important factor.

Furthermore, the principles of organization are designed to reduce the flow of paper to the top and to see to it that decisions are made at the lowest appropriate level. Decisions about who should be consulted are in the main pragmatic and flexible. The officers in question are supposed to use their common sense and to ask someone with greater experience when they are in doubt. It is significant for the Foreign Office's internal relations that one regards it as a courtesy not to burden people unnecessarily.

This system produces considerably more independence of judgment than would be permissible in most other foreign offices. For instance, when a question can be decided by a single department, this will be done, as a rule, at the lowest appropriate level. Junior officers are encouraged to assume responsibility and to submit questions to superiors only when they are at a loss as to the best course of action. There will be errors, but a few mistakes by junior officers are looked upon as less harmful than persistent shirking of responsibility. There is one qualification: One must always ensure that a Minister be informed if a proposed course of action is likely to be criticized in Parliament. When, within a single department, a question has to be referred to the higher echelons for decision, a submission is made by the head of the department. It sets forth the problem, the pros and cons and the alternative courses of action and recommendation. These submissions may be acted upon by the Under Secretary, but in most cases by the Ministers.

When departments other than the Foreign Office are concerned, decisions have to be made by mutual agreement. As a result, there is a vast amount of informal daily or *ad hoc* consultation on current business. But for recurring and difficult problems, or for unexpected issues that need to be dealt with, the Cabinet Office (whose responsible Minister is the Prime Minister) runs a system of Ministerial and Official Committees. The committee system is flexible; when one of the committees has outlived its usefulness, it is dropped. New ones are created as needed. Membership is determined by the principle that only those concerned should be selected. In general, problems are first discussed in Official Committees and afterwards submitted to the Ministerial Committees, always keeping in mind that matters should be settled, if possible, on the lowest possible level.

Ministerial Committees are regarded as cabinet committees. They are supposed to settle as many questions as possible among themselves in order to reduce the flow of business to the full cabinet. Decisions tend to be based upon a consensus, formulated by the Chairman, which is recorded in the minutes. This system has succeeded in reducing the agenda of the full cabinet; the disadvantage is that the cabinet no longer keeps an eye on the entirety of foreign affairs problems.[22]

As in the U. S. Department of State, the political, economic and functional detail work is done chiefly by experienced desk officers. Since the personnel of the Foreign Office and that of the Foreign Service are interchangeable, desk officers usually are assigned to areas which they know from personal experience. There is a great deal of close and interlocking cooperation between the desk officers of various departments. Organizational flexibility has developed to a greater degree than formerly; the changes in the world situation have not been lost to the administrators of the Foreign Office. Its setup is functional and compact and almost certainly efficient as an organization.

To sum up, it appears that, compared with the period prior to World War I, the authority of the Foreign Officer has diminished. More account has to be taken of the views of other government departments, and the weight of internal politics has increased. At the same time, the cabinet committee system and multiplying interdepartmental consultations have resulted from this situation. Furthermore, foreign policy involves far greater expenditures than formerly, a fact which strengthens the Treasury position. Thus the Foreign Office is most careful to secure Parliamentary opinion on its side, even though Parliament has no where near the power over the Foreign Office that Congress has over the U. S. Department of State.

National Security Policy. As we have seen in the case of the

---

[22] The consequences of this system are discussed by R. H. S. Crossman in his article "Machine Politics," *Encounter*, London: April 1963, pp. 17, 21-26.

United States, the formulation of security policy depends upon coordination of all government departments and upon an integrated formula resulting from such coordination. In Great Britain, the cabinet already symbolizes coordination but for special tasks the British government uses powerfully staffed committees. The most important of these is the Defence Committee which may be likened to the American National Security Council. However, the Defence Committee is far more powerful because it can make decisions, whereas the NSC can only advise. The reason for this is that the U. S. President, although Chairman of the NSC, listens to the views of the Council but makes up his own mind regardless of the Council's views. The Prime Minister of Great Britain, on the other hand, strong as his position may be, is not the actual chief of state as is the U.S. President, but—under the monarchy—"merely" the chief of the government and *primus inter pares* in the cabinet. Since he works hand in glove with the other ministers, the Defence Committee is really a reinforced cabinet. Membership is limited to the Minister of Defence, the Lord President of the Council, the Chancellor of the Exchequer, the Foreign Secretary, the First Lord of the Admiralty, the Secretaries for War and Air, and the Ministers of Labour and Supply. Military leaders are invited as advisers. This committee, successor to the Committee of Imperial Defence, considers and decides all problems of vital security, combining political and military issues.

The Minister of Defence, whose office, as in the United States, was established only after World War II, is Deputy Chairman of the Committee. His office coordinates the armed services and apportions "available resources between the three Services in accordance with the strategic policy laid down by the Defence Committee."[23] It is important to observe that the Minister of Defence is also the administrative head of the Joint Intelligence Committee, another parallel with the American security organization in which both the NSC and the CIA are part of the security mechanism set up by the same law.

However, the Foreign Minister's role in the Defence Commit-

[23] Stout, *op. cit.*, p. 332-3.

tee is considerable, scarcely less important than that of the Defence Minister. One might speculate that the most influential voices heard in the committee meetings are those of the Prime Minister, the Defence Minister, and the Foreign Secretary. At the same time, it cannot be forgotten that the Foreign Secretary's influence depends greatly upon his personality, political judgment, and diplomatic skill.

France

Constitutional Issues Regarding the Conduct of Foreign Affairs. The Constitution of the Fifth French Republic was adopted by referendum on September 28, 1958, and promulgated on October 4 of that year. It shifts responsibility for the conduct of foreign affairs from the parliament to the Prime Minister and, even more, the President. Like many other developments in the Fifth Republic, this, too, demonstrates the effect of Charles de Gaulle's towering influence.

The Constitution of the Fourth Republic of 1946, which threw out that of the Third Republic (1875), was short lived. Internal and external events had created so great an instability that France seemed unable, with existing basic laws, to reorganize its government machinery and revitalize its handling of political and economic issues. The 1946 Constitution, which contained only five articles concerning foreign relations, clearly expressed its framers' desire to increase popular control of French foreign policy by shifting responsibilities to the National Assembly. In so doing, they brought it under the supervision of the political parties which supposedly represented the will of the people in matters concerning France's position in the world. The 1875 Constitution gave the President of the Republic control over treaty negotiation and ratification, "subject only to the requirement of informing the Chambers of all treaties affecting peace, commerce, territory, finance and the personal and property rights of French nationals abroad."[24] The 1946 Constitu-

---

[24] F. L. Schuman, *War and Diplomacy in the French Republic*, New York: McGraw-Hill Book Co., 1931, p. 19.

tion curtailed these presidential powers. Art. 31 stated that the President "will be kept informed about international negotiations," but apart from the ceremonial duties of receiving foreign diplomats and accrediting French envoys, there was no further reference to his activities in foreign relations. War-making and treaty-making power was clearly vested in the parliament (Arts. 26-28).

The new 1958 Constitution not only provides that the President be kept informed of "all negotiations leading to the conclusion of an international agreement not subject to ratification," but also empowers him to "negotiate and ratify treaties" (Art. 52). Such treaties which in the Third Republic required ratification by the Chamber, "may be ratified or approved only by a law" and then "shall go into effect only after having been ratified or approved" (Art. 53). Cessions or additions of territories must be validated by the population concerned rather than the National Assembly.

It is no longer the political parties which determine the nation's policy, but the government. Its responsibility to the parliament is indicated in Articles 20, 49 and 50, but there are certain strictures which prevent the parliament from taking hasty action. For example, the President can send messages to the two assemblies of parliament and "cause" them to be read, but the reading "shall not be followed by any debate" (Art. 18). The President also "shall appoint the Premier" (Prime Minister) and can "terminate the functions of the Premier when the latter presents the resignation of the government" (Art. 8). There is no provision that his choice must be approved by the parliament. Even more important, the President "shall preside over the Council of Ministers" (Art. 9), which, according to the previous constitutions, was the responsibility of the Premier, then called President of the Council of Ministers. The President is the commander in chief of the armed forces and as such will preside "over the higher councils and committees of national defense" (Art. 15).

Under the new Constitution, the "government shall determine and direct the policy of the nation" (Art. 20). This obviously embraces foreign policy. Furthermore, the government "shall have at its disposal the administration and the armed forces." (Art. 20) Since the President is the commander in chief of the armed forces and has the right to select the Premier, it is clear that he is the actual source of power. Add to this the provision that the Premier "shall direct the operation of the government" and "shall be responsible for national defense" (Art. 21). The delegation of powers to other ministers is the Premier's responsibility, under the same Article. But in the highest councils of the government the chairmanship remains the President's, and the Premier is permitted to substitute for him only "by virtue of an explicit delegation for a specific agenda" (Art. 21).

Thus, the Foreign Minister's relationship to the Premier or the President bears little resemblance to that of the 1946 Constitution and far less to the relationship of the Foreign Secretary to his Prime Minister. Nor can it be compared profitably with the line of command which exists between the President of the United States and the Secretary of State. In fact, the position of the French Foreign Minister carries less influence than that of any other foreign minister in the West. Most of the powers for dealing with foreign nations are undoubtedly held, directly or indirectly, by the President, assisted by the Premier, who can function only as long as he enjoys the President's confidence.

Thus, while the Parliament of the Fourth Republic had an enormous actual and potential power over the government of France—which it abused—the Fifth Republic is notable for having curtailed this power more than any other Western country. In a sense, the Fifth Republic of France has become a "guided democracy."[25]

The Foreign Minister and the "Quai d'Orsay."[26] Like his U.S. and British colleagues, the Foreign Minister is a political

---

[25] See also J. Chatelain, *La Nouvelle Constitution et la Régime Politique de France*, Editions Berger-Levrault, Paris, 1959.

[26] The most important offices of the Ministry of Foreign Affairs are situated at 37 Quai d'Orsay in Paris. The name of this street on the banks of the Seine has through the years become identified with the Ministry.

appointee. But, since the Premier chooses him, almost certainly with the advice and consent of the President, it is doubtful that under the Fifth Republic a Foreign Minister will be appointed who has only political and no technical qualifications. On the other hand, his influence has diminished considerably in comparison with his postwar position. His responsibility toward the parliament (National Assembly) is practically non-existent; the Premier is responsible. His policies must withstand the scrutiny of the Premier and the President. In cases of particular importance, he functions as an adviser rather than a policy maker. The Foreign Minister thus is a diplomatic representative of the President, but less so than the U.S. Secretary of State. His initiative is greatly restricted and his influence on foreign policy formulation hard to assess; perhaps his status is comparable to that of the Soviet Foreign Minister.

As in former governments, the French Foreign Minister has at his disposal a "Cabinet" headed by a director, a deputy director, and a chief of cabinet who are assisted by departmental chiefs and diplomats experienced in foreign affairs. However, the importance of this Cabinet, in contrast with that of the Fourth Republic, appears somewhat diminished. It still is designed to ease the burden of the Minister, but, as a cushion between the Minister and the parliament, it is no longer of major importance. Its functions include arranging press conferences, dispensing information, and coordinating official foreign travel. Attached to the cabinet are a separate Bureau of Visa and Diplomatic Passports and secretariat.

The second-ranking official in the Foreign Ministry is the Secretary of State. A political appointee, who may or may not be named acting Minister, his primary role is that of high-level liaison officer between the Minister and the National Assembly.

More important in the administration of the Foreign Ministry is the office of the Secretary General of the Ministry, who is comparable to the Permanent Under Secretary of the British Foreign Office. He is the highest career expert in the Ministry and his advice is heavily relied on by the Minister. Most political, eco-

FRENCH MINISTRY OF FOREIGN AFFAIRS POLITICAL

SUB-DIRECTORATES

EUROPE

Southern Europe
Italy
Vatican
Portugal
Greece
Turkey
Monaco
San Marino
Andorra

Eastern Europe
USSR
Albania
Bulgaria
Hungary
Poland
Rumania
Czechoslovakia
Yugoslavia

Central Europe
Germany
Switzerland
Austria
Liechtenstein

Western Europe

Great Britain
Ireland
Belgium
Luxembourg
The Netherlands
Sweden
Norway
Denmark
Finland
Iceland

ASIA AND OCEANIA

South Asia-Oceania
India
Pakistan
Ceylon
Nepal
Afghanistan
Burma
Thailand
Malaysia
Singapore
Australia
New Zealand

South Pacific Territories
New Hebrides
Indonesia

Far East

Republic of China
Chinese Mainland
Hong Kong
Mongolia
Korea
Japan
The Philippines

FRENCH MINISTRY OF FOREIGN AFFAIRS POLITICAL SUB—DIRECTORATES (*Continued*)

AFRICA-LEVANT

Saudi Arabia
Iraq
Iran
Israel
Jerusalem-Jordan
Kuwait

Lebanon
Syria
United Arab Republic
  (Egypt)
Yemen and various small
  sultanates

AFRICA

South Africa
Burundi
Congo
  (Leopoldville)
Ethiopia
Gambia
Guinea
Kenya
Liberia
Nigeria
Uganda

Federation of Rhodesia
  and Nyasaland
Ruanda
St. Helena
Sierra Leone
Somalia
Southeast Africa
Tanganyika
Portuguese Territories,
  Islands in Indian Ocean

NORTH AFRICA

Morocco
Tunisia

Lybia
Algeria

AMERICA

North America
USA
Canada
Jamaica
Trinidad
Caribbean Countries
Autonomous and dependent
  American Territories
Latin America
Central America

Mexico
Cuba
Haiti
Dominican Republic
Venezuela
Brazil
Argentina
Chile
Uruguay
Paraguay

UN AND INTERNATIONAL ORGANIZATIONS
TREATIES AND SPACE AFFAIRS
(including atomic affairs)
PRESS AND INFORMATION SERVICE

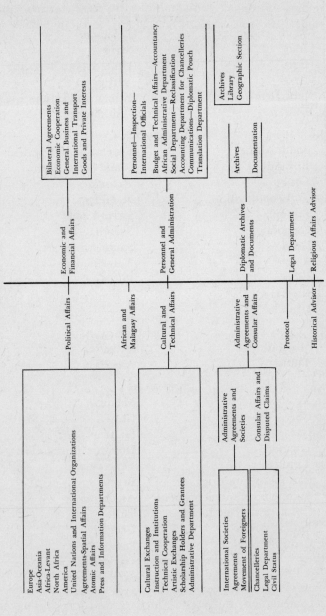

FRENCH MINISTRY OF FOREIGN AFFAIRS
(1963)

SECRETARY OF STATE

SECRETARY GENERAL

Political Affairs

Europe
Asia-Oceania
Africa-Levant
North Africa
America
United Nations and International Organizations
Agreements-Spatial Affairs
Atomic Affairs
Press and Information Departments

Economic and Financial Affairs

Bilateral Agreements
Economic Cooperation
General Business and International Transport
Goods and Private Interests

African and Malagasy Affairs

Cultural and Technical Affairs

Cultural Exchanges
Instruction and Institutions
Technical Cooperation
Artistic Exchanges
Scholarship Holders and Grantees
Administrative Department

Personnel and General Administration

Personnel—Inspection—International Officials
Budget and Technical Affairs—Accountancy
African Administrative Department
Social Department—Reclassification
Accounting Department for Chancelleries
Communications—Diplomatic Pouch
Translation Department

Administrative Agreements and Consular Affairs

Administrative Agreements and Societies

International Societies
Agreements
Movement of Foreigners

Consular Affairs and Disputed Claims

Chancelleries
Legal Department
Civil Status

Diplomatic Archives and Documents

Archives
Documentation

Archives
Library
Geographic Section

Protocol

Legal Department

Historical Advisor

Religious Affairs Advisor

nomic, functional, and administrative offices of the Ministry are under the Secretary General's supervision. His bureau is staffed by experts who deal with issues of concern to the following six specialized secretaries: the personal secretariat and the secretariats for study missions, coordination of nuclear questions, and liaison with the ministries of the Sahara, Algeria, and National Defense. These responsibilities constitute a major change from those of the previous General Secretariat which was divided into three parts: One handled "particular problems" outside routine business; another arranged conferences and liaison between the French government and the United Nations, including UNESCO; a third dealt with administrative business of the Foreign Ministry. Except for administrative functions, the Secretary General's responsibilities seem to have been adjusted to new international problems.

The organization chart of the Ministry of Foreign Affairs has also changed to cope with the intricacies of contemporary international relations. However, like other Western foreign offices, the Quai d'Orsay may be divided roughly into top-echelon offices, political and economic offices, cultural affairs (greatly emphasized in France) and administrative bureaus.

The Press and Information Service Sub-directorate listed in the chart on *pages 176* and *177* is set up both geographically and functionally. Its responsibilities are: relations with the press and the public, editing telegrams of information, analysis and study of the French and foreign press and press agencies, radio and television broadcasts; publication of daily bulletins for the press, liaison with the Ministry of Information, accrediting of foreign journalists and documentation for information services and French diplomatic missions abroad.

It is significant that, in addition to this large organization of Political Affairs, there is another separate directorate on African and Malagasy Affairs. The intense preoccupation with African areas is expressed in the organization of this directorate. Its Sub-directorate I contains two offices working on inter-African relations and groupings, implementation of cooperation agreements, documentation, and participation of the African states in international organizations; Sub-directorate II is concerned primarily with economic and financial problems; Sub-directorate III deals with political problems of Central Africa, West Africa, Madagascar, the Cameroons and Togo; it also takes up questions of defense and religion.

According to official statements, the political offices are responsible mainly for correspondence with and political work on the countries and organizations within the jurisdiction of the various bureaus. However, questions of national defense and international law are also examined, together with economic, administrative, and cultural questions. The military attachés appear to be supervised by the political rather than the military departments. [27]

The Directorate of Economic and Financial affairs has undergone considerable changes. Its four major sub-directorates are charged with responsibility for (a) bilateral agreements, (b) economic cooperation service, (c) business and international transportation, and (d) service for private interests and goods. In Sub-directorate (a), Section 1 keeps a watch on economic and financial relations with African countries, including Morocco, Tunisia and the Near East; Section 2 is responsible for economic relations with the countries of America and deals with such matters as sales of armament and airplane parts, international fairs, technical assistance, economic expansion abroad, and customs agreements. Section 3 works on economic and financial relations with countries in Southeast Asia and the Far East, including North and South Vietnam, Laos and Cambodia, Australia and New Zealand. Section 4 does the same with countries in North and West Europe and Section 5 with East Europe, the USSR, plus Greece and Turkey.

Sub-directorate (b)'s three sections have the following duties: 1. participation in the economic and financial organizations of the United Nations, the General Agreement on Tariffs and Trade (GATT), the International Bank, the International Monetary Fund and other such bodies; 2. participation in the organization of economic cooperation and development; 3. par-

[27] *Administration Centrale, Ministère des Affaires Etrangères,* Paris: Imprimerie Nationale, 1958, 11 ff.

ticipation in the European Economic Community as well as the Common Market and its associated countries.

Sub-directorate (c)'s three sections deal with 1. control over export of strategic goods; 2. international transportation on sea, land and in the air; 3. implementation of the Pact of Paris, the Austrian Treaty and other peace treaties, war damage, defense of French rights and interests abroad and motion picture exchanges.

Finally, the sub-directorate on property and private interests, war damage and nationalization is divided into geographic sections which denote those areas where French interests are specifically at stake: North Africa; Germany, Austria and the United States; Cambodia, Laos, Vietnam, Congo (Leopoldville), Guinea and other countries.

Apart from the offices concerned with administration and personnel, it remains for us to review the Directorate of Cultural and Technical Affairs. Great interest in these fields has always been evident in France, and the 1958 reorganization, as well as subsequent reshuffles of the Foreign Ministry, have reconfirmed this interest in its elaborate provisions for areas of work. Therefore, the Directorate is endowed with a full staff and a detailed organization. The service for Cultural Exchange is the first of numerous bureaus and is responsible for dealing with the United Nations and other international organizations; in addition, it handles books and publications; motion pictures, radio and television; literary, scientific and technical exhibitions; exchanges with Eastern peoples; and cultural missions and conferences.

The Service of Instruction and Studies is charged with dissemination of the French language and instruction abroad, exchange of university professors, archaelogical missions and the establishment of hospitals. This section is organized along geographic lines, specifically Morocco-Tunisia, Africa-Asia, Europe-America. The Service for Technical Cooperation also is geographically determined and the Service for Artistic Exchanges deals with theater, music and art exhibitions abroad as well as foreign programs in France.

Thus it appears that the over-all concept of the French Ministry of Foreign Affairs is one of many-sided, perhaps somewhat over-organized activity. The chart of the Ministry shows the desire to incorporate the principles of a new approach (which was missing prior to 1958) in adapting foreign policy making to new conditions and France's aspirations in a divided world. But former habits are still recognizable, and the result is an organization that comprises both old and new ideas. Since the advent of the Fifth Republic and its presidential system, the Foreign Ministry probably is less exposed to the many intra-governmental influences which formerly prevailed. The general responsibility for policy formulation lies with the Premier and the Foreign Minister, but it is the President who has the primary influence on foreign affairs and makes the final decisions.

National Security Policy. The American concept of coordinating and integrating national security with foreign policy has also been adopted by the Fifth Republic. It is referred to in the official announcement of the new Defense Organization.[28] Its most important aspects are the creation of two committees: The Defense Committee and the Restricted Defense Committee. The former committee's task is the formulation of *basic* defense policy which is not only military but also political in nature. The President is chairman; members are the Premier, the Foreign Minister, the Ministers of the Armed Forces, the Interior, and of Financial and Economic Affairs. The Restricted Defense Committee, also presided over by the President, is convoked by the Premier for the discussion of *specific* defense policies. Participants are selected by the Premier according to the problems to be discussed.

The result of the efforts of these committees remains to be seen. They have been in existence for too short a time to permit any informed judgment. The basic thought appears sound and certainly is a novel development in the history of the French Republic; the crown councils of the kings are hardly comparable, since their function differed and their voice under the absolute monarch was weak. The position of the President in the Fifth

[28] *Journal Officiel*, January 7, 1959.

Republic is very strong; it will be fascinating to watch the highest policy makers steer between presidential influence and constitutional safeguards.

Unquestionably, the President's position in the new Constitution has been tailored to fit General de Gaulle. If future Presidents of France are able to maintain his standards, the constitutional provisions concerning foreign affairs will remain effective. If not, the entire edifice of the 1958 Constitution may be shaken, for it depends upon the personality of one man. Should a future President abdicate some of his power to the Premier, the parliament might become correspondingly stronger and make its weight felt, possibly by disrupting political life and international relations—thereby defeating the purpose of the new Constitution. France's 12-year experience with constant governmental changes and an ungovernable National Assembly has enabled General de Gaulle to obtain a victory in his referendum regarding the new Constitution.[29]

THE EAST

The Union of Soviet Socialist Republics

The Communist Party and the Soviet Constitution in Foreign Affairs. The controlling factors of policy making in the Soviet Union differ greatly from those of the Western democracies. Certainly, among them is neither the Ministry of Foreign Affairs (*Minindel* in Russian abbreviation) nor the Foreign Minister. The Constitution of 1936 provides guidance in form, but not in content. For example, it decrees that the Supreme Soviet, as the leading legislative body of the USSR, has war- and peace-making functions. Article 14 of the Constitution says that "the jurisdiction of the USSR, as represented by its higher organs of state power and organs of state administration, embraces:

[29] For a new French interpretation of foreign affairs organization see Jean Baillou and Pierre Pelletier, *Les Affaires Etrangères*, Paris: Presses Universitaires de France, 1962.

(a) representation of the Union in international relations, conclusion, ratification and denunciation of treaties of the USSR with other states; the establishment of general procedure governing the relations of Union Republics with foreign states;

(b) questions of war and peace;

(c) foreign trade on the basis of state monopoly.

The Supreme Soviet is the parliament of the USSR, led and presided over by a Presidium which carries out the Supreme Soviet's legislative functions when the latter is not in session.[30] Since the Supreme Soviet is convoked only on very important occasions, the Presidium is responsible for ratification of international treaties. It also "appoints and recalls plenipotentiary representatives of the USSR to foreign states" and "receives the letters of credence and recall of diplomatic representatives accredited to it by foreign states" (Art. 49, p and q). The Presidium can also proclaim "a state of war in the event of armed attack on the USSR, or when necessary to fulfill international treaty obligations concerning mutual defense against aggression . . ." (Art. 49, m.) .

In practice, however, the Supreme Soviet is a rubber-stamp parliament, convoked for the purpose of passing measures taken by the leaders of the Soviet hierarchy. During the decades of its existence, no opposition has ever been voiced, unless prearranged. Instead of a parliamentary organization, it serves as a sounding board for important statements by the Soviet leaders. In other words, the Supreme Soviet is a parliament in form but not in substance, despite the principle of "public control" proclaimed by Soviet leaders. When the Supreme Soviet is not in session—which is most of the time—the Presidium conducts its business. But it is not a real force either. Power emanates from only one source—the Communist Party of the Soviet Union.

The Supreme Soviet is, of course, a part of the Soviet government organization. So is its Presidium and the Council of Minis-

---

[30] The chairman of the Presidium of the Supreme Soviet is the nominal head of the USSR, but his functions are chiefly ceremonial.

ters. Both bodies are interlocked with the Party organs: the Presidium, the Secretariat of the Central Committee and the Bureau for the RSFSR (Russia) of the Central Committee. Their sounding boards are the Central Committee and the Party Congress. The Party's organizational power base is the Central Committee. But the Presidium is the distillation of this power, and a number of its members also hold positions in the Secretariat of the Central Committee, the Council of Ministers and, in a few cases, the Presidium of the Supreme Soviet. Over this interlocking directorate of the Soviet Party and Government reigns the Party Presidium and it is this body which initiates or formulates Soviet foreign policy. In this light, the Constitution misrepresents the actual power relationship when its says, in Article 68, d., that the Council of Ministers "exercises general guidance in the sphere of relations with foreign states." For it cannot be stated too clearly that the Party, through its leading organs (Presidium, Secretariat, and Central Committee), rules the country. It determines all aspects of policy and implementation in both the internal and external spheres. Governmental agencies merely carry out the party line.

During the Stalin era, the dictator himself determined policies, internal and external. Whenever he sought information, it was apt to be tailored to his point of view; he laid down the party line and reports thus suffered from a lack of objectivity. The result was a scarcity of realistic information and the production of falsified documents which placed Stalin in a kind of intellectual isolation. What he would not accept, he either discarded or conveniently forgot. The refusal to believe Allied information on the impending Nazi German aggression demonstrated this attitude. Since Stalin's death, there is far more sophistication: The Chairman wants to be properly and factually briefed and, consequently, the Soviet estimate of the capitalist world has changed considerably. It is still influenced by ideological preconceptions, but it does not ignore the realities.

From the beginning of the collective leadership period following the death of Stalin and Beria, decisions probably were no

longer unilateral. There is some evidence of differences of opinion which were quite pronounced before the anti-party group
led by Molotov was isolated. Even then, the views of the members of the Presidium and the Central Committee were taken
into consideration. While Khrushchev was in power, his pragmatic and realistic approach to foreign affairs probably caused
the Presidium to listen more than ever before to the views of
the Council of Ministers in general and to the Foreign Minister
in particular.[31] Nevertheless, final decisions on foreign policy
are made by the Chairman and must rest partly on ideological
considerations because the Presidium as the highest organ of
the ruling Soviet Communist Party, must maintain its ideological stance either by fitting policy into the Marxist-Leninist
pattern or by adjusting the pattern to fit the rapidly changing
world. For example: The three chief concepts of Soviet foreign
policy are: 1) unity of the communist states, 2) peaceful coexistence with states of different social systems and 3) support of the
"national liberation movement" in the new and underdeveloped
Afro-Asian and Latin American states. All three objectives are
unthinkable outside the Marxist-Leninist concept, which suggests
that the Soviet or any other communist foreign policy is, at the
same time, international communist policy.

There is still another aspect of the organization and control of
Soviet foreign policy—the position of the Union Republics. Since
the establishment of the USSR, the status of these republics with
regard to participation in international relations has changed
twice. Before 1923, each of the republics was permitted to conduct its own foreign relations. After 1923, an All-Union Foreign
Commissariat took over representation of the entire Union,
including the republics. The republics were empowered to present their views through emissaries to the Commissariat. In
reverse, each emissary instructed his government about possible

[31] Cf. *National Policy Machinery in the Soviet Union*, Report of the Committee on Government Operations, U.S. Senate, U.S. Printing Office, Washington, 1960, p. 21 and pp. 40-42.

obligations concerning international treaties that might be of special interests to the republics.

In 1944, the system again changed, probably under the impact of war, and the Union Republics were permitted to enter into direct negotiations with foreign governments. When they did, they acted as the mouthpiece of the All-Union government. Since there was no Party decentralization, the local Party machinery was perfectly synchronized with the local governments.

In theory, there exist sixteen Union Republic foreign offices. It would be chaotic to permit all these republics to develop "normal" international relations; this could not be tolerated by any central government no matter what its ideology. By law, all treaties concluded between the Republics and foreign powers must be approved by the Supreme Soviet of both the Union Republics and the USSR. Thus one may conclude that the autonomy of the Union Republics is a fiction, used tactically when it suits the purposes of the Party whose control point is in the Kremlin. The decisions of the Party's Central Committee are binding for all Central Committees of the Republics. However, the "autonomy" of components of the USSR has affected Soviet foreign relations in several ways. First, it has created a larger representation of Soviet views in the international forum of the United Nations.[32] Second, it has relieved the Soviet Foreign Ministry of minor issues or embarrassing problems that could be sidetracked through Union Republic intervention. Third, it has emphasized the "independence" granted by the USSR to its constituent republics in the field of foreign relations, foreign trade, and national defense. Fourth, it has provided attractive domestic propaganda by arousing ideological fervor and by fostering loyalty to the regime.

These are, in brief, some of the more significant aspects of Soviet management of foreign affairs. There have been changes in the methods and approaches, and more are likely to occur. But "the summit of Communist hopes and aspirations is, in the last analysis, today as in Lenin's time, a complete change of the

[32] As agreed upon at the Yalta Conference in 1945.

world's political, economic, social and cultural setup, and at the
base of Soviet foreign policy lies the desire to make the world safe
for Communism and Sovietism."[33] In this sense, the machinery
of Soviet foreign relations is geared for the tactical implementation of its two main objectives: to overtake the West and to
achieve a bloodless victory of world communism. These are the
goals of the CPSU. The goals of the Kremlin are not only
national; they are primarily determined by those of the international communist movement. It is not the country but the
Party that determines these goals and their methods of implementation. This is true not only of the USSR, but also of Communist China and all other states under communist rule.

   The Soviet Foreign Minister and the "Collegium." The Soviet
foreign minister, unless he ranks high in the Communist hierarchy, is not a very important official. He is, of course, the administrator of the *Minindel,* the Soviet Ministry of Foreign Affairs,
but his influence on policy making is minor. This has been
underlined by several remarks of Khrushchev which seem to be
almost contemptuous of his foreign minister, Andrei Gromyko.
When Molotov was foreign minister, his influence was far
stronger, because of his high standing in the Party. But then Molotov was a member of the former Politburo; in other words, he
was strongly entrenched in both state government and party
government while Gromyko has never held a high party post. A
Soviet foreign minister is in actual fact the executor of the Presidium's will and cannot undertake actions without the Kremlin's
express orders. It is almost certain that not only policies but also
methods of implementation are planned by the Presidium, not
by the *Minindel.*

   Next to the Minister, the First Deputy Foreign Minister is the
most important official in the *Minindel.* His position may be com-

   [33] *Trends in Russian Foreign Policy since World War I,* prepared by the
Legislative Reference Service of the Library of Congress, U.S. Government
Printing Office, Washington, D.C., 1947, p. 65. See also *National Policy
Machinery in the Soviet Union.* Report of the Committee on Government
Operations, U.S. Senate, U.S. Government Printing Office, Washington, D.C.:
March 29, 1960, Parts II and III.

pared, to some degree, with that of a U.S. Undersecretary of State. His influence, too, depends upon his standing in the Party, and it is conceivable that he could have more actual power than the Minister himself. This, incidentally, is a general characteristic of the Soviet government hierarchy: An official's actual rank may have little relation to his real influence. Soviet defectors have revealed that minor employees could terrorize high officials by virtue of their affiliations with the KGB or their standing in the Party.

A unique feature of the *Minindel* is the Collegium. Presided over by the Foreign Minister, the Collegium comprises the Deputy Foreign Ministers and those additional experts whom the Council of Ministers may appoint. Its influence is not regarded as strong but its long existence demonstrates its usefulness in the eyes of the Kremlin leaders. Although it has been claimed that the Collegium is the directing staff of the Ministry,[34] it has also been compared with the U. S. Department of State's Planning Council.

The Collegium is said to enjoy certain prerogatives. For example, if the Foreign Minister sees fit to reject its recommendations, it may appeal to the Council of Ministers which, in turn, may sustain the Collegium and nullify the Minister's decision. It is unlikely, however, that this contingency has arisen often, if at all. Furthermore, to a considerable extent the argument is academic. The Party makes the final decision, voiding either the Minister's or the Collegium's view, or both. In any event, the Collegium may well be the only body of the Soviet government whose views are heard by the Presidium. Its existence tends to demonstrate that the Kremlin leaders are not given to hasty decisions but increasingly are relying on carefully planned policies. In the effort to think through problems such institutions as the Soviet Academy of Sciences and the Academy of Social Sciences, both arms of the Party, collaborate.

After Stalin, one may assume, the Presidium and the Council of Ministers paid more attention than before to expert analysis

[34] "National Policy Machinery in the Soviet Union," *op. cit.*, p. 41.

and evaluation of all available information. Even so, the value of this work, and perhaps that of the Collegium in particular, is prejudiced by the necessity for Soviet representatives abroad and officials at home to conform with the principles of Marxism-Leninism, in the contemporary interpretation, and apply them as touchstones to Soviet estimates and world views.

The Organization of the Soviet Ministry of Foreign Affairs (Minindel). According to the *Great Soviet Encyclopedia*, which often indicates Soviet political trends, the responsibilities of the *Minindel* are the following:

> Diplomatic protection of the political and economic interests abroad; establishment and maintenance of diplomatic relations with foreign countries; supervision of Soviet diplomatic activities abroad; preparation of international agreements and the conduct of negotiations for such agreements as well as the supervision of their proper execution; protection of Soviet citizens abroad and establishment of close cultural relations with foreign nations. [35]

Western nations have never regarded foreign office organizations as a secret. The Soviet government, however, has never published a chart of the *Minindel*'s organization. Nevertheless, by collecting bits and pieces of information, the organizational picture can be revealed with fair accuracy, particularly since no major reorganizations seem to have been undertaken for a long time or, more exactly, since the demise of the Comintern made necessary a strengthening of the foreign affairs machinery.

Apart from the top echelon and the Collegium, the *Minindel* consists of the conventional groups of geographic, functional, and administrative offices. While even the names of the department heads of the geographic divisions are known, the activities of the economic and administrative offices are not available. As far as international economics are concerned, it is reasonable to assume that the main work in this field is the responsibility of the State Committee for Foreign Economic Relations which "has ministerial rank and operates under the aegis of the Council of Min-

---

[35] Translated from *Bolshaya Sovietskaya Entsiklopediya*, Vol. XLI, p. 207.

isters."[36] It maintains economic contacts with foreign countries and supervises grants and credits as well as technical assistance and scientific cooperation with states outside the communist orbit. Within the orbit, the Council for Mutual Economic Assistance (COMECON) is the appropriate agency. However, economic policy is determined by the Presidium and this determination is influenced primarily by political considerations and only secondarily by economic needs. This fact has rarely been sufficiently understood in the West.

There are fifteen political divisions, six of which deal with European affairs: Western Europe (France, Italy, the Benelux countries and Switzerland); Great Britain and the commonwealth nations (except those in South and Southeast Asia); Central Europe (Austria and East Germany); East-Central Europe (Poland and Czechoslovakia); Southeastern Europe (Hungary and the Balkans, Yugoslavia); and the Scandinavian countries. The non-European world is divided into the following regional divisions: the Near East; the Middle East; South Asia, Southeast Asia; the Far East; two African divisions; two offices dealing with international organization, political and economic; the Latin American countries, and the United States.

The functional divisions contain most of the traditional administrative foreign office bureaus such as the treaty and legal section, protocol, consular and archives, servicing the diplomatic corps and press. The press section, probably highly specialized, is a mere cog in the wheel of the gigantic Soviet propaganda machine which permeates every government agency. The *Minindel's* training facilities, considered essential for the development of education of future Soviet diplomats, are located in the Institute for International Relations and the Higher Diplomatic School. The former offers a six-year course, open only to secondary school graduates recommended by such organizations as the Komsomol (communist youth). An important part of this course, which features languages and the more traditional subjects in the

[36] "National Policy Machinery in the Soviet Union," *op. cit.*, p. 45.

SOVIET UNION
MINISTRY OF FOREIGN AFFAIRS
1 MAY 1963

COLLEGIUM	
	MINISTER
	FIRST DEPUTY MINISTER
	DEPUTY MINISTERS
	COLLEGIUM MEMBERS

SECRETARIAT

FUNCTIONAL DIVISIONS	GEOGRAPHIC DIVISIONS		FOREIGN MISSIONS
PROTOCOL	INTERNATIONAL ORGANIZATIONS	INTERNATIONAL ECONOMIC ORGANIZATIONS	UNITED NATIONS
TREATY & LEGAL	USA	LATIN AMERICAN COUNTRIES	71 EMBASSIES
			10 AMBASSADORS
PRESS	1ST EUROPEAN	2ND EUROPEAN	5 AMBASSADORS
CONSULAR	3RD EUROPEAN	4TH EUROPEAN	2 LEGATIONS
PERSONNEL	5TH EUROPEAN	SCANDINAVIAN COUNTRIES	
SERVICING THE DIPLOMATIC CORPS	1ST AFRICAN	2ND AFRICAN	
ARCHIVES	NEAR EAST COUNTRIES	MIDDLE EAST COUNTRIES	
ECONOMIC	SOUTH ASIAN COUNTRIES	SOUTHEAST ASIAN COUNTRIES	
ADMINISTRATIVE	FAR EAST COUNTRIES		

field of international relations, is the study of Marxism-Leninism. The Higher Diplomatic School probably trains personnel already in service; its curriculum is not known. Foreign affairs training is also provided by the Ministries of Defense and Foreign Trade.[37]

It should be noted that the use of qualified personnel seems to be extremely flexible. It goes without saying that any member of the *Minindel* may be sent overseas, but so can persons from other ministries or institutions. They simply transfer to the *Minindel* or perhaps do not need even a paper transfer. Certainly, MVD personnel are assigned to posts abroad with or without the Ministry's blessings: They receive their travel orders and, according to the nature of their assignment, go under *Minindel* sponsorship or are attached to less conspicuous components. Similar flexibility governs appointments to higher level positions: There is a constant interchange between Ambassadors and Division Chiefs. In other words, owing to the highly integrated nature of the Soviet party and government apparatus, the *Minindel* is utilized as circumstances require, without regard for the bureaucratic standards which loom so large in the West.

National Security Policy. In view of the concentration of power in the Presidium, which holds sway over all branches of Party and government, questions of national security policy are easily coordinated. One of the chief characteristics of totalitarian systems is their striving for integration, covering all aspects of political life. There is no division of power; the one and only party rules the entire administrative apparatus which is its creature. Thus the leading organ of the CPSU, the Presidium, holds all the strands of policy. "In this sense, the USSR had a coordinated security policy long before the United States established its own . . . Metaphorically speaking, the Presidium of the Soviet Communist Party *is* a Security Council. In fact, it is much more, since it does

---

[37] Cf. *Staffing Procedures and Problems in the Soviet Union*, A study submitted to the Subcommittee on National Security Staffing and Operations to the Committee on Government Operations, U.S. Senate, Washington, D.C.: U.S. Government Printing Office, 1963, p. 60 ff.

not differentiate between internal and external policy problems."[38] One might add that in the communist understanding, foreign policy has always been security policy. The concept of the militant class struggle and the party as a quasi-military organization, the view of the non-communist world as suspect and hostile —all this brought about a political attitude that mistrusted normal diplomatic relations and conceived of foreign policy as a tactical instrument to achieve security for the base of world communism.

The People's Republic of China (Communist China)

The Communist Party and the Constitution of Foreign Affairs. Communist China's constitution of 1954 is the result of the Common Program of the Chinese People's Political Consultative Conference (CPPCC) in 1949. The CPPCC met in Peking, September, 1949, to create a semblance of legality after the communist take-over. The constitution itself was published about five years later. It differs from that of the Soviet Union in a number of aspects, particularly in the emphasis on what the Preamble calls a "people's democratic dictatorship" and on the "attainment of a socialist society." However, although the general tone of the constitution appears to be more belligerent than the 1936 Stalin constitution, the importance of the Communist Party of China (CPC) is not codified in this organic law. Furthermore, in implementing the law, some state agencies or committees seem to have more actual impact on the conduct of Peking's affairs than have comparable Soviet state bodies.

The National People's Congress, according to the constitution the highest governing organ of the country, is as much a rubber-stamp assembly as the Supreme Soviet, but the Presidium of the Supreme Soviet is not nearly so influential as the Standing Committee of the National People's Congress. Among the duties listed for this committee in the field of foreign affairs are ratification or

---

[38] K. London, *op. cit.*, p. 222.

abrogation of treaties with foreign states (Art. 31, 11), decisions "on the proclamation of a state of war in the event of armed attack against the state or in fulfillment of international treaty obligations concerning mutual defense against aggression when the National People's Congress is not in session" (Art. 31, 15), and decisions on "general or partial mobilization" (Art. 31, 16). The supervision of the conduct of relations with foreign states is, nominally, vested in the State Council, the Soviet Council of Ministers "opposite number." The State Council also controls foreign and domestic trade (Art. 47, 8), "directs work concerning Chinese residents abroad" (Art. 47, 11) and directs the "building up of the armed forces of the country" (Art. 47, 14).

The importance of the state government offices and committees depends upon the influence of the chairman or, rather, on his position in the CPC. The interlocking directorate does not appear to be so obvious as in the USSR but the Chairmen of State Council and the Standing Committee are also high officials in the CPC. Indeed, they are members of the Politburo, the highest governing body of the Party. Within the Politburo, there is also a small standing committee of the seven most powerful men in Communist China and one might speculate that it is these seven men who rule the country and the Party. This means, of course, that, as in the USSR, the policy-making body of the Politburo determines foreign policy and most likely specifies its implementation.

Two additional organs should be mentioned—the Supreme State Conference and the National Defense Council. Both are under the supervision of the Chairman of the People's Republic of China. The former, set up in Article 43, may have been designated for purposes of top-level coordination of the State Council and the Standing Committee of the National People's Congress. There is evidence, however, that this body has lost much of its initial influence. The National Defense Council, too, has been in eclipse since the CCP's Military Affairs Committee has taken over the reins of the defense machinery. It should be noted again that the Party organization, which parallels the state organization, remains the decisive factor. The unaware observer should not accept the illusion of state power at face value. The Party rules the state and the governmental organization simply carries out its orders. As in the USSR, the interlocking directorate provides the Party with control of the state organs. Indeed, at the highest level, the merger of Party and state leaders is consummated because the top echelon consists of men who function in both capacities. It will be remembered that for a long time Mao was chairman of both the Chinese People's Republic and the two highest Party organs, the Central Political Bureau (Politburo) and of the Central Committee of the CCP. Although he relinquished chairmanship of the state to Liu Shao-ch'i, he retained the Party leadership and thereby the key to his power. In order to concentrate the organizational aspects of this power, a Standing Committee of the Politburo was established in 1956, consisting of Mao and six of his closest collaborators. It is a compact politburo. This is all the more significant since the Politburo consists of only nineteen full members and six candidates. It appears that even such a small *gremium* was too large for Mao's taste, and its Standing Committee is a demonstration of a deliberate narrowing down of the locus of power to six men, most of whom are presumably loyal to him. Whether, after Mao's demise, a body such as the Standing Committee of the Politburo will continue to function is questionable, for nobody in the well consolidated top leadership group can command as much cult of the personality as Mao Tse-tung.

While the Standing Committee exists, however, "the breadth of responsibility entrusted to the men in the nation's top policy-formulation council . . . means that there is less tendency toward lowest-common-denominator policies. Men like Mao Tse-tung, Liu Shao-ch'i, and Chou En-lai have responsibilities that cross departmental lines, and they do not bring to policy-making sessions the parochial views of particular departments."[39] This

---

[39] *National Policy Machinery in Communist China*, Report of the Committee on Government Operations, U.S. Senate, made by its Subcommittee on National Policy Machinery, Washington D.C.: U.S. Government Printing Office, 1960, p. 9.

applies to both internal and external policies which almost certainly are conceived as parts of a whole as is customary in all communist regimes. Unquestionably, it is this standing committee which establishes Peking's policies toward the USSR and the other members of the "socialist camp" as well as toward the world. It may also be assumed that in view of Mao's dominant personality, Communist China's policies are those of Mao Tse-tung.

The philosophical base of Marxism-Leninism does, of course, provide for the motivation of Chinese Communists, and there can be no doubt that the leaders are following the catechism of chairman Mao. One might say that mainland China's credo has been shaped by what is commonly called the "Thought of Mao Tse-tung." The doctrine contained in this "Thought" is rooted in the CCP statutes and is far more important than the constitution. But with the exception of Mao's militarily significant doctrines on guerrilla warfare, his theories have little originality.

The "Thought of Mao-Tse-tung." In essence, Mao's rationale is the adjustment of Marxism-Leninism to Chinese conditions. It cannot be too strongly emphasized that Mao's China was never a Soviet satellite nor was it a copy of the Soviet Union, Stalinist or otherwise. It is easy to compare certain character traits of the aging Stalin and the aging Mao. There are similarities between dictators long in power. But there can be no question that before his conquest of mainland China, Mao followed Stalin's party line as a matter of Communist discipline. Yet once in power, he carried out his long-held view that the European-born Marxist-Leninist ideology had to be modified to suit Chinese conditions. Liu Shao-ch'i's statement to Anna Louise Strong in 1946, prior to Mao's take-over, is revealing: "Mao Tse-tung's great accomplishment has been to change Marxism from a European to an Asiatic form. . . . The basic principles of Marxism are undoubtedly adaptable to all countries, but to apply their general truth to concrete revolutionary practice in China is a difficult task, Mao Tse-tung is Chinese. . . . He uses Marxist-Leninist principles to explain Chinese history and the practical problems in China. He is the first that has succeeded in doing so . . ."[40] Although this may be a partisan statement, it does contain some truth.

It is perhaps the sense of contrast between the European and Asian versions of Marxism which stimulated Mao's own version of dialectics. The very concept of contradiction has, of course, its own opposite in unity. Perhaps with this in mind, Mao's version of forced unification of the country was explained in his essay "On The People's Democratic Dictatorship." He borrowed the concept from the Eastern European "People's Democracies" and somewhat enlarged it. The proletariat and the peasants automatically became members of the new society while the petty and national bourgeoisie (but not the international *compradores*) had to prove first that they were worthy of acceptance.

The concept of a four-class state, symbolized by the four stars on the Communist Chinese flag, the so-called new democracy, was basically a projection of revolution in several stages. This was nothing new: "Thirty-five years before Mao, Lenin taught the same doctrine, with this difference: he had not used the term 'new democracy'."[41]

It has been contended that Mao's attempts to modify Marxism "represent an adaptation of Marxism to Asian conditions rather than a Sinification of Marxism."[42] Although his theoretical contributions were, first of all, caused by his experience in China, "to the extent that they represent genuine theoretical innovations, they must have a larger relevance and therefore cease to be purely Chinese."[43] There is little doubt that Mao, as a convinced Communist, must have thought along lines that trans-

[40] Anna Louise Strong, "The Thought of Mao Tse-tung," *Amerasia*, XI, No. 6, June 1947, p. 161. See also Stuart R. Schram, *The Political Thought of Mao Tse-tung*, New York: Frederick A. Praeger, 1963, p. 56.

[41] Klaus Mehnert, *Peking and Moscow*, New York: G. P. Putnam's Sons, 1963, p. 156.

[42] Schram, *op. cit.* p. 60. See also Arthur A. Cohen's excellent analysis of Maoism in his book, *The Communism of Mao Tse-tung*, Chicago: The University of Chicago Press, 1964, *passim*.

[43] *Ibid.*

cended national boundaries. Asia, and not China alone, must have been included in his concepts and, beyond Asia, the former "colonial and semi-colonial" world. His theories on guerrilla warfare belong in this category of reasoning; they proved their mettle in the Vietnamese war, which led to the French catastrophe at Dienbienphu, and they remained active in the Viet Cong's operations against South Vietnam.

Finally, convinced that his technique of organizing Communist action is sounder (in non-European areas) than that of the successors to Lenin and Stalin, Mao seems to have believed, at least since the late thirties, that one of the most urgent missions of Chinese Communism should be to lead the underdeveloped areas toward "liberation." Again, this was not an original thought, for Lenin had emphasized the importance of a "national liberation movement" even before he came to power. In the 1920 Party Congress the Soviet leaders underwrote a revolutionary action in what they now call the "zone of peace," but could not carry out their policies, first, for want of strength and then because of the interruption of World War II. When the USSR had become a nuclear world power, the strategy of "peaceful coexistence" and the nuclear stalemate served as deterrents to the execution of revolutionary actions that could have led to local wars which, in turn, might have escalated into a world war. Clearly, in such an event, Moscow would have more to lose than Peking. The Kremlin cautiously shunned the harsher views of the Chinese Communists on instigating "national liberation wars" in Asia, Africa, and Latin America, although it must be understood that the warlike words of Peking are probably deceptive. Indeed, the Chinese leaders have emphatically repudiated Soviet accusations of being war lovers. The Mao regime is not really in a position to provoke a war; nor is there evidence from their behavior that they want it. What they do want is more revolutionary action, including guerrilla warfare which, they presumably calculate, can be contained.

The relatively temperate policies of the post-Stalinist leaders— which probably do not signify a change of heart but rather an accommodation to prevailing conditions—appear to have become familiar to the leaders of the Western alliance. This is not necessarily true of the "Thought of Mao Tse-tung," the fountainhead of Communist Chinese political and ideological motivation. Peking's foreign policy cannot be understood without consideration of this Thought.

The Foreign Minister and the Ministry of Foreign Affairs. The Foreign Minister's role is strictly limited to that of foreign affairs spokesman of the Chinese Communist Party and administrator of his Ministry, which is no more than an "executive instrumentality for carrying out policies decided by the party."[44] In view of the over-organized bureaucracy, of ubiquitous Party monitoring, and of the extreme caution with which the Party's general line must be carried out lest a mistake wipe out the careers of those responsible, this is no easy job. But it is not creative; it is merely administrative.

When Chou En-lai was Foreign Minister (until 1958) and concurrently Premier, the status of his position increased greatly, owing to the fact that he also belonged to the top echelon of Party leaders.

His successor, Ch'en Yi, played a lesser role although he became a member of the Politburo (but, significantly, not the Standing Committee). Under him work five Vice Ministers and four Assistant Ministers who are probably doing the major policy work.[45] It is impossible to estimate the influence these top ranking groups are exerting, through the Foreign Minister, in the Politburo. The fact that Peking has recalled its representatives abroad for consultation when important policy decisions were in the making seems to indicate that the Politburo will give some consideration to the views and estimates of its foreign affairs officers.

---

[44] *Staffing Procedures and Problems in Communist China,* Subcommittee on National Security Staffing and Operations, U.S. Senate, Washington, D.C.: U.S. Government Printing Office, 1963, p. 21.

[45] Donald W. Klein, *Peking's Evolving Ministry of Foreign Affairs,* The China Quarterly, London, October-December 1960, p. 30.

PEOPLE'S REPUBLIC OF CHINA (COMMUNIST)

GOVERNMENT ORGANIZATION

```
┌─────────────────────────────────────────────┐
│       STAFF OFFICE FOR FOREIGN AFFAIRS        │
│                  Director                      │
│  ─────────────────────────────────────────    │
│              Deputy Directors                  │
└─────────────────────────────────────────────┘
                      │
┌─────────────────────────────────────────────┐
│          MINISTRY OF FOREIGN AFFAIRS          │
│                  Minister                      │
│  ─────────────────────────────────────────    │
│               Vice Ministers                   │
└─────────────────────────────────────────────┘
                      │
┌─────────────────────────────────────────────┐
│    COMMISSION FOR CULTURAL RELATIONS          │
│         WITH FOREIGN COUNTRIES                 │
│                 Chairman                       │
└─────────────────────────────────────────────┘
```

DIPLOMATIC REPRESENTATIONS

(All ambassadors known or presumed to be
members of **Chinese Communist Party**)

Country

Afghanistan	Hungary	Pakistan
Albania	India	Poland
Bulgaria	Indonesia	Rumania
Burma	Iraq	Somali
Cambodia	Mali	Sudan
Ceylon	Mongolia	Sweden
Cuba	Morocco	Switzerland
Czechoslovakia	Nepal	USSR
Denmark	Netherlands	United Arab Republic
East Germany	North Korea	United Kingdom
Finland	North Vietnam	Yemen (Minister)
Ghana	Norway	Yugoslavia
Guinea		

As far as we know, the Foreign Ministry is organized in five geographic and seven functional departments. The geographic departments are divided as follows: USSR and Eastern Europe; Asian Affairs, subdivided into two departments dealing with communist and non-communist oriental countries; West Asian and African affairs comprising the Middle East and Africa, both north and south of the Sahara; West European affairs, concerning non-communist Europe; and the department for American and Australian affairs, charged with responsibility for the Western Hemisphere, Australia and New Zealand.

The functional offices feature the departments of Protocol, Treaty, Law, Consular Affairs, international organization, personnel and a General Affairs Office thought to have coordinating functions.

There has also been, since 1958, a new Office in Charge of Foreign Affairs, a staff bureau under the State Council. It consists of ranking Communists and is headed by the Foreign Minister. It is believed that this office's "responsibility involves coordination of international activities among all ministries whose work touches international areas. This includes the Ministry of Foreign Trade, perhaps the Overseas Chinese Affairs Commission, and the Committee for Cultural Relations with Foreign Countries."[46]

The body supervising the Foreign Ministry is the State Council which "directs and coordinates the work of thirty ministries, plus a number of commissions and special agencies."[47] In this sense, the State Council is the most important bureau of the state government and the Premier's foremost administrative instrument. Supervision by the Party is ensured by participation in the Council of members of the Politburo and the Central Committee.

Foreign affairs is an important sector of the Council's work. It is barely possible that Foreign Ministry experts may, as time passes, be consulted by the Party. This probably depends on the Party's—specifically Mao's—evaluation of the Ministry and its

⁴⁶ *National Policy Machinery in Communist China, op. cit.* p. 18.
⁴⁷ *Ibid.*, p. 17.

personnel. There is, at present, no evidence that men well versed in world affairs have been consulted or, if they were, whether they would dare to contradict the views of Mao, who, knowing little of the outside world, almost certainly has a narrow and unrealistic opinion of conditions and attitudes outside China—the countries of the socialist camp not excluded.

In addition to the official Ministry of Foreign Affairs there is an unofficial body, the Chinese People's Institute of Foreign Affairs which seems to be a combined protocol and propaganda organization. Guided by high-level Ministry officials, it may serve to extend Chinese Communist influence into those countries where Communist China either has no embassy or where its interests in a given area or country are especially strong. The Institute also sends unofficial "ambassadors" abroad, specialists in many fields of endeavor, whose tasks may be the promotion of Chinese policies into desired channels.[48]

National Security Policy. The problem of national security policy in Communist China is a simple one. There is, through the Politburo, the Supreme State Conference, and the State Council, full coordination of the various Party and state organs responsible for foreign and security policy. Indeed, despite the complexity of ChineseCommunist party and state government, coordination due to interlocking directorates and positions is fully established.[49] In comparing the Communist Chinese organization with that of the USSR, it seems that Peking has overstaffed its state and party apparatus. It is to be expected that as time goes by simplifications will be introduced if the machinery is to attain a greater degree of efficiency. One might say that right below the Politburo and its Standing Committee, the "second level" organizations, particularly in the state government, have proliferated to such an extent that there must be inordinately much cross-cutting in functions and responsibilities. We have no way of

[48] See chart on "Interlocking positions of selected Chinese Communist leaders', in *Staffing Procedures and Problems in Communist China, op. cit.* p. 3.

[49] Cf. Klein, *op. cit.* pp. 37-39.

knowing whether this would affect security policy formulation, but it cannot possibly ease the job of the Politburo—unless all these organizations are set up merely as recipients of internal dissemination of party policies. Conceivably the men determining Communist China's internal and external course need such high-powered groups for spreading Mao's gospel among the teeming masses of bureaucracy.

5. Formulation of Foreign Policy

DECISION MAKING

A nation's fundamental attitude toward foreign countries is conditioned by history and experience; its particular situation and resources determine the range between its minimum and maximum aspirations. In times past, it was not too difficult to adapt policies to needs and conditions. For example, French policy frequently was motivated by the quest for protection against Germany; the United States' foreign relations during most of the same period were characterized by the determination to avoid "entangling alliances" while guaranteeing the safety of the Western Hemisphere against possible European infringments.

The fundamental changes in world politics resulting from two World Wars and a variety of revolutions have rendered obsolete many traditional policies and compelled all nations, including the United States, to revise their viewpoints in world affairs. The formulation of new or modified policies to cope with these changes is exceedingly difficult—more so for statesmen who seek to maintain traditional political standards than for totalitarian party chiefs whose approach to international relations is as unorthodox as their social and economic systems.

The men who ultimately determine policy cannot be constrained to follow routine procedures, such as may be in force for research workers, administrative employees and, to some degree, area experts. Policy makers, however, must anticipate history. This presupposes not only factual knowledge, deductive capacities, and a talent for synthesis, but also much human understanding, psychological finesse, an astute sense of socio-political climates and, above all, courage. It requires an intuitive sense which enables a statesman to tune in on his opponent's wave length while retaining a cool objectivity. It is the scarcity of such talents that leads to so many political miscalculations. Such mistakes affect not only the country of the blundering statesman but other nations as well: Significant political actions produce chain reactions.

The techniques and habits of democratic decision making differ from those of the totalitarian countries. The Soviet leaders face little internal opposition to their policies. There may be some differences of opinion within the Central Committee of the Party, but the Party Presidium, and particularly the First Secretary, usually have little trouble keeping the members in line. The Supreme Soviet is properly coached and votes for any proposal set forth by the Party Presidium. The executive branches of the Soviet government are charged with the implementation of the policy and told what methods to use: There is no recourse; the orders of the Party will be obeyed. Since the funds necessary to carry out the policy have been earmarked by the Party, there is no further discussion of monetary matters.

In Communist China, the role of the Party appears to be even more dominant, probably because of the less complex society of China. In fact, the country is ruled by the Politburo's Standing Committee even though there is evidence of differences of opinion over such questions as agricultural policies and the professionalization of the armed forces. However, there is no question but that this Committee, which is dominated by Chairman Mao, enforces its will through the ranks of the Party and state bureaucracy with all the means at its disposal, allowing far less, if any, discussion.

Getting things done is not so easy for the governments of democratic states where the legislature controls the purse. Major policies announced by the chief of state or the government can be carried out only after the parliamentary body has agreed to make available the necessary appropriations. Even if money is not immediately needed, parliamentary consent is highly advisable. Congress or Parliament may overrule the executive branch of the government. Theoretically, this is more possible in the United States than in Great Britain: The Prime Minister controls the Parliamentary majority while in Washington the legislative and executive branches of government have been known to disagree.

There is no hard and fast answer to the question of how decisions are made except that the technique varies and the imponderables cannot be measured or systematized. Decision makers are only human. Not only are they subject to pressures within their own frontiers and public reactions all over the world, they are also products of their civilization, environment, upbringing, and their physical and psychological constitution. This should be kept in mind during the following discussion on methods of developing policy formulas. The idiosyncrasies of the decision makers—their mental and physical makeup—play a vital role in the final determination of policy. Their decisions may depend in part upon their attitudes toward foreign statesmen they know.[1] Decision making will be influenced greatly by their ideological conception of the world. It may be upset by little tricks of fate, which, through human error, play havoc with decision making: a breakdown of the messenger service; a missing or misrouted document; the failure of inter-office coordination; or the absence of an important adviser. Decisions may be affected by a physical indisposition or by family arguments. A statesman worthy of the title will keep aware of the real problems confronting him and will do his utmost to solve them.

Decision making, then, is filled with intangibles and no foolproof system exists by which they may be forseen. The evolution of foreign policy from an original idea to final formulation can

[1] The personal antagonism between Mao and Khrushchev has unquestionably exacerbated if not characterized the Sino-Soviet conflict. This may have been one of the reasons for Khrushchev's political demise in October, 1964.

be systematized and its progress described in detail. But behind the decision of the final arbiter of foreign policy, the chief of state or government, on whether to use the formula, whether to modify it or ask for the creation of a new one, are many imponderables. In this respect, the differences between East and West are not too outstanding. Certainly the Communist Party line permits the chiefs of the Party and the government less freedom of movement. Still, the intangibles of their backgrounds and psychosomatic changes can contribute to the substance of their decisions on how best to interpret the over-all policy determined by the Party. (In cases of critically important policy decisions, even the methods of implementation are strictly outlined.) This leaves us with the hard fact that final policy decisions, however carefully prepared, are, so to speak, an "act of God," communicated through carriers of power, beset by all the turns of fate and human frailities to which men are inevitably subjected.

In one of the series of reports, *The Administration of National Security,* issued in June, 1964, by a U.S. Senate subcommittee under the chairmanship of Senator Henry M. Jackson, Democrat, of Washington, officers testified that foreign policy is not really made at all, only managed, on an *ad hoc* basis at best.[2] Witnesses before the subcommittee pointed to organizational and individual difficulties. The structural complexities involved in most policy issues are indeed enormous in that not only politics but also intelligence, economics, international organization, cultural affairs, legal issues, Congressional relations, research and administration play their parts. All these problems, at one time or another, are reflected in the operations of the 274 United States embassies, missions or specialized offices throughout the world.

Such problems are not limited to *American* foreign policy making; most other countries involved in foreign affairs are bur-

---

[2] *The Administration of National Security: The American Ambassador,* staff study by the Government Operations Committee, Subcommittee on National Security, Staffing and Operations. U.S. Congress, Senate, Government Printing Office, Washington, D.C. June, 1964.

dened with similar problems. Thus it is exceedingly difficult to outline the policy-making process in terms of routine procedures. Only an approximation can be given, with the reader bearing in mind the ever-present minor and major crises that can change conventional processes and break through the neatly drawn organizational charts.

It must be added that decisions can be made only after the establishment of policies, or policy formulas, which seek to relate political realities to national capabilities and to bridge the frequent gap between ends and means. This is a problem that preoccupies all policy makers; it sets the scene and provides the context for the various policy operations described in the following chapters. The scene is determined by the factors contributing to foreign policy making (see Chapter 2); the context is provided by national (or international) objectives and ideologies; the background for political thought is affected by historic developments and the formulas developed are affected, more or less, by prevailing domestic trends.

It might be said that the detailed policy work, influenced by the over-all position of the government, strives to develop certain formulas which, in turn, lead to policy formulation. As formulas change, so do policies. For example, the United States position toward Communist China grew out of a formula under which it would be impossible to recognize and deal with a power whose behavior was considered hostile and altogether irreconcilable with political ethics and popular sentiments. With the hardening of this formula that rejected Communist China as a compatible member of the international community, officials who did not want to commit political suicide found it difficult, or impossible, to suggest changes leading to recognition of or UN membership for China. Therefore no new policy formulations were evolved. However, possibly as a result of the temporary *détente* between Moscow and Washington, the Soviet preoccupation with economic problems and the Sino-Soviet conflict, a slight change seemed to be forecast when the then Assistant Secretary of State for Far Eastern Affairs, Roger Hilsman, in a

speech on December 13, 1963, indicated with great caution that
U.S. policy was not rigid but that there was an "open door" for
those who wished to negotiate in good faith. Despite the strict
safeguards expressed in this speech and the emphasis on the
unchanged attitude vis-à-vis Chinese Communist misbehavior
and belligerent policies, the formula seemed to indicate a trace
of a thaw, thus enabling policy officials to consider alternatives
which in the past were not feasible. In other words, the framework of U. S. policy toward China had been imperceptibly
modified, probably in anticipation of possible Chinese concessions and the increasing chances that Peking may become a
member of the United Nations in the foreseeable future. Thus
the nod was given to the devising of new policies.

It is such reconsideration and revision of policy that sets the
scene and influences the context within which area and regional
experts must operate.

GENERAL ROUTINE OF POLICY WORK

The normal process of policy formation in foreign offices and
related agencies has four phases: recommendation, modification,
crystallization, and final decision. The area experts or desk officers recommend courses of political or economic action; upon
review by their superiors, these ideas are modified, rejected,
returned for rephrasing, or even recast by the reviewing officials
themselves. When an agreement in principle has been reached,
the recommendation will be worked into final form and thereby
crystallized into concise prose for submission to the high-level
policy officials. After possible additional changes, the policy is
finally formulated. Its fate is as yet undetermined; it may be
approved, modified, rejected, or tabled. It may become "law"
and be transmitted to the appropriate missions abroad; it may
remain secret or be announced officially. The more significant
decisions will not be made in the foreign office but turned over

to the chief of state or government, or the parliamentary organizations, for final disposition.

This procedure, which occurs daily, has many variations; sometimes prolonged, sometimes shortened or combined. It is simplified if the decisions to be made cause no change in the over-all picture of established foreign relations. It may be far more complex if the issues at stake concern the welfare and future security of a nation and its allies.

It is hard to say where new, creative, and significant policy ideas are born. More than is realized, they originate at the working level, that is to say, in the middle and lower ranks of specialists and area desk officers. If an idea proves successful, it will be named for the chief of state, the chief of government, or the foreign minister. Frequently, top-level officials work out new approaches with the specialists furnishing supporting research, evaluation, and field investigation. Regardless of whether these ideas originate from below or above, they rarely retain their original form. Suggestions, criticism, additional facts, and multi-sided analyses add or subtract substance, effect changes, and finally translate the idea into specific programs.

Occasionally, policy changes are introduced that are so radical as to upset the normal course of events in the foreign office. Despite this, agreement on policy formulation is produced by a team; a small one in totalitarian countries, a much larger one in the democracies. This process is bound to exist everywhere because no sane man would dare to formulate his country's foreign policy all alone.

The evolution of policy from recommendation to acceptance or rejection cannot be entirely systematized; it changes because the nature of policy issues changes constantly. In the most routine business concerning international relations, almost no two problems are alike; the description of procedures that follows is a generalization aimed at furnishing an approximate idea of political work in the foreign offices and related agencies.

Foreign policy problems that originate in a particular country cannot be examined in the light of their own merits alone; they will have to be considered in relation to the entire region within which the country is located. They must then be weighed within the framework of connected areas and finally evaluated in accordance with global policies. Although presumably both East and West follow a similar procedure, the communist policy makers far more than non-communist statesmen apply ideological and organizational yardsticks to measure and classify their findings in order to plan political strategy.

AREA WORK

We have mentioned the great variety of source material that is routed to the desk of the country specialist. The bulk of this material is informational and does not require immediate action. Cables from missions abroad are more important. Written by the diplomatic and consular staff, including the envoy, they are a running account of events, conditions, and developments in the country to which the mission is accredited. They also include evaluations of that country's relations with other nations. Within the range of these reports fall the messages of the attachés, sent to their respective agencies (Defense, Commerce, Agriculture, etc.), copies of which go to the foreign office area bureaus.

Cable messages that frequently include brief press surveys are supplemented by despatches, transmitted by couriers, which contain more detailed reports and analyses on current problems or specialized matters which rarely require action but keep the foreign office staff informed on pertinent issues. As can be seen, the foreign office procedure resembles that of the intelligence offices in so far as the study of information material is concerned. It begins to differ in the application of such information to the political scene. It cannot be as intensive for the foreign service officer as for the intelligence officer because studying incoming reports is only part of the former's responsibilities.

Desk officers, of course, must be familiar with the mass media of the countries involved. They are in touch with that country's diplomatic staff and, when feasible, develop personal relations beyond office hours. They confer with knowledgeable travelers and fellow diplomats recently returned from the area. They talk to foreign journalists and those of their own press. They make efforts to keep their information up to date. They must know the area's past in order to appraise its present; knowing the present, they are in a better position to anticipate the future. Policies are formulated upon assumptions of future developments.

Finished intelligence reports, radio and press surveys, and the estimates of the embassies probably are among the most important source material. The influence of an envoy of recognized experience and sound political judgment is usually strong, but his advice is not always accepted. Should policies be determined against his recommendations, the reason may well be that, being concerned with one area exclusively, he has lost his sense of proportion with regard to regional or global policy formulation. In any event, serious consideration is given to the envoy's messages.

As for all other information, the area expert has to evaluate, with care and objectivity, the reliability of the sources and the soundness of the envoy's political analyses. Most foreign affairs officials have developed, after years of practice and experience, shrewd judgment and good analytical ability. The steady flow to their desks of reports and documentary evidence produces a full enough picture to enable them to distinguish between reliable, questionable, and unreliable information. Accumulated evidence of past mistakes in judgment or accuracy in deduction further helps them to arrive at a close familiarity with their area.

Let us now imagine one of the most routine events in any foreign office—the arrival in the mail center of a cable from one of the embassies abroad. In most cases, it is a classified message and therefore in coded form. Consequently it has to be decoded before transmittal to the geographic office concerned. The higher the classification, the smaller the list of distribution. It is of utmost importance for every foreign office to avoid leaks since lack of security constitutes a grave danger to any nation's world position.

In a hypothetical case, a cable arrives in the foreign office of Country A, written by that country's ambassador accredited to Country B. It contains information concerning impending changes in the government and political composition of Country B, indicating a move from moderation toward radicalism. As a result, it forecasts the shift from free to state-controlled economy. The cable therefore concerns both the political and economic area experts of the foreign office and, in some countries, those of the ministries of overseas trade. Obviously, it will be brought to the attention of the top-level policy makers, who must be informed about such important and pertinent developments. It also is of interest to the intelligence sections of the armed forces since the indicated changes may be expected to modify the defense policy of Country B by way of new alliances or new enmities. For the time-being, however, the politico-economic aspects of the message appear to be the most important ones. Since the basic considerations are political, the cable should be answered by the political area division concerned.

The reaction to the ambassador's cable differs according to Country A's political and economic ideas. If that country happens to be a liberal democracy devoted to a free economy, the possible changes in Country B would raise serious questions of a political and economic nature. A deterioration of relations between the two countries may be expected. This era of ideological crusades has left little opportunity for compromise between diametrically opposed ideologies. Thus the officials of Country A's foreign office must determine whether the change in Country B requires a change in Country A's policies toward Country B in particular and its geopolitical region in general. It may well be that the policy makers of Country A have relied upon a long standing friendship between A and B and made this relationship the cornerstone of their regional and perhaps even global policies, which now may have to be changed. On the

other hand, if Country A were a defender of a controlled economy and inclined to applaud the introduction of political radicalism in Country B—with whose previous governments it had
not felt especially sympathetic—the shift in Country B's concep-
tions would clearly initiate a period of closer cooperation
between the two countries on the basis of ideological affinities.
If Country A is a capitalist democracy, it may cancel credits; if A
is ruled by a socialist or communist regime, it may grant credits
to Country B. If Country A is democratic, it will tend to discourage state monopolies and be reluctant to deal with them; a
leftist-totalitarian Country A will do all it can to further nationalization and state trade monopolies in Country B.

In either case, the responsible desk officer of a foreign office
receives the cable for his immediate attention, thinks the matter
over—if he has time to think—and then consults with his opposite numbers in the economic or functional divisions. He
requests detailed background material from the research bureaus
and finally discusses the matter with his superiors. In some foreign offices, country or area committees are set up for the clarification of current policy; in this case he would consult them to be
informed and to inform them. Eventually, having reached certain conclusions, he drafts an answer to the cable, if a specific
answer is required at this juncture. The envoy's message need
not, however, specify immediate action. He may have sent it for
the purpose of clarifying and detailing previous information, or
to contribute new information and thereby keep his government
on the alert for major political and economic changes in Country B. On the other hand, he may feel that the impending crisis
will necessitate a new policy approach or different methods of
executing existing policies, and he may request instructions on
which course to follow should the predicted change occur. He
may himself recommend definite policies or suggest the general
direction of policy he considers advisable.

In studying the ambassador's cable, the country specialist
needs to be objective and discriminating in judgment. Neither
he nor his superiors are obliged to accept the ambassador's analy-

sis as infallible, even though they consider his situation report reliable. In fact, the officials of the area division concerned may find themselves in disagreement with the envoy's interpretation and overrule him.

If the country specialist does not consider the situation urgent or wishes to await further developments, he may merely acknowledge receipt of the cable, possibly indicating whether or not the foreign office is taking appropriate action, and when. If, on the other hand, action is considered necessary, a variety of ways and means is available to the officials concerned. Subject to approval of the high-level policy officials, the following steps to be taken may be recommended: (1) publication of an official policy statement by the government of Country A; (2) announcement of the cancellation or granting of a loan according to the political beliefs of Country A; (3) a note of protest from the government of Country A to Country B or a note of encouragement and offers of moral support or actual assistance; (4) dissemination of inspired stories by radio or newspaper. These are but a few examples; the variety of political action is as great as the variety of circumstances with which policy makers must cope.

It is understood that in most of these cases, the recommendations of the area experts must be approved by the foreign minister and his advisers, if not by the chief of government. Nevertheless, the range of action for desk officers, at least in democracies, is considerable, although it is up to the foreign minister whether he wants to utilize expert advice. But even under the most favorable circumstances, the area experts are not under the illusion that their work is more than preparatory or that they furnish more than an indicator of the direction that a foreign policy may ultimately take. They know that it cannot be more than that, not because their recommendation may be lost in the channels of protocol, but because they must concern themselves with strictly specialized areas. This means that their findings and suggestions must be looked upon as part of a more comprehensive policy issue, that of regions, continents, and the entire globe. Only when coordinated with the broader policy issues, and with domestic capabilities and temper, can their policy recommendations be appraised—can they be either used, modified, or rejected.

The entire procedure may produce much nervous tension and emotional strain. In an organization as complex as a foreign office, whose recommendations may be of vital importance to the welfare of the nation and the peace of the world, frustrations of the staff members are daily experience and may affect everybody from the foreign minister down to the lowest clerk. The area specialists are probably subject to the greatest frustrations. They are exposed to pressures from above and below. Their work may be affected by cumbersome bureaucratic machinery, which may deprive them of important documents. Their ideas may be watered down by their superiors, if only because local recommendations must be subordinated to regional or global considerations. Protocol may prevent the area specialists from defending their views in the front offices; and they may encounter a lack of cooperation and understanding in other bureaus of their office or other governmental agencies.

REGIONAL COORDINATION

Recommended policies toward individual nations must be adjusted to over-all regional policy and, in some cases, to a policy of global validity. The area department heads, who supervise the country specialists, usually have administrative responsibility for a group of countries located in the same general area and therefore are concerned with similar political problems. In all probability this system of coordination is also the rule in totalitarian countries where socio-political ideologies influence general policy. It is a question whether the desk officers in the Soviet Foreign Ministry submit policy recommendations or whether their chief duty is rather to work out the details of a policy line dictated by the Party leadership and to submit it to the Collegium.

In any event, the Soviet area specialist is probably less inclined to go out on a limb than his Western counterpart. No one in a governmental bureaucracy wants to assume responsibilities of some magnitude unless his position is so high that accepting blame or plaudits is part of his job. Totalitarian officialdom has even more reason for caution than bureaucrats in a democracy. The worst that can happen to the latter if they are incompetent or too individualistic is dismissal. Although democracy praises individualism, mavericks in government are not appreciated. The worst that can happen to the former is disgrace or banishment (an improvement over the penalty of slave labor or death during the Stalin era).

In order to coordinate the recommendations submitted by their country specialists, the chiefs of a geographic region confer with the next higher officials in the hierarchy, those in charge of continents or wider areas such as Europe, the Near and Middle East, or the Far East. It is doubtful that important disagreements are brought out in the *Minindel* since area policies are part of the international communist global strategy which is determined by the Party Presidium with the possible advice of the Council of Ministers of the USSR and the Collegium. Other communist states coordinate their policies accordingly. The exception is Communist China, which has retained its own approaches to regional problems. In the event of internal disagreements in a democratic foreign office or security council, the highest ranking officials have the last word prior to the final decision, but minority opinions are heard and given serious attention. Obviously, some decision must be reached, but not before all aspects of the problem are considered. In the end, a decision will be recommended by the foreign minister to the chief of state.

In a shrinking world, matters of regional policy are often concerned with world politics and certainly are far more intricate than policies at the country or area level. For example, Western policy toward an Eastern European satellite cannot be separated from issues affecting the USSR and thereby East-West relations. Policy toward Greece has to be considered in the light of questions connected not only with the Balkans, but also with the Middle East and the Mediterranean area in general. Policy toward France is linked not only with Western Europe, NATO, and the Common Market, but also with basic approaches to East-West relations. Policy toward India or Communist China must be looked upon as pertaining to the whole of Asia as well as the Middle East and the USSR, not to mention the crucial problem of Sino-Soviet relations and the consequences of the nature of these relations for the communist and the non-communist world.

This necessitates the close and constant cooperation of a great number of officials and offices, both inside and outside the foreign ministry. It requires what might be called an interdisciplinary effort. Since the policy line under a totalitarian regime is much narrower and more specific in detail, interdepartmental and interoffice boundaries are probably less sharply drawn in the East than in the West, where, unfortunately, vested interests sometimes lead to subjectivism. On the other hand, the broader and vaguer outlines of policy in the West should encourage original thinking and imagination unless interfered with by traditionalist and routine-minded administrators. But it must be taken for granted that there will be no fundamental digression from national (or international) ideologies which ultimately determine the character of policies adopted. The policy makers and their aides on all levels must be presumed to accept the ideologies. If they deviate, even with the best intentions, their usefulness to the policy machinery ceases. For this and other reasons one might state the maxim that the more clearly basic policy objectives are defined, the better will the policy advisers be able to synchronize their thinking about local and regional policies with the great scheme of national political philosophy.

GLOBAL POLICIES AND NATIONAL SECURITY

Policies of a global scale can rarely be devised by small states. Countries that once were regarded as powers of the first class and still behave as if they were, can affect global policies passively rather than actively: While they cannot actually formulate such policies and be taken seriously, they can influence positively or negatively the course of relations between the superpowers.

In the West, the British Commonwealth, although no super-power, still has formidable reserves of strength. De Gaulle's France is seeking to achieve first-rank power status with second-rate power resources; whether its influence will be more destructive than constructive remains to be seen although De Gaulle's return to nineteenth-century nationalism does not augur well for the unity of the West. The Federal Republic of Germany, which has developed a new European power base of great actual and potential influence has so far followed a sound course of cooperation toward Western unity and contributed more than France toward a positive and constructive policy.

In the East, Communist China, while not yet a super-power, has the potential of becoming one some decades hence, provided it succeeds in marshaling its natural resources, controlling its explosive population growth, creating a great industrial establishment and bringing order to its agricultural chaos.

This weighing of power ratio is necessary if we are to realize where global policy originates. It is also important in bringing to mind the enormity of formulating global policy which cannot be devised by one man or even by one agency. Even the monolithic Communist parties of the Soviet Union and China cannot devise their global schemes without complex organizations to prepare for the "transition to communism." Much less can a democracy make decisions of so great a range without relying on a many-sided conglomerate of experts and committees.

It has become a truism that national self-interest can no longer serve as the only yardstick by which to develop global policy. The interdependence of the nations within the two great power groups does not permit one state, be it a super-power or not, to pursue its own goals without regard to its responsibilities to the community of states to which it belongs. This confronts the policy makers with formidable difficulties. They have to create a common denominator of both national interests and international obligations. Another problem with which statesmen have to deal when pondering global issues concerns the interests of their nation and those of their allies in relation to the requirements of the United Nations, which was created to solve disputes peacefully.

The difference between totalitarian and democratic attitudes in coping with these tasks is striking. In the light of its ideological objectives, a totalitarian government compromises with trends toward international cooperation only so long as it feels that in this way it can serve its purposes. A dictatorship can never be expected to recognize the rights of majority opinion. It vetoes any distasteful compromise and boycotts decisions that cannot be vetoed.

Under democratic constitutions and governments, policy decisions of worldwide import require the approval not only of governments but also, directly or indirectly, of parliaments. This is particularly so in the Anglo-Saxon democracies, where consultations between the executive and legislative branches of government are the rule. However, the initiative and primary responsibility remain in the hands of the policy makers. Their recommendations are influenced by the views of their political and economic advisers, the attitudes of the chiefs of state and their parliamentary bodies, and the opinions of the mission chiefs abroad. Inevitably, they also are affected by the intangible human elements and the aforementioned turns of fate.

Yet policy on a global scale goes beyond routine policy formulation. It is a matter of national concern and not exclusively the domain of the foreign ministry. Its elements consist of both foreign and security policy. When decisions are reached at conferences between the cabinet ministers, military leaders, and the chief of state, foreign affairs experts and administrators can only advise and recommend. The issues at stake are larger than those concerning one country. In trying to attain the best possible deal for his nation, the decision maker is bound to consider the consequences of his policy on the fate of his allies as well. He must keep in mind the strength and unity of his "bloc," for if he does not, its strength may diminish and thereby jeopardize the security of his group of states vis-à-vis the opposing group. This means coordination on a large scale, which is also a problem in the communist orbit where national interests supposedly are subordinated to the common ideology and the common enmity toward the non-communist world. It would seem that the aim of Western global policy making in a nuclear age should be, first, a subordination of "national interests" to the needs of priorities in the defense of mutual security against military and ideological aggression and, second, the accumulation and exploitation of the best brains to cope with the requirements of the cold war, hidden in the deceptive concept of "peaceful coexistence."

International politics and national security are confronted with issues which have no precedent. If statesmen and area experts are bound by tradition, it is difficult for them to grasp the elements of a new political organization whose reality they are inclined to deny. It is just as difficult for democratic governments to contemplate changes in their social organization for the sake of national defense in depth. Thus the formulation of global policy and its implementation require an integration of both external and internal planning. The communist leaders know this and act accordingly; the noncommunist statesmen all too often insist upon compartmentalization and continue to make a complete separation between foreign and domestic politics, hoping to combine political struggle on a global scale with "business as usual" at home.

To summarize: The process of developing and formulating foreign policy in the West is faced with the need for a change in thinking habits. The contest of political ideologies requires as much research in the social sciences as in technological developments. The study of international relations is no longer a standardized field but needs as much investigation and experimentation as any of the natural sciences. Existing Western facilities for such research are as yet insufficiently exploited. Governments and academic institutions might well consider the possibility of supporting workshops in which foreign affairs officers and academicians could undertake interdisciplinary studies and gradually eliminate outdated approaches to new problems.

6. The Conduct of Foreign Affairs

DIPLOMACY, THEN AND NOW

Diplomacy is an ancient institution. The maintenance of relations between monarchs, or sovereigns, and heads of suzerain or vassal states through itinerant ambassadors was already a time-honored custom in the ancient Egyptian, Roman, Hellenic, and Far Eastern empires. As a rule, the envoys in those distant eras were dispatched for special purposes and not stationed permanently. Much later, during the Dark Ages, the development of temporal institutions was slowed down rather than stimulated by the clergy, though it continued to be important in non-Christian areas of the world. In Europe, the end of scholasticism gave new impetus to commercial and cultural contacts. City-states such as Venice and Florence developed a vigorous program of official contacts with both Christian and Moslem countries, and Marco Polo's exploits fell roughly into the same category. Certain bilaterally accepted principles concerning the status of ambassadors, for example their inviolability and immunity, anticipated later agreements which, between the Peace of Westphalia and the Congress of Vienna, grew into international law. However, the law of nations was by and large restricted to Europe and, to a limited extent, the Near East. Not for a long time did such far eastern countries as China and India recognize the existence of an international law, although they did grant restricted privileges to foreign envoys.

The regulations covering diplomatic ranks and privileges which were signed in Vienna in 1815 and in Aix-la-Chapelle in 1818, have remained in effect ever since, with only minor adjustments to the changing world. But although the organization of the diplomatic hierarchy has remained more or less static, the character and technique of modern diplomacy have undergone profound changes owing to constitutional, technological, and organizational developments.

For thousands of years, envoys were personal representatives of their monarchs, accredited to foreign sovereigns. They were "plenipotentiary" not only in name but also in substance. Once they had left their countries, they were on their own. With communications poor and travel hazardous, they had to determine policies and carry them out. While trying to adhere to their sovereign's political and economic designs, they often were compelled to change policies when they found conditions to be different from what they had expected. But they were not in a position to consult their rulers without great delay, and there was always possible exposure if the messenger—the only available instrument of communications—was caught and his papers seized.

As communications improved, the importance of envoys decreased. Still, during most of the nineteenth century, they remained key political figures in the political chess game. More than their sovereigns or governments, they were the creators of history. Indeed, their actions could contribute to decisions involving war and peace. But as the invention of the telephone and telegraph spawned twentieth-century electronics, as modern means of transportation broke down obstacles to long-range communication, the envoys found themselves exposed to ever-closer scrutiny by their headquarters and no longer able to exercise the full prerogatives of a plenipotentiary. Moreover, heads of governments and foreign ministers found personal meetings with their opposite numbers more satisfactory than using envoys as relay stations. When they met, they brought with them a staff of experts, relegating the envoys to a mere advisory capacity.

Thus the role of the envoy has changed from that of policy maker to the more menial one of an implementer; even the methods of implementation more often than not are prescribed. Nevertheless, an envoy's tasks are difficult and complex. Conducting negotiations for limited objectives and approaches is thankless work. Being the chief administrator of an embassy adds to the burden of responsibility. Adjusting headquarter's directives to prevailing conditions in the host country may require the agility of a juggler. Interpreting events and information puts the envoy on the spot: If he is right, it is taken for granted; if he is wrong, he is criticized and his career may suffer. Finally, the glamor which once surrounded diplomats has faded. Most social activities are humdrum affairs. Thus it might be said that the profession of diplomacy requires a great deal of personal sacrifice; much is demanded and little given in exchange. It is interesting to note how the U.S. Department of State describes the model of an efficient member of its diplomatic staff. This ideal diplomat should be able

To create good will and common understanding, and, with restrained and critical leadership born of mature experience and profound knowledge of men and affairs, use these as instruments for enhancing international confidence and cooperation among governments and peoples.

To promote and protect the interests of the United States and its citizens. To negotiate with tact, sound judgment and intimate knowledge of conditions at home and abroad, protocols, conventions and treaties, especially regarding international intercourse, tariffs, shipping, commerce, preservation of peace, etc., in strict conformity to Government instructions. To establish and effectively utilize personal contacts in farsighted ways for the benefit of his Government and of American citizens.

To analyze and report on political and economic conditions and trends of significance to the United States.

To exercise skill in following prescribed form and routine procedure when possible; and display discriminating judgment, as may be necessary in more complicated situations requiring investigations, careful accumulation of information, or professional understanding of laws, customs, conditions, etc. To administer an office in a business-like and efficient manner.[1]

This American description of an ideal diplomat could be applied universally. Harold Nicolson, defender of "moral" diplomacy, pictures an ideal diplomat as having the specific virtues of "truthfulness, precision, calm, good temper, patience, modesty and loyalty."[2] This list omits traits the author takes for granted: "intelligence, knowledge, discernment, prudence, hospitality, charm, industry and even tact."[3] It is doubtful that in the annals of diplomatic history there has ever been a man so endowed. Had there been, the trait of prudence might well have neutralized the virtue of truthfulness. In the era of a world divided into Western, Eastern, and neutralist blocs of states, the vitally important characteristics of an envoy are "sound political judgment, talent for quick acquisition of area knowledge, ability to adapt to a country's social and psychological climate, and understanding of the problems concerning the general area in which the country is situated.[4]

Several causes have led to the decline of traditional diplomacy since the Vienna Convention in 1815 established the ground rules for the organization of the diplomatic corps, its immunities, and behavior. First is the division of the world into ideological groups. For, while it is possible to reach certain limited agreements such as the suspension of nuclear tests, it is doubtful that common ground can be found for both sides to achieve more than "peaceful coexistence," which is not synonymous with genuine peace and world disarmament. Such common ground exists only among statesmen of like-minded groups of nations regard-

[1] *The American Foreign Service,* State Department Publication 235, pp. 4-6. Cf. also State Department Publication 6608, January 1958.

[2] H. Nicolson, *The Diplomat,* New York: Harcourt, Brace & Co., 1939, Chapter 5.

[3] *Ibid.,* p. 126.

[4] London, *op. cit.,* p. 261.

less of pluralism in the West and polycentrism in the East. For example, while the United States and De Gaulle's France do not agree on world politics in principle, they belong to the same group and would, in the event of open conflict, undoubtedly stand together. The Sino-Soviet conflict and the end of monolithic communism have created sharp conflicts in the communist camp but should the Soviet Union or Communist China be involved in war, we cannot discount the possibility that they would help each other.

Second, modern communications enable diplomats to maintain daily contact with their home bases so that as a rule, dangerous situations can be ironed out speedily at the highest level. The "hot line" between Washington and Moscow, established in 1963 to enable the U.S. President and the Soviet Premier to be in direct contact in emergencies, is an intriguing example of the bypassing of summit meetings and diplomatic channels. Little room or time remains for diplomatic maneuvering, and diplomats have become a rather technical arm of foreign affairs organs in all countries.

Whether diplomacy will regain its former influence as a result of prolonged nuclear stalemate and recognition by the two superpowers that thermonuclear war means mass annihilation remains to be seen. International affairs, conducted with the knowledge that peace must be maintained—even on a cold war basis—in preference to a nuclear world war, may require new diplomatic techniques; the need for these new techniques, as it stimulates maneuvering, may revitalize the diplomatic arts.[5]

ORGANIZATION OF THE DIPLOMATIC CORPS

Before 1815, the problem of diplomatic precedence in political and social affairs caused much feuding and often brought dynasties to the brink of war. Ever since a semblance of diplomatic

[5] See *The Administration of National Security: The American Ambassador*, cited in Chapter 5 *passim*.

activities existed, as early as the sixteenth century, strict orders of precedence were *de rigeur* for negotiations or ceremonies. Usually, the representatives of the Pope came first, those of the Holy Roman Emperor and his heir apparent next, followed by the envoys of the Kings of France, Spain, Aragon, Portugal, Britain, and Denmark in that order.

In modern times, particularly since the few remaining monarchies have been constitutionally limited, these problems are no longer taken quite so seriously. Countries are created and vanish; the political power of existing states changes. Today protocol must be flexible, accommodating itself quickly to prevailing conditions, and setting up precedence accordingly. Furthermore, round-table conferences make the seating order illusory; and the realistic attitude of contemporary diplomats precludes their taking serious offense should errors in protocol occur. Diplomacy has become less ceremonial and more businesslike.

Nevertheless, the *corps diplomatique,* as it is called in the former language of diplomacy, is still subject to certain accepted customs. The *corps* consists of the heads of the missions and their counselors, secretaries, attachés, and, in certain cases, consuls. The honorary head, the *doyen* (dean), is usually the oldest of the envoys present or the one who has served longest in the particular capital; however, if there is a papal nuncio he is frequently made *doyen* regardless of his age or the time he has served.

The *doyen* represents the diplomatic body at important functions that do not involve problems of political relations between the countries but concern the *corps* itself. He is the "supreme guardian of the immunities and prerogatives of the whole corps . . . but in all other matters his authority is limited."[6] Before speaking for the *corps,* he must consult with its leading members.

In accordance with international conventions the members of the mission are given a number of privileges, the most important of which are: extraterritoriality, inviolability, and immunity. Extraterritoriality is the concept of regarding the premises and

----

[6] R. Genet, *Traité de Diplomatie et de Droit Diplomatique,* Paris 1931/32, Vol. I. Chapter 370, p. 398.

equipment of the diplomatic establishment as being outside the territory to which it is accredited and the notion that its compound constitutes part of its home territory. Consequently, diplomats are exempt from direct taxation by the receiving government. Inviolability means that even in the event of war between the sending and receiving powers, the safety of diplomats is guaranteed. Immunity signifies the diplomats' exemption from criminal and civil courts of the host country and extends to their families. All these privileges are based upon reciprocity.

An often-debated question is the "right of asylum" for political refugees in extraterritorial missions. Opinions vary concerning this right; no clear-cut international agreement is subscribed to by all civilized nations. In certain areas such as Latin America the right of asylum is customary, possibly as a relic dating from the medieval right of asylum in churches. The United States in the past has not encouraged universal acceptance of this right but, on the other hand, has not hesitated to grant asylum to victims of political persecution. This happened in the United States Legations in Sofia, Bucharest, and Budapest in 1946 and 1947 when moderate political leaders sought U.S. protection against persecution by their respective Communist-dominated governments. Similarly, Cardinal Mindszenty was granted asylum following the Hungarian revolution of 1956.

The appointment and recall of envoys is handled in accordance with internationally recognized procedures. However, every state appoints envoys in its own constitutionally determined way. Except in the United States where Congressional ratification of the appointment is required, the approval of the chief of state suffices in the West; in the East, the appointment is made officially by the Council of Ministers, but in reality by the Party Presidium; the parliaments need not be notified formally. In the United States, the presidential nomination is not valid until the Senate confirms the appointment by simple majority. There have been cases where nominations were turned down or aroused such antagonism in Senate ranks that the nominee preferred to withdraw his candidacy.

Even before the candidate has been officially approved by his authorities, a so-called *agrément* is sought from the government to which he is to be accredited. No government need accept an envoy it does not want. If an *agrément* is refused, no choice remains but to seek a new candidate; and relations might well become temporarily strained. In such a case, the envoy-to-be is *persona non grata*. However, if it is granted, he may proceed to his post. Since a nomination normally is made public only after the nominating authorities have made certain of the *agrément*, one may presume that the publication of a new envoy's candidacy implies consent of the government to which he will be accredited. That government may reverse itself and request recall of the envoy, or any member of the diplomatic staff, should it consider that his activities have made him *persona non grata*.

Once domestic and foreign provisions have been fulfilled, the new envoy officially begins his work by conferring with the head of his state, his foreign minister, and the chiefs of the political divisions of his foreign office. He reviews the foreign office file material concerning the country or area in which he is to be accredited. He then awaits the return of his predecessor and, if possible, confers with him before departing. On his arrival in the capital of the receiving country, he seeks an audience with the head of the receiving state in order to submit his "letter of credence." This state visit was once a most elaborate affair; today, it is comparatively simple. The envoy, in presenting to the head of the receiving state a letter from his own head of state, makes a brief speech, stressing his desire for friendly and peaceful collaboration. In accepting the credentials, the head of the state, in the presence of his foreign minister, replies in a similar vein. The speeches rarely have political significance since it is considered bad form to touch upon political problems or disputes during the ceremony.

Presentation of his credentials and acceptance by the head of state constitutes full accreditation of the envoy. A copy of his letter has already been sent to the foreign minister, and it is he who receives the first of the new envoy's calls. Other required visits are made to the most influential leaders of the receiving government and, of course, to his colleagues in the diplomatic corps.

The recall of an envoy is less ceremonial. Whether or not the resigning envoy pays farewell visits to the leaders of the host government depends upon the circumstances of his recall or resignation. He may travel home "for consultation" and not return; he may be withdrawn for political reasons and leave the capital during a period of tension. As a rule, however, he considers it politic to say goodbye in person to prominent government leaders. No formalities are customary for foreign service personnel. None require accreditation except the consul.

THE DIPLOMATIC HIERARCHY

The *règlement*, initiated nearly a century and a half ago, defines the hierarchic ladder of diplomatic personnel. It is still the basis of contemporary classification. The *règlement* distinguished between four classes of heads of missions:

1. Ambassadors, legates, and nuncios.
2. Envoys and ministers accredited to the sovereign.
3. Ministers resident, accredited to the sovereign.[7]
4. Chargés d'affaires (*ad hoc* or *ad interim*), accredited to the foreign minister.

In modern times, this list has been reduced to three categories. Ambassadors still rank highest. Legates and nuncios are papal envoys; a legate, always a cardinal, is sent for special missions; a nuncio, never a cardinal, is a permanently accredited diplomat.

A merger of the second and third grades has developed gradually through the past century. Ministers, who rank under ambassadors, are usually called "envoy extraordinary and minister plenipotentiary." The former distinctions between envoys, min-

---

[7] A minister resident's duty was observation rather than negotiation. There is presently no need for a minister resident. His responsibilities have been taken over by the envoys and their staff.

isters, and ministers resident, the latter being lowest in rank, were created for the sake of precedence. The words "extra-ordinary" and "plenipotentiary" were added to enhance the dignity of the title and thereby achieve precedence but since this method was emulated by almost every state, these adjectives became meaningless stereotypes. Moreover, the number of lega-tions, headed by a minister, has dwindled. Formerly, only the larger powers exchanged embassies, headed by an ambassador, but now most of the smaller states also insist on having embas-sies. As a result, the word embassy has lost much of its former prestige and has become a generic name for foreign diplomatic headquarters.

There are two types of *chargés d'affaires*. A *chargé* may be assigned to do a special job (*chargé ad hoc*, or *en titre*); he may also substitute for the envoy during the latter's absence (*chargé ad interim*). Usually a counselor or first secretary takes over the duties of the envoy when the latter is absent or incapacitated. He also heads the embassy or legation during the interim between the resignation of the old and the arrival of the new envoy.

Political necessities have added two types of high-level diplo-mats to the ranks of diplomacy. One is temporary, and called "chief of mission," with the rank of ambassador or minister. He may be found in countries where embassies or legations have not as yet been established but where diplomatic relations seem de-sirable. The other is the minister-counselor, second-ranking mem-ber of the more important embassies, who helps to ease the burdens of the ambassadors and deputizes for him. With the growing pressure of work, more and more of the ranking foreign service officers became minister-counselors when it was con-sidered desirable that they be given special status in their own right.

The rank of ambassador or minister is often conferred for a limited time on persons who are sent abroad to fulfill important tasks of a specialized nature. They may be accompanied by their own staff, but, since they do not fall within the categories of the *règlement,* any special status granted them is a matter of courtesy rather than of international law. Such envoys are not required to present their credentials. The United States in particular has appointed quite a few men to such posts. The heads of delegations to the United Nations also carry the rank of ambassador or minister.

Below the chiefs of diplomatic establishments, the following diplomatic ranks are internationally recognized and used:

Counselors. They are the highest ranking officers of the foreign service staff after the ambassador or minister. They often serve as *minister-counselors,* as noted above, and will be *chargés d'affaires* if the envoy is absent or incapacitated.

Secretaries. They usually rank as first, second, or third secretaries, according to their length of service, experience, and age. However, their actual importance to the mission does not depend upon their personal rank. First Secretaries may become *chargés d'affaires* and Third Secretaries may function in a key post of the diplomatic organization.

Attachés. They may be specialized experts as indicated above or junior officers of the mission. In some countries, newly appointed foreign service officers begin as attachés although this custom appears to be on the wane. Today attachés are usually seasoned specialists. Experts in commerce, agriculture, information, labor, science and the armed services, "attached" to the mission and under general supervision of its head, are more or less independent observers in their fields and are charged with maintaining personal and professional relations with their opposite numbers in the receiving countries. Usually a commercial attaché is responsible to the ministry of commerce rather than to his foreign office; an agricultural attaché to the ministry of agriculture and the military, naval, and air attachés to their respective services. They are, however, obliged to submit to the mission's discipline and general practices, and copies of their reports are transmitted to their government's foreign office.

As for the special functions of the attachés, the commercial attaché is expected to collaborate with the consular services that specialize in matters of commerce, trade, and transportation. Thoroughly familiar with his own country's economy, the commercial attaché explores the economy of his host nation, reports on its aspects and tries to discover how his own country's economy may profit by collaborating with that of the foreign country. In this way, he furthers good relations between the two nations and works toward the economic well-being and prosperity of each.

Agricultural attachés keep informed about the development of food production of the receiving country and are ready to exchange views and techniques with foreign agricultural experts. They may advise or receive advice; like the commercial attachés, they foster relations between the two countries by cooperating to mutual advantage. This post became increasingly important after World War II, when food production suffered a severe setback.

Labor attachés are stationed mainly in industrial countries where the labor force is of great social and political significance. They report on working conditions, activities of the Trade Unions, labor relations with management, governments and the people, and labor's strategic and current potential.

Science attachés form a new category and are stationed only in countries where scientific developments have become of special interest in the bipolar technological competition. The field of science comprises questions of technological, political, social, economic, and strategic import. A somewhat different type of science attaché operates in underdeveloped countries, where he is assigned to offer technical assistance, as are some of his agricultural colleagues.

Military, naval and air attachés are primarily technical advisers to the chief of their mission. The state of the armed forces at home and abroad must be known to the ranking diplomats, for the strength of armies, navies, and air forces—along with the estimate of the willingness and ability to use them—often determines the character of diplomatic negotiations. Second, these attachés report to their respective ministries on the conditions, strength, and morale of the armed forces in the receiving country. It is their responsibility to obtain such information. They use official information but also try to acquire source material from personal contacts. As mentioned before, every government is well aware of the nature of their activities and accepts them on the basis of reciprocity. They represent their country at official military displays and attend whatever conferences are concerned with problems of the armed forces. They are expected to study the general organization of the receiving country's armed forces and agencies of defense; the development of new weaponry on land, sea, and in the air; the system of recruiting and how it works; the public attitude toward national defense; the ways and means of military instruction; the morale of the armed forces; approaches to strategy and mobilization; the current defenses of the national territory and the military geography.

Among other specialized officials of the mission, the cultural and press counselors or attachés have come into prominence. Since the importance of foreign information and cultural exchange as a new arm of foreign policy has been universally recognized, most governments have created organizations to cover these fields. Prior to World War II the Congress of the United States did not see fit to maintain such services on a significant scale, whereas many other nations had elaborate informational and cultural service organizations. Because of the importance most countries attach to these affairs, personnel for such activities have now become part of the missions and have been granted diplomatic status.

Although there is no official limitation on the number of officers and clerks accredited to the diplomatic or consular establishment, prudence dictates that the size of embassies, legations, and consulates be kept in proportion with the significance of and relations with the host country. However, the complexities of international relations are greater than ever before; more fields must be covered since the bipolar aspect of world politics has moved toward integration of political matters with economic, social, cultural, and scientific affairs, all of which have become part of foreign policy. Consequently, foreign representation has swelled its ranks far beyond former complements. The size of diplomatic staffs is a matter of reciprocity, particularly in relations between East and West. Communist establishments in noncommunist countries are particularly large, containing as they do agents of propaganda, the secret police, and espionage organizations.

Theoretically, the rank of the missions varies with the importance attributed to the receiving country by the sending government and its potential or actual value in the political scheme of things. Embassies are highest ranking; then follow legations, and finally the temporary, specialized missions. The former two establishments are located in the capital of the host country. (The only exception is Israel, whose government, contrary to UN stipulations, transferred its seat to Jerusalem, supposed to be an international city but divided between hostile Arabs and Jews. All diplomatic offices have remained in Tel Aviv in order not to recognize officially the legality of the Israeli move.)

THE CONSULAR SERVICE

The history of the consular service reaches far back into the Middle Ages in what is today Italy and France. It came into being for purposes of settling disputes on commerce and transportation of goods. The great European powers did not set up permanent consular services until the early nineteenth century; Great Britain, in 1825, was the first to organize one. As early as 1792, the United States defined the duties of consuls as related to the protection of United States citizens and their property.

Since the end of the nineteenth century, the consular and diplomatic services in Europe have gradually merged; the United States followed this trend as late as 1924. Nevertheless, the duties of consular and foreign services are distinct. A foreign service officer can be assigned to consular duty, but his responsibilities vary considerably from those of his colleagues in the diplomatic posts. As the duties differ, so does the international status.

Strangely, despite the vital importance of consular work, international law treats consuls less well than diplomats. Whatever immunities are accorded them are either based upon mutual agreements between governments exchanging consuls or are granted by courtesy. While the extent of consular immunity has always been debatable, consuls are well enough protected; in certain cases, where diplomatic personnel is unavailable they receive all the privileges of diplomats. (Those in the merged foreign service carry diplomatic passports.) Unquestionably, consular officers and archives are regarded as extraterritorial and most of them enjoy exemption from taxes and customs duties. No such immunities are granted, however, to non-career consuls.

As a rule, consular services have no part in diplomatic work, but their reports may shape their government's commercial policies and, in turn, affect over-all foreign policy. Reporting is only a small part of consular duties, among which are: replies to private inquiries regarding trade and commerce; assistance to nationals of the sending state if their business is to be transacted in the respective consular district; the creation of conditions favorable for exports from the consulate's country and the promotion of their sale if such promotion is possible or necessary; the protection of fellow citizens, particularly those who become stranded, entangled with foreign courts, or land in foreign jails; the authentication of documents, registration of births and deaths of nationals, and issuing of visas and passports; decisions concerning citizenship; jurisdiction over vessels and seamen of the home country when in a port belonging to the consular district. Consular services, in fact, include nearly every problem arising within their district.

There are two kinds of consuls: career consuls and honorary consuls. Only the career consuls belong to the foreign service. There are four ranks of consular career officers: consul general, consul, vice consul, and language officer (interpreter). Honorary consuls are often called consular agents; they may be nationals of the receiving or sending countries and receive only a token salary. They are neither extraterritorial nor inviolable but subject to the laws of the land in which they function.

The consul general, being the principal career consular officer, is in charge of all his government's consulates in the country to which he is accredited. For example, the U.S. consul general in London supervises all United States consulates in the British Isles. In some oriental countries, the consul general may also fulfill diplomatic functions provided no diplomatic mission is present. Should there be other consulates general in important cities of the same country, they come under the supervision of the ranking consul general.[8]

The duties of consuls are similar if they are in charge of the consular offices in a country where there is no consulate general; also, they may be subordinate officers in charge of specialized work. If there is a consulate general in the country, the jurisdiction of consulates is limited to certain districts.

Vice consuls are usually junior foreign service officers but, although young and on the threshold of their careers, they may well be assigned to responsible work, particularly in the smaller consular offices. (There are also non-career vice consuls, promoted from the ranks of clerical personnel to execute specialized duties.)

Before a consul takes office, the government to which he will be accredited must agree to receive him and grant him the privileges he may claim. This agreement, called *exequatur*, is for the consul what the *agrément* is for the envoy. An *exequatur* must also be granted to an honorary consul or consular agent who is a national of the receiving state. As in the case of envoys, inquiries are made to determine whether the consul to be named is *persona grata* in the receiving state before the appointment is actually published. The request for an *exequatur* is sent by the foreign office to the envoy accredited to the receiving state who, in turn, transmits it to the foreign office of that state.

An amalgamation of diplomatic and consular duties often occurs in places where the diplomatic staff is smaller or non-existent. While a government may refuse to recognize such a combination of activities, in practice, most of them do not object.

---

[8] Cf. H. Nicolson, *The Evolution of Diplomatic Methods*, London: Constable & Co., 1954, p. 72 ff.

In places where there are consular representatives from other nations, there exists a consular body (in the manner of a diplomatic body) headed by a *doyen*. A newly appointed consul gets in touch with the *doyen* for reasons of international courtesy just as his diplomatic colleagues address themselves to the diplomatic corps.

THE FOREIGN SERVICE

In the free world, the diplomatic and consular personnel assigned to diplomatic missions are drawn from the foreign ministries. It is the rank and file of officers and clerks who make possible the work of the envoy, thereby helping to carry out their country's foreign policy. The governments of the civilized world, being well aware of this fact, try to select the finest from among the young men and women candidates for their foreign service organizations.

Until World War I, this profession was universally regarded as the prerogative of wealth and noble birth. There were historical traditions for such discriminations; the diplomatic representative of monarchs were wealthy aristocrats who could afford the heavy ceremonial expenses involved. Diplomatic salaries, if paid at all, were insufficient, and the envoys invariably spent more than they received. They were willing to pay for the resultant prestige and power. A telling example of this condition was pre-World War I Britain, where candidates for the foreign service examination were admitted only if they could prove a minimum independent income of at least £2000 per year. They received no salary whatsoever during the first two years of service. Although restrictions were less severe in the United States, even before the Rogers Act of 1924 introduced a modernized American foreign service, salaries were small. Family, political connections, and independent means were as important to aspiring young men as intellectual achievements and character. In the France of the Third Republic, the foreign service remained more or less in the hands of the

wealthy upper middle class and aristocratic families who had
maintained themselves despite the Revolution. In Imperial Germany, diplomatic careers were open only to the titled aristocracy
and high reserve officers of the army and navy; neither the
France of the Fourth Republic nor Weimar Germany did
enough to correct this inequity. In Czarist Russia, even the sons
of the wealthy bourgeoisie were discouraged from seeking entry
into the Ministry of Foreign Affairs if they had any ambitions to
become higher level officials: The foreign service remained the
exclusive preserve of the aristocracy.

This situation changed radically between the World Wars, and
after World War II further progress was made toward eliminating discrimination. In the United States, these changes were
demonstrated in the Foreign Service Act of 1946 and the amendments of 1956 and 1959. Training facilities, higher pay scales,
and the integration of Foreign Service and departmental personnel are among the many new features of the amendments. With
the passing of the 1956 amendments concerning integration, the
United States joined the other countries whose foreign office
personnel and foreign service corps were interchangeable.

In Britain and France, liberalization measures also have been
introduced. The qualifications for foreign service in the new
German Federal Republic appear to have been democratized
beyond the accomplishments of the Weimar Republic. Still, the
foreign service in these three countries continues to attract
mainly members of the upper classes. Perhaps traditions die
hard; perhaps the income remains too low for the materialistic
urges of the new generations; perhaps the prospect of leading an
itinerant life, interrupted only by a few years of service in headquarters, is not universally appealing. The foreign service officer
has a limited choice of assignments; he may be able to pick one
station in preference to two or three others, but often must
accept an assignment which does not suit him at all.

In the communist countries, the situation is entirely different.
As noted before, there is complete interchangeability between
the personnel of the foreign office and that of other agencies. A

person who appears promising for foreign service is drafted, regardless of age, position, or experience. He is sent to a training institution for substantive and language training. He may be given brief special missions to test his abilities. Should he prove successful, he will be given a long-term assignment abroad. However, even though appearing to be one of the Secretaries reporting on political or economic events, he actually may engage in political activities in the embassy (where even the ambassador is subject to KGB supervision) or try to organize espionage networks. He could become the leader of the embassy staff's "Activ," whose members are encouraged to excel in work useful to the Party and the government. He is, of course, a member of the Communist Party.

The Soviet government can handle with ease and certainty the selection of young, unproven candidates. The life of Soviet citizens is an open book to the authorities; since peoples' reactions and tendencies are recorded from the time they enter the day nursery or kindergarten, it is easy enough to determine a candidate's character and loyalty in terms of Party requirements. Of course, scholarship is also required. Candidates will probably have completed the equivalent of a college education and thorough language training; if appointed, they will attend Party schools and area study courses so as to be prepared for the country of their destination. Only the most promising students will be given this opportunity.

DIPLOMATIC COMMUNICATIONS

The most ingenious policy is only as good as its application. Political thought of the highest intellectual caliber remains idle theory unless it becomes a living principle of one nation's relations with other nations. The value of a policy formula is determined not only by the depth of its perception and its accurate foresight, it must also be founded upon its workability. On the other hand, the failure of a policy to meet with response need not imply that the policy makers have come to the end of their resources. It is rare indeed for a policy, once introduced, to find immediate success in its envisaged form. As a rule, modifications in substance and method occur gradually; sometimes an entirely different approach will have to be tried. In general, policy substance is treated flexibly in the West and rigidly in the East, while methods of application change slowly in the traditional West and rapidly in the revolutionary East.

At one time the execution of foreign policy was the domain of diplomats. This period of classic diplomacy developed after Richelieu, when the French diplomatic fashion and language were adopted throughout Europe. It reached its climax during the Congress of Vienna, then gradually deteriorated. Old fashioned diplomacy, according to Harold Nicolson, was "courteous and dignified; it was continuous and gradual; it attached importance to knowledge and experience; it took account of the realities of existing power; and it defined good faith, lucidity and precision as the qualities essential to any sound negotiations."[9] This picture is highly idealized. There have always been rascals in the diplomatic profession who had a great gift for smooth talk and an even greater talent for deception. They were masters at couching vituperations in polite language. However, diplomats knew what and whom they had to face; above all, they shared a common platform of culture and civilization which made eventual understanding possible. Their work (but not their play) was protected from the glare of publicity; the problematic Wilsonian concept of "open covenants, openly arrived at" had not yet been introduced.[10]

It is quite possible that the lack of secrecy in negotiations resulting from the ever-widening demand for public information accelerated the decline of old-fashioned diplomacy which functioned best under conditions of confidential negotiations.

[9] H. Nicolson, op. cit. 72 ff.
[10] Cf. J. Poorterman, "Des diplomats et de leur statut," International Review of Administrative Sciences, Vol. XXIV, No. 4, Brussels, 1958. See especially pp. 431-432.

According to Harold Nicolson, covenants should be open, but not openly arrived at. Yet, of the factors contributing to the shrinkage of diplomacy during the first half of the twentieth century, this was only one. More important were the ideological divisions of the world and the arrival of the nuclear age. Furthermore, the communications system enabled the chiefs of states and governments to be very mobile and much less dependent upon the envoys. Thus the more traditional diplomatic activities were overshadowed by the trend toward multilateral high-level conferences.

In special cases which seem beyond the range of diplomatic competence, trouble shooters are called to the scene. Combining the prestige of an official representative of the chief of state with that of a high official from the foreign office, they have frequently proved to be of great consequence in settling thorny problems. The ramifications of such new diplomatic communications are vast.

Nevertheless, for handling routine day-to-day international affairs, traditional diplomacy remains irreplaceable. Both East and West use its facilities, with this difference: In the East the trappings of diplomacy are mere means for accomplishing objectives; in the West, form and content are inseparable. This is explained by the fact that totalitarians consider diplomacy and propaganda to be one and the same while the free world clearly differentiates between the two.[11]

In carrying out government policies and maintaining routine relations between officials and peoples of the sending and the receiving nations, traditional diplomacy uses essentially two forms of communication: written documents and oral representations. Documents are passed by the host government to an ambassador for transmission to his foreign offices. Vice versa, the ambassador receives for transmission to his host government either the full text of a note or the general outline of one which he is responsible for drafting in accordance with his first-hand

[11] See below, p. 293ff.

experience of the prevailing political climate. Similarly, the ambassador is instructed to visit the foreign minister so as to outline his government's point of view for the latter's consideration. Although the envoy's natural point of contact is the foreign minister, he may also see other government officials connected with foreign affairs. He uses social gatherings—as does his staff—to establish personal relations with these officials, taking advantage of whatever opportunities arise to discuss the affairs of state in the relaxed atmosphere of pleasant and non-official surroundings. Often more is achieved in this informal manner than during long periods of strenuous official conferences. Only political fanatics or those acting under orders of a regime such as Communist China deny themselves the human urge to find a bridge of understanding. The communists discourage more than superficial contacts, although they sometimes order their diplomats to appear congenial for reasons of their own. No diplomatic purpose would be served by their cultivating personal contacts since the Party's policy line is fixed, even though the methods of implementation change with circumstances. Therefore, any effort to create such contacts is dictated by the desire to proselytize or to obtain intelligence.

There are two types of diplomatic notes: the *note* and the *note verbale*. The *note*, in the form of an official letter, is sent under the signature of the envoy to the foreign minister or is sent by the foreign minister to the envoy for transmission to his headquarters. The *note verbale* is a memorandum, bearing the official seal of the sending government but unsigned and directed to no particular person. It is customary for diplomatic communications to be channeled through the respective diplomatic establishments rather than sent directly from one government to another. This is often true in the United Nations, where members' communications are transmitted through either the Secretary General, the Committee Chairman, or the Chairman of the Security Council of the General Assembly. Personal letters exchanged between heads of states are not in the same category. Although they are diplomatic documents, they are officially regarded as "private" correspondence regardless of their possible importance or the fact that they may be published.

In addressing a foreign minister or a political or diplomatic agency, certain formalities of style and phraseology are still observed. Notes begin and end with standard phrases, slightly varied in accordance with the degree of good or bad relations between the corresponding countries. Although meaningless in themselves, their omission would be regarded as a breach of diplcmatic etiquette. The composition of a note is no simple literary task. It requires much substantive and aesthetic capability to translate political thought into an intellectually and diplomatically acceptable language.

The length of notes appears to have increased. Communist diplomacy, especially, has produced lengthy tracts which are designed to combine political points of contention with propaganda lines. This "literary" output is reminiscent of the marathon speeches delivered by communist leaders. Traditional governments, unless compelled to be explicit in answering communist notes, are much less wordy. They sometimes prefer to send memoranda, called *aide memoire,* or *exposé.* Customarily, a memorandum may forego the courteous language of a note and be limited to facts.

The *collective note,* now rarely used, is a document signed by several or all members of the diplomatic corps accredited to the government to which it is sent. Such a note may contain a complaint regarding non-observation of the corps' privileges. Collective notes also may be sent by several allied governments who desire to express simultaneoulsy their coordinated position on policy. However, these have come more and more into disuse. Instead, allied governments usually send identical notes, thereby demonstrating both their similarity of views and their sovereign freedom of action which may be expressed by minor differences in the text of the note.

The most severe of all diplomatic notes is the *ultimatum.* It stipulates a definite time by which the receiving government must either take certain action specified by the sending nation or

face the prospect of a state of war. Since national pride or a
nation's adherence to what it believes is a righteous position
usually prevents the addressed government from complying, an
ultimatum is tantamount to the proclamation that war is imminent. However, few ultimata have been issued since World War
I. They have been replaced by public statements of warning,
followed by a declaration of war when war was already a fact.
Such declarations are sent as *notes* or *notes verbales* through regular diplomatic channels. If no direct communication exists
between the hostile governments, the declaration may be broadcast; as a rule, countries at war request the services of a neutral
power to safeguard their interests.

Since World War II, a curious aversion seems to have developed to the use of the term war to denote military conflict.
Instead, such euphemisms as "police action," "liberation movement" or "revolutionary war" are used as substitutes for the hard
truth. If there is no war, there need be no declaration of war; a
shallow half-truth provides the seemingly logical reason for a
violation of international law. Even worse, hostilities have been
initiated without declaration in order to utilize the element of
surprise. The North Korean aggression belongs in this category,
as does the British-French-Israeli attack on Suez. One may speculate that, in the future, advance announcements of aggressive
intentions will be less and less frequent. An abundance of
"warnings" has been issued by both East and West. The Chinese
Communists, who have issued scores, have the unique system of
numbering their "serious warnings"—which has the character of
psychological warfare. Any power sufficiently daring to initiate a
conflict in the nuclear age would hardly announce its plans, but
would stake everything on a surprise knockout.

Generally, the number of written communications is held to a
minimum. First, it is easier to deny spoken words than written
ones. Second, the art of diplomacy can best be applied in personal contacts. Elimination of misunderstandings, clarification of
policy, and negotiation of treaties are most often conducted
orally. One example of combining oral and written communica-

tions is the "summoning" of an envoy by the foreign minister to receive a *note* or *aide memoire* with oral explanation—which may consist of a dressing down and exhortation, or take the form of an emphatic plea.

Treaties, which are usually regarded as the crowning work of policy execution, are of many types and of varying importance. Not all treaties appearing as such are termed treaties by international lawyers. For example, "protocol" may be a preliminary draft review or simply minutes of a treaty negotiation. The "agreement" is a somewhat more informal type of treaty but not necessarily less important in its political implications. The joint "declaration" of two or more contracting states commits the signing parties to definite policies or actions toward the world. The "concordat" is a treaty between a national government and the Papal Curia. The treaty itself, like most other agreements or declarations, has to be ratified in accordance with constitutional law. Treaties and agreements may cover any aspect of political, economic, military, or cultural problems. They may be bilateral or multilateral; they may be regional arrangements or international covenants.

Traditionally, contracts between nations have been regarded as the foundation of international relations. Respect for the sanctity of treaty structures was tantamount to respect for international law and therefore treaties were considered a basic part of the body of law regulating relations between governments and nations. Unfortunately, the extreme opportunism of totalitarian policy has lessened the respect for covenants. Frequent violations of agreements and treaties have greatly weakened their value in the eyes of both statesmen and peoples. They tend to guard against too much reliance on written agreements, not to mention oral promises, because both are only as effective as the intention of the "high contracting parties" to fulfill their stipulation faithfully.

Here again it must be emphasized that the diplomat's real task is directed far less toward attaining signed promises than toward maintaining routine relations with the officials of his host government and with as many private individuals as possible. It is now recognized that one of the foremost duties of an envoy and his staff is to try to understand the people of the country. As a consequence of his efforts, his advice to the home office is sounder and he becomes more popular among the people who unconsciously transfer their feelings for him to the country he represents.

DIPLOMATIC SANCTIONS

War is the conduct of organized military operations to carry out a policy or to press demands by force of arms. Cold war is the conduct of international relations between basically hostile nations by all means short of military warfare. Between these two stages of enmity is a twilight zone of diplomatic sanctions. Developing after strenuous attempts to compromise have failed, it leads to the deterioration of relations. At such time, several possibilities for action short of war are open to the governments concerned. There is, in view of the nuclear stalemate, a long way between a political deadlock and imminent danger of war. There is also much diplomatic territory to be explored between the deadlock and the development of full-fledged cold war.

A mild way of showing displeasure is the diplomatic protest, usually transmitted by the envoy's personal "representation," accompanied by a *note* or an *aide memoire* detailing the grievances of the complaining government. Most protests are rejected by written note. In order to refute statements or rumors, a government may send a note denying the facts stated or rumored. Such an action used to be called *dementi,* a term which has virtually disappeared in diplomatic usage and, in English at least, has been replaced with denial. Protests and denials are routine occurrences in international relations. More serious is a protest by action, such as the recall of an envoy. This does not necessarily signify a break in relations between the nations at loggerheads. The mission's work continues under a chargé d'affaires. Officially, the envoy is called home "for consultations;" he may or may not return to his post. Such a recall may imply to the host country that a serious situation has arisen and measures must be taken to resolve controversial issues before further deterioration sets in. A recall also may set in motion an ambassadorial reshuffle. Should the sending government consider that the recalled envoy failed to interpret policy correctly or lacked adequate methods for coping with existing difficulties, he might be replaced by a man whose background and approach have definite bearing upon the mission to be fulfilled. On the other hand, the embassy might purposely be left under the care of a chargé *ad interim,* for a long period of time, which would clearly downgrade its status. Such was the case when after the Hungarian uprising in 1956, the U.S. ambassador was recalled and not replaced for several years. Theoretically, an embassy can function without a chief for long periods, but host governments have little appreciation for such a hiatus, being well aware of the implied snub.

The recall of an envoy may also signal the initiation of new headquarters policies. In such cases the recalled envoy is unlikely to return to his post. Politically and psychologically, it is wiser to introduce a new man to implement a new policy. Most governments recall an envoy who has consistently failed. In the West, he may be sent to another post or be given another headquarters position; in the East his career as a diplomat is almost certainly over.

In the event of a break in relations, the entire mission must be closed. Although another nation's embassy may take over the outgoing mission's interests, it can deal with little more than the protection of nationals. If there are bonds of friendship and mutual interests between these two nations, reports and information may be available. While nothing can replace the "eyes and ears" of a diplomatic establishment, a complete blackout of communications is thus avoided.[12]

---

[12] As a result of insulting accusations against the United States by the Bulgarian Communist regime, the government of the United States broke off relations with Bulgaria in 1950. Only ten years later, as a result of Bulgarian efforts, were relations restored and an American Minister sent to Sofia.

A further means of expressing disapproval is the refusal to grant recognition to a new government (installed, for example, after a successful revolution) or the withdrawal of recognition from a previously recognized government.

There are two types of recognition: *de jure* or *de facto*. (Recognition includes not only governments but also acts of government, such as the annexation of territory.) *De jure* recognition means that a government, a new state of affairs, or a new policy is formally recognized by official diplomatic action. *De facto* recognition means that whether or not an official statement of recognition is issued, the new situation has been accepted as inevitable. Silence, in this case, denotes consent or toleration, and it matters not whether this consent is implied with good grace or with misgivings. No particular diplomatic method is prescribed for recognition or non-recognition. It may be "granted expressly by a formal document or an oral declaration, or implied by the indication of entering into diplomatic relations" with the new state or government.[13]

Usually a government is reluctant to withdraw recognition from the government of a state with which it has maintained diplomatic relations. Such a withdrawal entails a break in relations and leads to the closing of missions in both countries. Withholding recognition from a new government which has come to power through violence, or from a newly formed state, presents a similar problem. There is always the danger that such decisions are made for emotional rather than pragmatic reasons, and the results are quite often undesirable. The American non-recognition of the Soviet government after the Russian Revolution lasted for fifteen years after that government's establishment, but such cases are relatively rare; their value is questionable from a *real-political* point of view, although they probably provide emotional satisfaction. Far more complex is the case of U.S. non-recognition of the Chinese Communist regime; first, because the pre-revolutionary government of the Republic of China still

[13] L. Oppenheim, *International Law, op. cit.*, 3rd edition, Vol. I, Sect. 82, p. 135.

exists in Taiwan and second, because the actions of the Chinese Communists have placed them outside the circle of civilized governments and made them ineligible to join the United Nations to whose principles they do not subscribe, and against whose forces they fought in the Korean War.

In the majority of cases, the government initiating non-recognition is bound to injure itself as much as it injures the government from which it withdraws or withholds recognition. One repercussion is the loss of official intelligence sources, a serious loss indeed. Nevertheless, during its diplomatic history, the United States frequently has applied the principle of non-recognition as an attempt at policy enforcement or political demonstration. Yet it has become manifestly evident that non-recognition is primarily a demonstration of political principles and a show of determination to stand by those principles regardless of the cost. The actual effectiveness of such a measure depends entirely upon its byproducts, such as freezing of assets, denial of credits, suspension of loans, trade embargoes, abrogation of treaties, exclusion of nationals of the non-recognized state, and stoppage of political, social and economic intercourse. The rigors of ideological disputes have, unfortunately, left moral principles in a weakened state. Political demonstrations such as non-recognition or the breaking of diplomatic relations are no longer effective in themselves. They must be backed by strength, determination, and domestic unity of purpose.

Non-recognition of a government's action or policies is possible without an actual break in diplomatic relations. For example, the United States did not recognize Hitler's annexation of Austria or his destruction of Czechoslovakia, nor did it recognize the Soviet Union's annexation of the three Baltic States. But it did not withdraw its diplomatic representation from either Nazi Germany or the USSR. This type of non-recognition may be useful and necessary for the political record.

Economic boycotts and embargoes are also included in the arsenal of diplomatic sanctions. However, they have heretofore been unsuccessful in breaking the will of a punishable nation.

The economic sanctions decreed by the League of Nations against Mussolini's Italy for its attack on Abyssynia failed to achieve their purpose. The blockade of Spain during its civil war only served to deepen the misery of the Spanish people: It did not help to end the war. No airtight system has yet been devised to isolate completely the nation to be punished; in a polarized world, such action is certain to be countermanded by one group or the other, as the case of Cuba demonstrates.

Recall of envoys, non-recognition, economic embargoes, and breaking of diplomatic relations—these are the primary tools of diplomatic sanctions. The choice is by no means adequate and sometimes there is no choice at all. "One can only conclude that traditional diplomacy no longer is able to cope with the over-powering problems created by ideological and doctrinally directed cold war; it must seek new means to execute foreign policy. It needs a new arm. This new arm exists. It has become enormously powerful and influential. It has caused a mutation of diplomacy and even foreign policy. It has left its imprint on world politics in indelible ink. The new arm is propaganda."[14]

[14] London, *op. cit.* p. 272.

7. Propaganda in International Politics

CONCEPTS AND TYPES

The making of propaganda is an intensely human trait. The oldest records of human history reveal efforts at propagandizing. What else are the heroes of Homer's *Iliad* doing when they engage in a battle of words before they fight one another with swords and spears? They are trying to weaken the resistance of their opponents by claiming themselves stronger, enhancing the righteousness of their cause, and thereby lowering the morale of the enemy. The chronicles of the ancient and medieval worlds are full of attempts at propagandizing, and it seems strange that some modern nations should have developed a self-consciousness about propaganda. The countries of Western civilization, in particular, seem to regard it as something illicit. The very term has become a dirty word. Yet it is a perfectly legitimate concept, derived from the Latin *propago,* meaning "to extend, increase, carry forward, advance or propagate, to make known, to spread an idea."[1] The Roman Catholic Church uses the term *congregatio de propaganda fide* to define a committee in charge of foreign missions whose task is to spread the gospel. Specifically, international propaganda "is addressed to people at large, or to a regional, national, racial, religious, or professional group . . .

[1] L. J. Hargrave, *Words Win Wars,* Wells, London: Gardner, Darton & Co. 1940, p. 31.

International propaganda takes place when the propaganda originates in the territory of one state and is received in the territory of another state, regardless of the citizenship of the person or persons issuing the propaganda."[2]

After the establishment of the Bolshevik regime in the Soviet Union in 1917, propaganda became an increasingly important factor in international relations. While traditional-minded governments abhorred the excesses of totalitarian propaganda, but did not altogether refrain from propagandizing other states, the communists, as well as the Nazis and Fascists, elevated propaganda to political and ideological principles. The character of such propaganda ranged from extreme vulgarity and roughness to the soft tones of cultural relations, designed to assist in the achievement of ideological, political or military objectives with no holds barred. Disregarding long-established customs and sidestepping diplomatic channels, revolutionary governments frequently addressed themselves to target peoples over the heads of their governments—an unforgivable *faux pas* in terms of traditional diplomacy and pre-revolutionary relations among nations.

The Fascist and Nazi regimes learned well from the Bolshevik vanguard. They understood that propaganda was essential for totalitarian states, both internally and externally. A comparison of propaganda activities during the two World Wars demonstrates the strides made by this new substitute for diplomacy. By the end of World War II, propaganda in all its forms had become an irreplaceable instrument of the cold war. But while the West still looked at propaganda disdainfully and clearly differentiated between political and propaganda policies, the East, aided by modern technology and communications systems, used propaganda for implementation of communist strategy and tactics and indeed for the furtherance of its ideological goals.

As propaganda became an essential factor in the East-West struggle as well as in the rivalry for the favors of the uncommitted nations, its apparatus grew ever more complex, both in

[2] L. J. Martin, *International Propaganda: Its Legal and Diplomatic Control*, Minneapolis: University of Minnesota Press, 1958, p. 16.

the use of propaganda media and in the difficult determination of targets. *Media* are the vehicles by which propaganda is disseminated, for example broadcasting or printed matter; they will be discussed later in this chapter. *Targets* are the peoples and governments of specified countries and, in particular, the various social and political strata of the population.

Propaganda may be ideological, political, economic, social, or cultural. Such differentiation automatically creates specific types of propaganda which may be classified as information, political (psychological) warfare, and cultural relations.

Information

This term is a euphemism. Informative reporting can in itself have strong propagandistic effects, even when truly objective. It can also appear objective but be loaded with slanted items, specifically designed to propagandize. This may occur through intentional "leaks" to reporters or broadcasters and become part of a psychological warfare issue. One also must consider the fact that *absolute* objectivity in news reporting is virtually non-existent. Every country observes from its particular vantage point and though it may lean over backwards to be honest by reporting issues that are detrimental as well as those that are advantageous to its own image, on balance, presentation, and especially the interpretation of news and events, cannot help but keep national interests in the back of the informant's mind. Moreover, the type of government or administration in power determines intentional or unintentional slanting of news. In the United States, information from a Republican Administration differs in many ways from information under a Democratic Administration. The same is true of Britain: Tory news and Labor information are bound to vary from one another despite the proverbial objectivity of British news media. French information released by General de Gaulle's government certainly looks different from that of the Fourth Republic.

It can be said, however, that information emanating from

Western media has preserved a degree of detachment completely missing from communist news reporting. At least the West is relatively honest in presenting its own civilization and cultural objectives; as a rule, Western news media have not evaded reporting shortcomings on the social and economic scene. American media, for example, have not tried to conceal news about the race issue although the communists have worked hard and rather successfully to exploit this grave problem for their own purposes.

In contrast, the communists have always found reasons to distort or minimize Western achievements. Only in rare instances have they admitted their own shortcomings and then only in internal matters. Outstanding Western successes which cannot be ignored are played down; Soviet treatment of its own space exploits and the minimum attention paid to the American space record are a good example of uneven treatment and slanting of news. Racial troubles in the United States are highlighted, but the efforts of the Kennedy and Johnson administrations to cope with these problems are played down.

It is thus clear that information is neither more nor less than a specific form of propaganda, perhaps the least obtrusive, but also potentially the most dangerous. The non-communist "man in the street" who is not too well-informed about the intricacies of international politics and has only hazy ideas of its importance in his own life and that of his children, and the communist man who has lived under the steady ideological pall for years or decades and thus lost much of his objective reasoning powers, might be an easier prey to information than to the more heavy-handed forms of propaganda. But the noble concepts of Elmer Davis,[3] who insisted on truth and propriety and whose ideals have continued to influence official American propaganda, may not be practical against opponents as steeped in agitation and propaganda as the communists. For them propaganda is a major

[3] Director of the U.S. Office of War Information during World War II and author of several books in which he exemplified an admirable integrity.

instrument for the promotion of world communism whether through armed conflict or "peaceful coexistence."

Psychological Warfare

This term comprises a variety of propaganda approaches in the ideological, political, economic, and social fields. It is at times difficult to differentiate between information and psychological warfare because, obviously, information is used as ammunition for psychological warfare, whose character is generally more aggressive than the primarily defensive information. It is conducted for the purpose of alienating the peoples in the target areas from their governments or beliefs. The communists have used it frequently within the context of specific issues—for example, peace and disarmament campaigns or campaigns on such problems as Berlin or Southeast Asian danger spots.

Psychological warfare "uses the means of mass communications in order to destroy the enemy's will to fight," [4] and, one might add, to fight either hot or cold wars. Political warfare, on the other hand, "adds the important idea that all instruments of policy need to be properly correlated . . ." with the other "chief instruments of policy in war and peace: diplomacy . . . economics, arms . . . Political warfare thus includes operations in relation to allies, neutrals, and the home audience . . ." while "psychological warfare includes propaganda directed against the enemy together with the use of arms to create the greatest impact upon the enemy's will to fight at the least cost of capability." [5]

Perhaps it is better to distinguish between propaganda in peace and war. Conditions vary with these two contingencies; if a nuclear holocaust should ever be permitted to occur, there would be little time and few technical means of communications left; furthermore, the minds of the survivors would hardly be

[4] H. D. Laswell, "Political and Psychological Warfare" in *Propaganda in War and Peace*, D. Lerner, editor, New York: George W. Stewart, 1951, p. 262.
[5] *Ibid.* p. 262/263.

open to attempts at propagation of ideas—except recommendations for survival. Therefore propaganda has become largely an instrument of the cold war or of attempts by governments to advertise their positions peacefully. In the future, the emphasis will be on ideological persuasion, economic competition, and technological predominance.

It is in this connection that propaganda's role has competed strongly with diplomacy. Although the more traditionalist Western diplomats still look upon it more or less contemptuously and hate to admit that policy can no longer be separated from propaganda, the Communist parties and governments, together with some of the new and less traditional-minded states, seem to have grasped the hard fact that a separation between political policy and propaganda policy is no longer possible but that an amalgamation between the two policies has occurred.[6]

As a result, non-communist diplomats have no choice but to revise their view of propaganda and to use it to the limit. Indeed the dissemination of propaganda by communications media must be supplemented and further driven home through resident diplomats. This can be done in all fields of political endeavor, from the more subtle pressures to the hammer blows of economic sanctions or a show of military strength. There are gentler (though relatively less effective) ways of political propaganda, generally called "cultural relations."

Cultural Relations

Of all types of contemporary propaganda activities, this is the oldest. Even before World War I, Germany, and particularly France, had initiated cultural propaganda; it was both a matter of cultural prestige and national pride in their cultural accomplishments. Between the wars, this type of propaganda was expanded. Great Britain, too, set up cultural programs. Even the United States, penetrated though it was with isolationism during

[6] Cf. "Politprop: The Amalgamation of Policy and Propaganda," in K. London, *The Permanent Crisis, op. cit.* pp. 283-295.

these years, followed Franklin D. Roosevelt's political "good neighbor policy" with a limited cultural program in Latin America. Japan had tried to develop a cultural relations program ever since the Meiji Restoration of 1868, and many smaller states throughout the civilized world became interested in demonstrating abroad their achievements in the arts and sciences.

The Communist-ruled states, particularly the Soviet Union, followed by Communist China, recognized the advantages of cultural exchange. It was a rather inexpensive way of making friends and influencing people among non-communists. It was this innocuous method of attracting attention to the fact that communist regimes fostered culture which no doubt led many political unsophisticates to the conclusion that governments paying so much attention to the arts could not be too bad. Thus music, theater, ballet and the like hid political designs behind their brilliant facades. For example, the Peking leaders, in their attempt to gain decisive influence over non-committed areas, sent out advanced guards of artists and jugglers; the Kremlin went much further and concluded cultural exchange agreements for an exchange of artists, scientists, teachers and scholars with the United States and many other non-communist nations.

There are considerable exchange activities between American and Soviet delegations in the fields of science and technology. Also agriculture, transportation, building, education, and the social sciences are subjects of mutual investigation. It is impossible to evaluate the substantive value derived from such exchanges. The advantage of cultural exchange probably is the contact it creates and the possibility that some stereotyped prejudices, old or new, can be eliminated. Furthermore, continuous direct contact on all levels helps prevent relations from becoming brittle. Impressive Western achievements in the arts, sciences and in technology have no doubt contributed to certain revisions in the minds of citizens under communist rule. Conversely, the West has been impressed by Soviet artistic achievements though it is increasingly aware of the restrictive influence of "socialist realism" on the arts.

But cultural exchanges between the United States and Soviet Union do not, as a rule, penetrate deeply to the masses. Expensive performances limit the audiences on both sides. Whether this limited audience can affect the minds of the Soviet people by proxy remains to be seen. In any event, cultural propaganda has become a real factor in East-West relations and must be regarded as one of the more practical avenues of influencing the intelligentsia in target areas.[7]

The West has not yet been exposed to the Chinese Communist style of such propaganda. Most of Peking's activities in this field have been directed toward the underdeveloped areas of Asia, Africa, and Latin America. Unlike the Soviets, who can offer achievements created after the revolution and do not have to rely on those from the pre-revolutionary times, Communist China has had no time nor has it given its artists and scientists much of a chance to present works that speak for its present civilization. Most of what Peking has produced represents China's cultural achievements over thousands of years and has nothing to do with Marxism-Leninism.[8]

From the point of view of Western foreign policy, cultural diplomacy is somewhat paradoxical: It is important as a political tool but ineffective as a propaganda weapon. On balance, it would seem that the advantage of cultural propaganda has been on the Soviet side because, owing to the nature of Western free society, Soviet offerings have had much greater publicity and accessibility to the public than American performances in the USSR. The exceptions are exhibitions and fairs. The intense curiosity of Soviet citizens probably has given rise to greater numbers of visitors to these events in the USSR than to Soviet exhibitions in the United States. In any event, one should avoid overestimating the impact of cultural propaganda.

[7] See Frederick C. Barghoorn's excellent analysis, *Soviet Cultural Offensive*, Princeton: Princeton University Press, 1960 and Herbert Passin, *China's Cultural Influence*, New York: Frederick A. Praeger, 1963.

[8] See Herbert Passin, *China's Cultural Diplomacy*, New York: Frederick A. Praeger, 1962, *passim*.

DEVELOPMENT AND ORGANIZATION

Propaganda media are government-controlled in most states. If the government does not control all propaganda output, propaganda policy cannot be well coordinated. The United States is, in fact, the only country that permits private organizations to conduct international propaganda; several of them will be discussed briefly below. Britain's two main propaganda organizations, the British Council and the British Broadcasting Corporation (BBC) are semi-governmental, that is, they are incorporated and licensed as non-governmental institutions, but are supported by government funds and are obliged to conform to Foreign Office policy guidance. Although they are not standard government agencies, they are nevertheless part and parcel of the British government machinery. No other countries are known to permit the operation of uncontrolled international propaganda media and they control their domestic communications media as well.

After World War II, most nations organized information activities. The lessons of totalitarian propaganda in the thirties and forties were not forgotten. Even small states allocated sizeable portions of the national budget for their information and cultural relations services. The democratic countries, which had disdained propaganda despite the totalitarian efforts, had to reconsider, however unwillingly. The postwar organization charts of the British and French foreign offices indicated the growing importance these states attached to propaganda. The United States most reluctantly decided to increase its efforts in this field but never appropriated sufficient funds to counter the gigantic efforts of the communist countries which spent billions for propaganda. Communist political organization was inextricably interwoven with an all-pervading propaganda apparatus geared to reach party members and sympathizers all over the world and try to convince neutrals and opponents of the superiority of their system. It seems strange that Americans, who are masters of commercial advertising, shied away from political and ideological advertising; even now United States international propaganda expenditures are only a fraction of what is spent for commercial promotion campaigns.

Radio broadcasting, the most important medium of international communication, is a comparatively new technique. Developed during World War I, it became popular during the early nineteen twenties before it was used for propaganda purposes. Unconventional iconoclasts like the Soviets, Fascists, and Nazis were needed to initiate regular programs, propagandizing listeners in specific areas.[9] Soviet radio propaganda broadcasts were first developed, designed to serve "long-distance relays in the Soviet Union" and, at the same time, "the radiation of programs overseas."[10] In 1938, two shortwave transmitters were constructed which were then the most powerful in the world. The programs, sponsored by the Comintern, were aggressively Bolshevist. The Soviet Commissariat for Foreign Affairs ostensibly had nothing to do with them. At this time, Soviet foreign policy was conducted by two agencies which seemingly worked at cross-purposes: The Foreign Commissariat sought to adjust Soviet aspirations to traditional international diplomacy; the Comintern prepared for world revolution without appearing to interfere with official Soviet foreign relations. In the years that followed, spurred by revolutionary fervor and increasing propagandistic opposition, the Soviet leaders perfected their propaganda machine without regard to cost.

During the early 1930's, Fascist Italy began to disseminate propaganda by radio. By 1936, when Ciano's Ministry of Press and Propaganda was established, Fascist "information" had become aggressive and expansionist. From 1932-1936, most programs were transmitted in Arabic languages; after 1935, the

[9] After World War II, the Allies broadcast special programs to displaced persons in various languages, beamed to areas where these languages are not spoken. For example, Polish language shows were offered to Polish displaced persons in Germany.

[10] See A. R. Burrows, "Broadcasting Outside the United States," *Annals of the American Academy of Political and Social Science*, Vol. 177, Philadelphia, January 1935.

broadcasts were translated into eighteen of the world's most important languages. Soon, however, Mussolini was outdistanced by Hitler, whose Ministry of Propaganda, headed by Joseph Goebbels, threw itself into psychological warfare with enormous vigor. It started foreign-language broadcasting in April, 1933, three months after Hitler seized power.

Needless to say, the Japanese government had followed the practices of its Axis partners long before the outbreak of the war but had directed its activities mainly toward the Far Eastern area where it concentrated on racial and religious "exchange." Its shortwaves, beamed to America, carried on psychological warfare with the aid of American-educated Japanese.

The Western powers, disdainful of such methods, remained silent for too long. Although in 1932 the Empire Service of the BBC was established, it was not until 1937 that the British Broadcasting Corporation began to transmit foreign-language programs in Arabic, Spanish, and Portuguese. In 1938, after the Munich catastrophe, there followed German, French, and Italian-language broadcasts. But not before the outbreak of World War II, when the Ministry of Information was established, did these programs assume the character of an organized propaganda effort. The French waited until the war had broken out before setting up a limited foreign-language broadcasting program; they concentrated on cultural relations as they had always done. The course of the war, unfortunately, gave them little time to develop a propaganda organization but their cultural program continued to function in one way or another, even under the Germans. The United States was the last great nation to join the broadcasting war in 1941; however, not until 1942 was a program established with the organization of the Office of War Information (OWI) for Europe, Asia, and Africa and the Co-ordinator of Inter-American Affairs (CIAA) for Latin America

Next to radio, the printed word and the picture are powerful instruments of persuasion. But dissemination may be greatly impeded by the need to obtain import licenses or to devise costly means of surreptitious distribution in opposing countries. Among friendly states, much literary and pictorial interplay exists; between ideological opponents, official distribution must be reciprocal (and controlled) or reduced to occasional forbidden import. In either case, circulation remains relatively limited.

Pamphlet and leaflet operations as well as book smuggling are frequently resorted to in war and cold war. One of the most celebrated cases during World War I, testifying to the potential effect of the printed word, was German novelist Leonhard Frank's pacifistic book *Der Mensch Ist Gut* (Man Is Good). The book, banned by German censors, was smuggled out to Switzerland, where its author had taken refuge. After being rebound inside innocuously titled covers, copies were sent secretly to persons in Germany, who, in turn, mailed them to soldiers in the front lines. It contributed greatly to the undermining of the German Army's will to resist.

If budget considerations or foreign exchange prohibit the printing of foreign-language books other than those published commercially, the dissemination by missions abroad of news bulletins and feature material may furnish some substitute, however insufficient in quality and quantity. The effect of a continuous foreign-language publishing program such as Moscow's Foreign Languages Publishing House, which sells its books for a nominal price or gives them away, is unique and can scarcely be offset by the far less impressive Western programs. Peking has set up similar facilities.

The governments of France have been pioneers in the field of cultural media. For decades their use of cultural relations and exchange has been a classic example of the importance and long-range effects of culture as a medium of persuasion. One might suggest that the gradual decline of France as a world power during the past century was hidden so well by its awe-inspiring cultural propaganda that even policy makers failed to realize that post-Napoleonic France had ceased to be a *grande nation* in all but cultural terms. By the same token, the long negligence of the

United States in acquainting the world with its growing cultural life has contributed materially to a false stereotype in foreign countries. The stereotyped American is further perpetuated by sensation mongers, uninhibited tourists, and unrealistic Hollywood films. How dangerous such misconceptions can become was clearly demonstrated by their effective use in anti-American propaganda, even to their being accepted as facts in many nations of the free world.

Great Britain, too, was slow to introduce cultural relations programs. The "British Council for Relations with Other Countries" began activities in Paris in 1934. Its task was described as culturally expanding the "national interpretation" of Great Britain.[11] The Council was "to promote abroad a wider knowledge of the English language, literature, art, music, science, educational institutions and other aspects of our national life, and thereby to encourage a better appreciation of Great Britain and to maintain closer relations between this and other countries."[12]

Prior to the war, a host of Axis cultural societies existed. Of particular interest were the many cultural relations bodies organized by Japan and representative of the powers which it befriended. There were German-Japanese and Italian-Japanese cultural associations in all three countries, not to forget the Japan-China Educational Association, whose primary purpose was to convert Chinese and Manchurian students in Japan to the Japanese viewpoint.

As early as 1925, the Soviet government established an organization called the All-Union Society for Cultural Relations with Foreign Countries, VOKS in the Russian abbreviation. Working with Intourist, the bureau which manages and supervises tourist traffic into the USSR, it encompassed a comprehensive field of interest. It handled cultural exchanges and distributed periodicals and books, some of which it published. Nor did it

[11] R. McMurray and M. Lee, *The Cultural Approach: Another Way in International Relations*, Chapel Hill: University of North Carolina Press, 1947, p. 138.

[12] *Ibid.*, quoting the *London Times* of March 20, 1935.

limit its activities to the non-communist world: Cultural relations with the satellites and the Far Eastern communist powers lay within the scope of its charter. VOKS was, of course, subject to supervision by the Party and the Ministry of Culture. In 1957, it was replaced by the State Committee for Cultural Relations with Foreign Countries. Other organizations handling foreign visitors are the Trade Union Council, the World Peace Council, the World Federation of Democratic Youth, international student organizations, a Slavic Committee of the USSR which allegedly fosters Pan-Slav movements, and many other front organizations.

The preceding sketch of propaganda development in certain leading nations raises the question of how this growing apparatus has come to be the new arm of foreign policy and international relations.

United States: Government Media

Missed opportunities characterize the position of the United States. Its elected representatives, deeply suspicious of any form of government propaganda or information, consented to the establishment of the OWI and the CIAA only under the duress of a total war effort. While the OWI's main objective obviously had to be the conduct of psychological warfare, it was frequently embarassed by Congressional mistrust and the State, War, and Navy Departments' reluctance to recognize it as an administration agency entering this new form of warfare.[13]

When the war ended, President Truman abolished both agencies. But, knowing well that certain services remained essential to the conduct of United States foreign policy, he set up, in 1945, a temporary organization, the Interim International Information Service (IIIS), to formulate plans for a new information agency under the supervision of the Secretary of State. The CIAA and OWI were merged into the new IIIS, to formulate plans for a new information agency under the supervision of the Secretary of State.

[13] Cf. Wallace, Carroll, *Persuade or Perish*, Boston: Houghton, Mifflin, 1948.

In 1936, the Congress had allocated a small sum for cultural relations with Latin American nations to help implement the Good Neighbor Policy. Hence the State Department created a Division for Cultural Relations to direct the ensuing activities. This office was eliminated when all information and cultural relations activities were merged into the Office of International Information and Cultural Affairs (OIC), which was established by a 1946 executive order as part of the State Department, under the Assistant Secretary for Public Affairs. However, the agency still operated on its own budget and lacked Congressional enabling legislation. Since it was a new type of operation, the Congress considered it necessary to pass upon the principle involved. A law authorizing the State Department to conduct information activities failed to pass in 1946 though money was appropriated to keep the agency alive.

In 1947, with the enabling legislation still in abeyance, the Congress overruled the administration by cutting the requested budget for OIC so extensively that the State Department was compelled to operate with a skeleton staff, weed out cultural exchange activities, reduce the "Voice of the United States of America" (foreign-language radio program) to scarcely more than a whisper and hope for better times to come. The increasing tension between the Soviet Union and the Western powers, the endangered prestige of the United States abroad, and the creation of the Cominform to coordinate Soviet and Soviet-satellite propaganda succeeded in changing the minds of many legislators, but did not immediately help to finance American propaganda more generously. True, in January 1948, legislation was passed authorizing the State Department to undertake informational activities in a reorganized Office of Information and Educational Exchange (OIE). But only at the end of fiscal 1948, did the Congress appropriate sufficient funds to permit the organization to operate on a very modest scale. The program's effectiveness was hamstrung, however, by the Congressional decision to separate information completely from cultural relations. Thereupon the radio, press, and motion picture media were organized in the Office of International Information (OII) while those concerned with educational exchange, American libraries abroad, and other long-range cultural branches were administered by the Office of Educational Exchange (OEX). Although policy coordination was envisaged and institutionalized in 1949 through the establishment of the office of a General Manager, the fact was overlooked that propaganda is indivisible: All media must dovetail.

The next reorganization led to the establishment of the International Information Administration (IIA) in 1952. Although still a unit of the State Department, this new office was the first step toward the administrative separation of propaganda from policy. In 1953, the Congress adopted President Eisenhower's plan to create an independent United States Information Agency (USIA) to take over the tasks of the IIA. It is by no means certain that this Agency will remain organizationally independent. (Policy guidance has always remained in the hands of the State Department.) Future administrations may well reverse the 1953 reorganization and again incorporate information activities into the Department. It is hard to say which course is better, particularly when measured against the reluctance of the Congress to overcome its deep-seated suspicions against propaganda activities at a time when conventional diplomacy alone can no longer hope to dislodge ideological offensives.

After many years of tortuous reorganizations, which severely curtailed continuity and professional development of the staffs, the organization of United States propaganda activities still remains divided into information and cultural relations. The former is administered by USIA, the latter by the Bureau of Public Affairs at the State Department.

The mission of the U.S. Information Agency, according to President Kennedy's statement of January 25, 1963, is:

> to help achieve United States foreign policy objectives by (a) influencing public attitudes in other nations, and (b) advising the President, his representatives abroad, and the various departments and agencies on the implications of foreign opinion for present and contemplated United States policies, programs and official statements.

The influencing of attitudes is to be carried out by overt use of the various techniques of communication—personal contact, radio broadcasting, libraries, book publication and distribution, press, motion pictures, television, exhibits, English language instruction, and others. In so doing, the Agency shall be guided by the following:

1. Individual country programs should specifically and directly support country and regional objectives determined by the President and set forth in official policy pronouncements, both classified and unclassified.

2. Agency activities should (a) encourage public support abroad for the goal of a peaceful world community of free and independent states, free to choose their own future and their own system so long as it does not threaten the freedom of others, (b) identify the United States as a strong, democratic, dynamic nation qualified for its leadership of world efforts toward this goal, and (c) unmask and counter hostile attempts to distort or frustrate the objectives and policies of the United States . . . . . [14]

To carry out these tasks, the USIA maintains 239 information posts in 106 countries of the Free World. (These 1963 figures are subject to frequent changes due to the fluidity of the world situation.) The overseas information posts are part of the U.S. Information Service (USIS) and are directed by a Public Affairs Officer who is subject to the envoy's supervision.

The organization of USIA is relatively simple. Under a Director, there are four layers of bureaus. The first consists of administrative staff offices and program services divided into an Office of Research and Analysis and an Office of Private Cooperation. The former is similar to the State Department's Intelligence and Research Office; the latter is a liaison staff of sorts, which attempts to coordinate non-governmental propaganda and information activities with government programs and policies. In this connection it is interesting to note that an Advisory Commission on Information has been established, comprising government representatives and private individuals of stature. The benefit of their advice is sought in matters concerning propa-

---

[14] The rest of the order concerns itself with the USIA's advisory function and the responsibilities of the overseas staff.

ganda policy and its technical implementation. One may assume, however, that the private sector of this Commission receives as much information as it gives. Besides, through the Commission, clashes between official and private interests in the fields of information and advertising may be averted. The Commission has three specialized Advisory Committees dealing with broadcasting, cultural information and public relations techniques.[15] Although the name of its Director is not on the Commission's roster, USIA's position on the organizational chart indicates its high standing.

The second layer of the Agency's organization comprises the Media Services, of which there are five: broadcasting, television, information centers, motion pictures, press and publications.

Broadcasting is the responsibility of the Voice of America (VOA) which transmits 761 hours weekly in 36 languages over a network of 99 transmitters located in the United States and abroad.[16] It also furnishes local stations with package programs, i.e., taped or recorded VOA material. For example, in Latin America, no less than 1,300 local transmitters use VOA programs. Broadcast relay bases for shortwave transmission exist in the Philippines, Okinawa, Greece, and Germany; standard wave programs are relayed from Munich, Germany. In addition, USIA operates RIAS (Radio in the American Sector) from West Berlin and Hof, Bavaria, beaming transmissions to Eastern and Southeastern Europe. RIAS, though under American guidance, exercises some autonomy in shaping its programs which have proved most effective ever since its creation in 1946 as a counterpoise to powerful Soviet transmitters. To add to this array of information broadcasting there is the Armed Forces Radio Network in Germany, set up by the U.S. Department of Defense primarily for the entertainment of servicemen with typically American programs, but now listened to by many local inhabitants. The offerings are not of high intellectual caliber but con-

[15] Lists of the members of the Commission and the Advisory Committee are published semi-annually in the USIA's *Review of Operations.*
[16] In 1963, according to USIA.

vey the flavor of average American life which is, after all, the objective of U.S. propaganda.

The television service, established in 1959, provides weekly programs to 2,000 television stations in 67 countries of Europe, Latin America, the Far East, and Africa. These package programs, similar to the radio tapes and disks, are tailored to suit the national character and language of the target country.[17]

Next to broadcasting, the Information Centers constitute the USIA's most ambitious undertaking. They consist of libraries, information centers and exhibits, both stationary and mobile. The 180 libraries in 86 countries sometimes operate in coordination with local administrations, as for example in Latin America. The Centers not only provide libraries but, by furnishing personal information to interested visitors, strive to develop contacts with individual citizens. They also arrange film showings, lectures and exhibits of art, science, and commerce. They bring bookmobiles and traveling exhibits to people in remote areas. In 1963, the Agency's book translation project circulated some 7 million books by American authors and distributed about 2.3 million U.S. books, published overseas in English, to key individuals and institutions abroad, not counting an additional 1.5 million paperback reprints and simplified editions. The Centers distribute these books, a number of which are issued at nominal prices. In countries where the buying of American books is impeded by dollar shortage, arrangements have been made by the U.S. government to enable American publishers to convert their foreign income into U.S. currency. The Centers also sponsor performances of American plays and classical music; they exhibit American paintings and sculpture, teach English and endeavor to present a broad and comprehensive picture of American arts and civilization.

The Motion Picture Service is not only in charge of film showings but also produces films in 50 languages. Many of these are filmed in the United States, but some are made abroad with

---

[17] All figures as of 1963.

local settings and actors. Being non-commercial, they cannot be shown in U.S. theaters; however, commercial theaters in foreign countries may perform them. Specialized subjects are viewed by selected audiences. USIA operates more than 100 film libraries abroad. Numerous 16mm projectors are available for loan free of charge to civic groups interested in showing these American films.

Through the USIS, the Press and Publication Service provides news and features to thousands of newspapers and magazines in the Free World. Since, after the war, the great press associations have refused to make their copy available to the U.S. government, the Service wires a 10,000-word news bulletin daily except Sunday to 107 posts in 100 countries. Important U.S. government statements are, of course, included. Still photographs, including cartoon strips, are also distributed. In 1961, the Service disseminated about 18 million pamphlets. In addition, the magazines *Amerika,* in the Russian and Polish languages, and *Al Hayat Fi America* in Arabic, are distributed. Edited abroad are *News Review*, a bi-weekly in English and Arabic, and *Free World,* published in Manila in eight languages.

Returning now to USIA's over-all organization, its third layer comprises the geographic offices, of which there are four: Europe, Far East, Latin America, and Near East-South Asia-Africa. These Offices are headed by Assistant Directors who maintain the link between the USIA Director and the Agency's overseas activities. They are, in effect, roving representatives of the Director and spend much of their time abroad. They do not make policy, but supervise the implementation of announced guide lines.

The fourth layer consists of the USIS posts, the radio centers, relay bases, and production centers, all of which are abroad.

The political principles which form the basis of its programs are not evolved by USIA but by the Department of State's Bureau of Public Affairs or, more precisely, by the Policy Guidance and Coordination Staff in that Bureau's Office of International Information and Cultural Affairs. The Staff provides USIA with all information pertinent to foreign policy and also assumes policy control over the Agency's output so as to ensure an accurate reflection of the Department's foreign policy position. The Staff also reviews the Agency's programs, plans, and budget, and keeps a close watch over its production. At the same time, the Staff surveys non-governmental overseas programs and advises the Assistant Secretary of State for Public Affairs on their impact. It serves as a focal point for coordinating the State Department's interests in propaganda—or, to use the diplomatic term, in public affairs. Significantly, it represents the public affairs point of view in inter-departmental groups such as the Operations Coordination Board, the National Security Council, and the various government intelligence bureaus.

Thus USIA functions as a technical arm of the Department, its autonomy is limited to programming along prescribed lines. Moreover, USIA is empowered to work on neither educational exchanges nor a variety of cultural activities which have been retained by the Bureau for Public Affairs. This Bureau is divided into two parts: the first, being responsible for domestic affairs, does not concern us; the second is the Office of the Deputy Assistant Secretary for International Information and Cultural Affairs. Apart from the Policy Guidance and Coordination Staff discussed above, the most important unit is the International Educational Exchange Service. It covers aspects of program development and operations in the field of international educational exchange. In addition, the Deputy Assistant Secretary has attached to his office an Executive Secretariat of the U.S. Advisory Commission in Educational Exchange, which examines such questions as the protection and restitution of artistic and historic property, the preservation of cultural institutions (the Arts and Monuments Adviser), and the facilitation of transport and performance of American artists, or artistic and athletic groups overseas (Cultural Presentation Staff).

The Public Affairs Bureau has yet another Staff coordinating cultural activities with USIA as well as with the Agency for International Development (AID), which engages in technical assistance to foreign countries, namely, the Cultural Planning and Coordination Staff. It maintains a UNESCO Relations Staff, which coordinates policies with the United States National Commission for UNESCO. Finally, there is the East-West Contacts Staff, an important attempt to initiate and develop proposals for exchanges and contacts between the United States and the Soviet Orbit. This Staff, undoubtedly, will become a focal office for implementing U.S.-USSR cultural agreements and will develop plans for further exchanges, recommending their scope and type.

This complex organism which produces fuel for the American propaganda machine is organizationally diversified; it operates with a spirit of respectability; it is not fully coordinated when one considers private propaganda outlets, but it nevertheless presents the world with a fairly accurate picture of the United States and its policies. However, owing to its very respectability and the ethical nature of American principles, it is not nearly so hard hitting as Communist propaganda, nor is it comparable quantitatively with the Soviet propaganda machine. Appropriations granted by Congress to USIA are around $100 million. It has been estimated that Soviet propaganda alone costs the equivalent of $3 billion, to say nothing of propaganda expenditures in such a growing power as Communist China. In other words, even if one assumes that the *entire* American information and cultural exchange apparatus costs about $300 million, this is a mere 10 percent of what the Soviets are believed to spend without taking into account the rest of the Orbit.

At a time when war is no longer a workable instrument in international relations, when the East-West contact is being fought along "peaceful" and "competitive" lines, propaganda in all its forms assumes an even greater importance than before. It is in the interest of the United States, as the leading nation of the Western world, to overcome its reluctance and recognize the fact that adequate funds for propaganda are as vital as those for military defense.

United States: Non-Government Media

The most important organizations carrying out propaganda are the Free Europe Committee and the American Committee for Liberation from Bolshevism.

The Free Europe Committee, through *Radio Free Europe* (RFE), engages in the most extensive activities. Founded in 1949, the Committee is financed by the Crusade for Freedom, which raises private funds through continuous campaigning. Some additional funds are reportedly contributed by the U.S. Government, but the organization determines its own plans and programs. Instigated by prominent exiles from the East European satellites and a number of outstanding American personalities, the Committee was set up in New York. Shortly after its establishment, a Radio Committee was organized to determine how the voices of the refugees could best be used. A few months later, Radio Free Europe began broadcasting to Albania, Bulgaria, Czechoslovakia, Hungary, Poland, and Rumania. The organization grew rapidly; in the Committee's report for 1954 the range of RFE was well determined and comprised all the aforementioned states except Albania. East Germany was excluded because it was well within the range and responsibilities of RIAS; the Soviet Union, because it had become the domain of Radio Liberation. The report emphasized that RFE is a private organization, that over its transmitters "Poles speak to Poles, Hungarians to Hungarians, etc., in their own name, not in the name of the U.S. Government or of the American people."[18] It further stated that Munich, West Germany, would be the center of operations, that 85 percent of the daily broadcasts would be prepared in Munich (the other 15 per cent in New York), and that relay services would be maintained in Lisbon, Portugal.

RFE is divided into two organizations, one in New York and the other in Munich. Over-all policy and long-range planning

[18] *Free Europe Committee,* President's Report for the year of 1954, pp. 4-5. See also R. T. Holt, *Radio Free Europe,* Minneapolis: University of Minnesota Press, 1958, pp. 9-16.

are controlled by the Director's headquarters in New York. His Plans and Policy Staff is responsible for this strategic aspect; it is assisted by the Guidance Staff, which issues daily tactical guidance. The Program Review Staff seeks to establish whether policy and guidance have been carried out. Substantive support is supplied by a Research and Information Division which has developed a comprehensive system of cross-referenced files concerning persons and events in the target areas.

The operating organization in Munich is more complex. The European Director is supported, first of all, by the Political Adviser who is one of the most important men guiding the political content of the broadcasts. The Adviser keeps in touch with the chiefs of the country services through daily morning conferences in which the leading issues are discussed. He is assisted by Audience Analysis, a public relations office and a bureau surveying station operations. The operating organization is divided into four departments: administration, engineering, news and information, and programming. The News and Information Services are responsible for news, evaluation of news, and research; they also maintain a staff which monitors broadcasts from the target countries. Programming handles the five satellite countries and in addition has a script control, a music library, production office, tape library, and various program activities.

The relations between New York and Munich are delicate. Headquarters dispenses both general and specific guidance; the more difficult or dangerous the situation, the more specific the guidance (as during the Poznan riots in Poland and the Hungarian revolution in 1956). There is, however, a difference between policy and daily guidances. Policy guidances are binding; daily ones are not, in the sense that the local autonomy of the Munich operations enables the policy adviser to modify them if need be. Programming is more or less the responsibility of the operating part of RFE, but here, too, events of magnitude stimulate more headquarters supervision.[19] Solutions decided upon

[19] Cf. Holt, *op. cit.*, pp. 30-43.

by the directors of the New York and Munich organizations concerning policy control are subject to change according to prevailing conditions. It is very difficult and sometimes impossible to establish whether policies and actions initiated by the Communist Orbit are short-term or long-range, tactical or strategic. One may surmise that New York is interested mainly in the strategic aspects while Munich must deal with the ever more flexible tactics. Whenever the two categories overlap, New York's competency for guidance must be recognized. Nevertheless, it is significant that they are guidances rather than directives. Since guidance leaves more room for interpretation than a directive, differences in interpretation probably occur frequently.

Another more important question is the nature of the policy guidances. The men in New York who determine RFE policies are Americans. They do not want to harm the foreign policy of the United States. On the other hand, they are private individuals and, as such, are not admitted to the State Department's councils. If they do receive advice, they may or may not follow it, for the government cannot issue orders to them. In particular, RFE is not subject to Congressional control as is USIA and will hardly be summoned to Capitol Hill for questioning. This independence from governmental control and bureaucracy has advantages, but whether they outweigh the disadvantages arising out of an autonomy that could harm or neutralize United States propaganda as a whole is open to question. Only in America is such a contradiction possible, and the freedom of a group of people to take action in a grand style to fight for an ideal is typically American.

Whatever the negative aspects of lack of coordination may be, positive ones unquestionably exist. The Voice of America, being the official government organ of the United States, has assumed a dignified, official tone of respectability. Its aspirations admittedly are the dissemination of true facts and the explanation of American civilization. This is excellent as far as it goes, but in the struggle against the voice of communism, it is not nearly effective enough. RFE, on the other hand, is much freer to deliver hard-hitting messages. The programs, conceived without regard to international niceties, often strike at the sensitivities of the satellite regimes and their supporters. While there are times when such an approach may not be in the best interests of American foreign policy, on other occasions it may be well to supplement diplomacy with brutal frankness.

Whether this dialectical propaganda, a "unity of opposites," can be maintained in a democracy remains to be seen. The fact that émigrés do much of the programming work may cause complications in the future. They have their political axes to grind; for the most part, they are not integrated into the life of any nation and have generally remained isolated. Because of this, implementation of guidances occasionally suffers. Émigrés are partisans, and although they work for an American-financed, American-directed organization, they retain their own domestic politics which might well clash with concepts held in the United States. Nevertheless, it must be recognized that, on the whole, RFE has done important work and contributed heavily to Western political warfare directed against the Iron Curtain area.[20]

Other activities of RFE include the publication of the journal *East Europe* and leaflet-dropping balloon operations. These have caused considerable excitement in the Orbit and must be considered quite successful. RFE also continues to maintain relations with the Eastern European exile organizations.

The *American Committee for Liberation from Bolshevism* has a history similar to that of the Free Europe Committee. Created in 1951, its stated objective is to "aid the world-wide Russian and Soviet national minorities' emigration in its efforts to sustain the spirit of liberty among the peoples of USSR, and work toward their liberation from Soviet tyranny, preserve and sustain the historic cultures of Russia and the national minorities, and aid the united emigration in hastening understanding of the worst within the USSR."[21]

[20] For a discussion on RFE as a "Nonofficial Instrument of Foreign Policy" see Holt, *op. cit.* Chapter 2.

[21] As quoted in Martin, *op. cit.*, p. 33.

The establishment of the Committee was plagued by political antagonism between the émigré groups which made a united undertaking almost impossible; there was much unwillingness to recognize the realities of the situation in the USSR. Only in March 1953, was the broadcasting organization *Radio Liberation* finally established and activated. The relationship between the Committee in New York and the operations offices in Munich may be likened to that of RFE. However, the New York Committee's radio division is a rather small body, consisting of about 10 Americans and 29 Russians; the Munich operations are maintained by 75 Americans, 175 émigrés from the Soviet Union and a number of German technicians.[22]

Following the Soviet campaign for international relaxation of tensions, Radio Liberation was renamed *Radio Liberty*. This probably went very much against the wishes of the émigrés manning the microphones, many of whom think in terms of a country no longer extant. The nationality problem in the Soviet Union, though by no means liquidated, has progressed toward unification; the Soviet melting pot gradually is producing a unitary state even though "cultural autonomy" remains official policy and the national languages, in addition to Russian, are still being taught and used. Thus, the viewpoints expressed by the nine language desks of *Radio Liberty* may not necessarily be consonant with the realities of Soviet life. The Committee's failure to establish a unified front at the outset of its organization— a factor which delayed the start of its operations—was a clear indication of the émigrés' local nationalism and lack of reality. Basically, they were more interested in obtaining the liberation of their own area than in seeking a *modus vivendi* between the Free World and the USSR. To continue to believe in "liberation" without considering war is unreasonable. In fact, the American Committee, expressing more realistic views than those of the émigrés, has stated frankly that liberation is not a direct goal of Radio Liberty and that the "Liberation movement is the interaction of pressures toward freedom in the Soviet orbit with

[22] V. Petrov, "Radio Liberation," *The Russian Review*, April 1958, p. 106.

the forces of freedom in the free world, looking to the displacement of the Communist despotism by a system of political liberty."[23]

The nine desks represent eighteen Soviet nationalities: Russian, Ukrainian, Byelorussian, Georgia, Armenian, Azerbaijanian, Tatar, Uzbek, Kazakh, Kirgiz, Turkmen, Tadzhik, Ossetin, Adyge-Kabardin, Karachy-Balkar, Chechen-Ingush, Avar, and Kalmyk.[24] About three-quarters of the entire broadcasting time is made up of Russian-language programs; the remaining quarter is divided among sixteen of the national languages. Radio Liberty has fourteen powerful transmitters in West Germany and Spain and four transmitters in Formosa.

Radio Liberty does not seem to have found its definite bearings. Whether it ever will, depends largely on the policies formulated by the Committee which has been accused of reflecting "the shortcomings of the American policy towards the Soviet Union in general."[25] However, it must be remembered that the Committee is a private, not a governmental establishment and that its policy decisions are hampered not only by over-all considerations of Soviet-American relations during a period of "relaxation," but also by the controversy among émigrés who refuse to take cognizance of the fact that the USSR is becoming more and more a unitary state.

The effect of Radio Liberty is very hard to assess. Most likely it is not so strong as that of RFE. However, the potential of both organizations is great if used properly and realistically. To what extent these organizations help or hinder United States policy is difficult to fathom. On the other hand, owing to USIA's official sedateness and the ensuing limitations of its impact, the greater freedom of movement enjoyed by the unofficial propaganda machineries of RFE and RL offers a useful counterpoint to more conventional information. Such differences might work at cross-

[23] "A Fresh Look at Liberation," American Committee for Liberation, New York 1957, p. 6. See also Petrov, *op. cit.* p. 110.

[24] Cf. Petrov, *op. cit.*, p. 108. Also see E. Hobbing, "Radio Liberation Speaks for the Silent", *The New Leader*, October 6, 1958, 21 ff.

[25] Petrov. *op. cit.*, pp. 109-110.

purposes and time alone will show whether decentralization of propaganda is possible without violating the principle of consolidation and integration.

Of some importance is the *Institute for the Study of the USSR* in Munich, Germany. Incorporated under German law, it is a research organization connected with the American Committee and staffed by some eighty to one hundred researchers in different languages; its *Bulletin* has become a respectable journal. The difficulties besetting this organization are again the divergencies among the national minorities and a certain lack of objectivity so essential to serious research. However, since the latter part of the nineteen fifties, production has gradually improved and, with the retirement of the older diehards, a more objective approach to questions concerning the USSR may be anticipated.

Great Britain

The United Kingdom was as slow and reluctant as the United States to accept propaganda as an instrument of international relations. Ideology and propaganda, the main elements of the bipolar struggle, are distasteful to the Anglo-Saxon mind; some of Britain's most outstanding old-school diplomats have expressed in no uncertain terms their displeasure at the penetration of propaganda into the diplomatic field.

Britain set up limited cultural relations activities in 1934, initiated limited foreign language broadcasting in 1938 and, during the war, created a Ministry of Information which it abolished in 1946. But the more definitive work of formulating the principles and practices of propaganda was undertaken by the Drogheda Committee, named for its chairman, the Earl of Drogheda, which was appointed in 1952. Its terms of reference were "to assess the value, actual and potential, of the overseas information work of the Foreign Office, Commonwealth Relations Office, Colonial Office, Board of Trade and Central Office of Information; the External Services of the British Broadcasting Corporation; and the work of the British Council; to advise upon the relative importance of different methods and services in different areas and circumstances and to make recommendations for future policy."[26] The full report of this Committee was presented to Parliament in April 1954 by the Foreign Secretary.

The Committee's general considerations present a vivid picture of the problems. Incorporated in Part III of the Report are the following propositions:

> The Information Services must today be regarded as part of the normal apparatus of diplomacy of a Great Power . . . Private enterprise is still the main source of the information and impressions by which foreigners judge this country. Government activity in information is a supplement to private effort and should be so regarded. . .
>
> . . . However, the United Kingdom Government will still require official propaganda in order to explain their policy abroad . . . The aim of the Information Services must always be to achieve in the long run some definite political or commercial results . . . Winning the cold war is but one of a number of the current aims of our information work. The Information Services of the United Kingdom have to deal with firm friends, dangerous enemies, wavering allies and the particular relationships of the Commonwealth and the Colonies—a variety of problems and relationships requiring separate treatment in each country . . .
>
> Propaganda is no substitute for policy; nor should it be regarded as a substitute for military strength, economic efficiency or financial stability. Propaganda may disguise weakness, but the assertion of strength will deceive nobody unless the strength is there . . . It is as easy to underrate the potentialities of propaganda as it is to overrate them. The effect of propaganda on the course of events is never likely to be more than marginal. But in certain circumstances it may be decisive in tipping the balance between diplomatic success and failure. . . A Great Power with world-wide commitments is therefore well advised to pay the comparatively small premium represented by cost of efficient Overseas Information Services."[27]

[26] *Summary of the Report of the Independent Committee of Enquiry into the Overseas Information Service*, April 1954, H. M. Stationery Office, London.
[27] *Ibid.* pp. 6-7.

These principles demonstrate admirably the British position and elucidate clearly the reasons for the British approach to propaganda. They also emphasize the requisite diversity of the United Kingdom's propaganda policies. Unlike the United States, Britain does not limit its targets to the free world and the Communist orbit, but also must focus attention on the Commonwealth states; nor does it separate the domestic and foreign functions of broadcasting. This places Britain's information system in a very different light, especially since all its information services, while not necessarily official establishments, are semi-official and under the guidance and support of government. There is no "private sector" which independently dispenses international propaganda.

The Drogheda Committee recommendations rejected the re-establishment of a Ministry of Information but advocated a decentralized organization of considerable complexity. This is explainable primarily by the participation in propaganda activities of the Foreign Office, the Commonwealth Relations Office, the Colonial Office and the Exchequer. To coordinate views among these Offices, an "Official Committee" was set up under Foreign Office chairmanship. However, since some issues could be decided only by the Ministers, the establishment of an Advisory Committee of "independent persons" to survey regularly the operations of the Overseas Information Services was suggested.

The *Overseas Information Service* comprises three essential units: the Central Office of Information, the British Council, and the British Broadcasting Corporation. These units whose organization is not interlocked, are directed or guided by the pertinent information departments in the Foreign Office.

The News Department, in addition to other duties, serves as the Foreign Office contact with the domestic, Commonwealth and foreign press as well as with the BBC overseas service. It provides material for the explanation of the British point of view, keeping in close touch with "British diplomatic correspondents and foreign journalists stationed in London and with represen-

tatives of the press at important international conferences."
Foreign Office communiques are written by the News
Department. [28]

The Cultural Relations Department advises the Foreign Secretary on all cultural and educational affairs, paying particular
attention to policies adopted by the British Council. It also
"issues instructions" to the British Council and watches over the
implementation of the cultural clauses of the Brussels Treaty.
Further, it apprises the Foreign Secretary on the activities of
UNESCO and other cultural establishments of which the United
Kingdom is a member.

The Information Policy Department's duties are important and
manifold. It oversees all information activity abroad and is
responsible for its implementation of British policy; it maintains
liaison between the Foreign Office and the BBC services, coordinates Foreign Office requirements for the Central Office of
Information, and represents the Foreign Office information viewpoint in inter-departmental committees. It supervises the flow of
publicity material to information officers in foreign countries
and is particularly interested in trade and tourist activities, in
collaboration with the Board of Trade and related offices.

The Information Research Department's activities are not
known but it may be presumed they include providing intelligence for the information services as does the USIA's Office of
Research and Analysis.

Although, through its chairmanship of the official committee,
the Foreign Office has primary influence on the British information services, other Ministries are vitally involved, particularly
the Commonwealth Relations Office and the Colonial Office.
The former's very small information staff is dwarfed by the information departments of the Foreign Office. Yet it not only maintains Commonwealth press relations in London but also informs
the British and foreign press on Commonwealth affairs and
supervises the activities of its representatives in the field. It has

[28] Lord Strang, *op. cit.*, p. 211.

staff offices in India, Pakistan, Ceylon, Canada, Australia and New Zealand, and South Africa. In Central Africa, it opened an information office in Salisbury, in consideration of the newly won independence of certain African states and the granting of future independence to others.

The Colonial Office, at the suggestion of the Drogheda Committee, has established small information staffs in Nigeria, Ghana, other East African countries, and the West Indies. The Board of Trade, which maintains no information service of its own, utilizes the facilities of the various overseas departments. It is interested mainly in commercial propaganda and, in that respect, collaborates with British industry. Interestingly, the Drogheda Committee suggests that commercial and industrial publicity be incorporated in the conduct of overseas services and refers to similar views expressed by the Federation of British Industries. The Committee apparently considers that the British Council "especially in regard to the teaching of English in Asia will be highly beneficial to our overseas trade."[29]

The decentralized, not to say scattered, British propaganda machinery points up the great difficulties involved in combining general overseas propaganda with information destined for the Commonwealth and the colonies. Indeed, the British Information Services are designed to a significant extent for dissemination to widely separated Commonwealth audiences. Considering that the propaganda targets extend beyond the United Kingdom and the manifold Commonwealth nations to include western, neutralist and communist peoples, the Services face the challenge of approaching a tremendously diversified audience with a minimum of contradictions.

We turn now to the three main agencies charged with the execution of these complicated tasks. The Central Office of Information was in an unhappy position, for which reason the Drogheda Committee recommended that the Office be given a charter and that its work, as well as the extent of its control by various

[29] Summary, *op. cit.*, p. 29.

ministries, be better defined. Apparently there was a lack of coordination between the Office and the overseas posts. The Information Services Department in the Foreign Office did many things the Central Office was supposed to do. Also, the responsibilities of the defunct wartime Ministry of Information were partially bequeathed to the Central Office, but its authority was not. As a result, the Office became a frustrated service organ, bypassed by ministerial departments. Yet there was need for a bureau of "common concern" for such information services as function at the media level in USIA. The Central Office's main activities comprise press services (the London Press Service) for overseas countries, films, book export arrangements, tours arranged for journalists, and such miscellaneous services as visual aids, provision of magazines and newspapers, etc. Very much different is the standing of the two chief organs of British propaganda—the British Council and the BBC.

The Council is a semi-official agency, financially backed by the government and subject to prevailing policy lines but relatively independent in carrying out policy by means of cultural relations. It was established in 1934; in 1940, it received a Royal Charter which charged the Council with promoting "a wider knowledge of the United Kingdom and the English language" and developing "of closer cultural relations with other countries . . ." The Council "is financed almost entirely by public funds, mainly through the Foreign Office. In the Commonwealth, the Council acts directly as the agent of the Commonwealth Relations Office and the Colonial Office. It is usually designated as the British government's principal instrument for the implementation of cultural conventions to which the United Kingdom is a party."[30]

It is of interest to note that the Council was first established as an unofficial body whose chief object was to counter Nazi and Fascist propaganda in the Middle East. During the war, it expanded to include Turkey, Iran, Ethiopia, Spain, Portugal, Sweden, China, certain Latin American countries, the West

[30] *British Council Circular*, January 11, 1955.

Indies, and West Africa. After the war, the Council sought to continue its expansion in Iron Curtain countries but gradually withdrew or was ejected, until only the Polish branch office remained. Owing to economy measures, activities have been cut in various areas, but are still quite extensive in Europe and in some Commonwealth countries.

The Council's organization is outlined in its charter, which stipulates that management shall be vested in an executive committee of not less than 15 or more than 30 members (Art. 4), that all powers of the British Council shall be vested in the Executive Committee (Art. 6), that the Committe may by special resolution amend or add to the charter (Art. 7), that the Committee may delegate powers to sub-committees (Art. 9), and that resolutions may be passed by no less than three-quarters of the Executive Committee's members (Art. 10). The Committee, which has one Chairman and one Vice Chairman, appoints a Director General—who may be the Chairman to supervise the Council's activities. In 1946, an Arts Council of Great Britain also was constituted and granted a Royal Charter. Its fifteen members are appointed on an honorary basis by the Chancellor or the Exchequer in consultation with the Minister of Education and the Secretary of State for Scotland.

The British Council maintains staffs in about sixty countries to provide regular information about British life and thought, foster English-language studies, and disseminate knowledge of scientific, artistic, and other achievements of the United Kingdom. These staffs maintain contacts with schools and learned institutions and process requests for scholarships. Furnishing of books, educational supplies, lecturers, and artistic performances are also arranged for by the Council which thus combines the work of some USIA bureaus and the educational exchange offices in the U. S. Department of State. Special emphasis is placed on cultural relations with the countries of the Western Union.[31]

The only privately endowed institutions of consequence which

[31] Cf. "Western Union Cultural Cooperation," UK Participation, British Information Services, I.D. 1013, March 1950.

deal with cultural relations are the Carnegie United Kingdom Trust, founded and chartered in 1917, and the Pilgrim Trust, founded in 1930. Both are American-endowed but their exclusive purpose is the furtherance of British arts and learning, and the preservation of British national heritage.

The British Broadcasting Corporation is the best known of the overseas services. After the Nazis overran the Continent, the BBC was the only radio voice of the West until the Voice of America was established. During the war BBC quickly expanded its facilities, but postwar economic weakness forced the British Government to reduce its grant-in-aid. As a result, program hours in the BBC's External Services were reduced from more than 100 a day in 1944 to 79 a day in 1952. The BBC has acquired a fine reputation of reliability, and it is the intent of the British government to maintain this reputation through objective reporting. The British directors of the BBC certainly agree with those of the Voice of America in stating that "the most effective propaganda to many countries consists of a factual presentation of the news . . ." but they add "and of British views concerning the news." [32] This appendix constitutes the great difference between the BBC and other broadcasting facilities and perhaps detracts somewhat from its "objectivity." For unless objectivity is considered an absolute, it is not a true expression of the term.

In the period of 1962-63, the BBC's External Services in English and 40 other languages were heard throughout the world for more than 86 hours every day.[33] They are organized into seven services. The General Overseas Service in English is directed toward the Commonwealth nations and the colonies but also to those British subjects living abroad who want to hear their home radio. The European Service comprises the languages of the East European communist bloc; however, the decision as to which of the other European languages are to be retained is fluid, depend-

[32] Summary, *Op. cit.* p. 44.
[33] *BBC Handbook*, which appears annually in London, gives a detailed description of the BBC organization and its broadcasting schedule.

ing on world political and economic conditions. The Drogheda Committee recommended eliminating some West European languages, but apparently was turned down because broadcasts are still heard in French, German, Spanish, Portuguese, Turkish, Greek, Hebrew, Finnish, Italian, and Serbo-Croat. Dutch and the Scandinavian languages are now omitted but may be re-introduced if conditions require.

The Latin American Service, which uses the facilities of local stations to rebroadcast programs in Spanish and Portuguese, has suffered severe economy cuts. More generous funds are at the disposal of the Middle Eastern Service; the Far Eastern Service with relay stations in Malaya for Chinese, Indonesian, Burmese, Thai and French language programs; the Service to India-Pakistan-Ceylon; and finally, the North American Service which broadcasts to Canada and the United States.

The BBC's programming difficulties stem from the need to regionalize English-language broadcasting since broadcasts to the Commonwealth countries are accessible also to Britons at home. However, available funds do not permit a truly regionalized series of programs. Therefore BBC shapes its English program to suit the Commonwealth audiences, without regard to other listeners. Regionalization also has been eliminated in other languages, including those of the Iron Curtain, so that identical programs are heard in various languages, whether they be beamed to the USSR, the Middle East, the Far East or Canada. By way of comparison, VOA has the advantage of not having to concern itself with American audiences and therefore can produce more foreign-angled and regionalized broadcasts than the British Overseas Services are able to transmit.

On the other hand, British broadcasting has the great advantage of ready access to its own foreign correspondents. It is known that the leading American radio networks have foreign correspondents all over the world. These networks are private enterprises and USIA, being a government agency, cannot avail itself of their services. The BBC correspondents not only obtain news but also help to corroborate news. In addition, BBC has a

small staff of "diplomatic correspondents" who cover the Foreign
Office, the Commonwealth Relations Office, and the Colonial
Office. They enjoy a high professional standing in the
journalistic community.

The BBC external services, linked as they are to the home services, have access to the full resources of the over-all organization which commands a common personnel pool, correspondents
serving both at home and abroad, and a logistics system rich in
resources.

France

France "first among modern nations recognized the advantage
of a large-scale program of cultural relations with other countries."[34] Of the many governments France has had since the
establishment of the Third Republic, none is known to have
repudiated the country's cultural propaganda activities. The
results of this policy have justified the efforts. During World War
II, not even the impoverished and compromised Vichy regime
ceased cultural propaganda, and when the French Committee of
National Liberation was founded in Algiers, it immediately
started a small program of cultural relations. The liberation
accomplished, one of the first acts of the new government was the
reinstatement of the cultural and information services. Considerable sums of money were allocated to rebuild confidence in
French cultural achievements and thereby help re-establish the
greatly damaged French prestige.

With the reorganization of these services came the establishment of further policy and administrative offices in the Ministry
of Foreign Affairs which have been outlined above.[35] Comparatively large funds have always been allocated for cultural relations and information. The French, who vie with the Scots for
the reputation of being the thriftiest people in Europe, believed

[34] McMurray & Lee, *op. cit.* p. 9.
[35] *Ibid.* see pp. 414-415.

that no expense was too great if it restored universal respect for French culture.

France has no centralized, coordinated propaganda apparatus. As in Britain, the different aspects of information and cultural propaganda are parceled out among various governmental ministries and bureaus. From a policy point of view, the organization of these activities has been discussed previously; the Ministry of Foreign Affairs plays a vital role in shaping the character of propaganda to suit its purposes. However, the Ministry of Information exercises coordinating control over the French radio, television and press services. The Ministry also is in charge of documentary film production and furnishes the media staffs with documentation from various ministerial departments. It must be kept in mind that all these responsibilities pertain to domestic as well as international information. In France, perhaps more than elsewhere, the borderline between internal and external propaganda is blurred.

The Ministry has instituted a Legal and Technical Service which is of interest: Its legal section is occupied with questions of legislation and over-all regulations; the economic and technical section is concerned with the press, press agencies, publishers, distributors, and statistics; the "international" section is engaged in general studies on the freedom of intellectual information everywhere. To some extent, the Ministry is comparable to the British Central Office of Information which inherited the debris of the British Information Ministry.

Radio and television is directed by *Radiodiffusion and Television Française* (RTF). Needless to say, these communications media are fully state-controlled as in most other countries. Although RTF maintains artistic control of transmissions, it must be emphasized that this control can by no stretch of the imagination be compared with Soviet Party control of the arts. Rather, it functions as a watch dog to guard the standards of good taste.

RTF's several directorates guide both internal and external

broadcasting. The Directorate of Short Wave Transmissions has a foreign section which supervises French overseas and Arabic language services; a second section handles over-all information and documentary material. Other directorates are responsible mainly for the press, radio, and television information services in France and the French overseas possessions.

Perhaps the most amazing yet characteristic governmental organization in France is the Ministry of State (Cultural Affairs). It unquestionably has a tremendous influence upon the cultural relations activities of the Fifth Republic. Significantly, its first Minister was André Malraux, the internationally known writer. This Ministry primarily serves France and the French *Communauté*, guiding and stimulating French arts and letters. Sensing that herein lies France's greatest strength in world prestige, the Republic is anxious to promote production in all the art forms, both traditional and modern. There are bureaus for theater, literature, music, artistic education, architecture, cinematography and museums. Government relations with artists are emphasized; general developments in the productive and reproductive arts actively supported, and treasures of the past cared for. The organization of the Ministry has two parallel layers, one for Paris and one for the provinces.

It is not surprising, then, that in French international propaganda, culture takes precedence over all else. This is easy since France has no need to embellish what it has: If it offers the world what it has produced and is producing; the *Civilisation Française* needs no comment, it speaks for itself. French policy makers know this well, as do the legislators. Centuries of culture have penetrated deeply into the French national character, and although it is true that even General de Gaulle cannot turn back the clock of history and make France a politically great nation again, culturally, it remains one of the greatest. Yet in most non-European and uncommitted nations, specifically the Afro-Asian countries, the culture of France probably has less meaning than the shrinking of its power. Nor is it clear whether its cultural propaganda has more effect than has that of other Western nations. Thus, despite the. magnificent achievement of French civilization, in the polarized power struggle, culture is not likely to be a decisive element. Even in propaganda, ideology and power remain the Alpha and Omega.

The USSR and the Communist Orbit

Turning now to the vital question of Soviet propaganda, we find its dimensions too vast to be fully encompassed here. The implications of its meaning and organization—insofar as the latter is known—can only be sketched in the broadest possible terms.[36]

It must be understood at the outset that communism, like all totalitarian forms of state management, considers propaganda one of the essential devices for achieving its objectives. Furthermore, domestic and foreign propaganda, though they sometimes pursue different objectives, must be regarded as an integrated whole, just as foreign and domestic policies are basically one. The reason for this approach can be found in the ideological concept of communism as a universalist movement. In previous chapters, it was mentioned that communist thinking eschews the nation-state and strives for an eventual world community of nationalities rather than an alliance of communist powers still endowed with national aspirations. This, admittedly, is a long-range goal but nevertheless it indicates the all-embracing concept of integration which pervades communist thinking and planning. Accordingly, there never has been a separation between policy and propaganda in the Soviet Union. One cannot even say that propaganda is always tactical because, in the communist scheme of things, strategic objectives, too, cannot be envisaged without long-term propaganda.

Even since the establishment of the USSR, propaganda has been considered of the utmost importance. For that reason, its direction was assigned to the Party's Central Committee. Those

---

[36] See Frederick C. Barghoorn, *Soviet Foreign Propaganda*, Princeton: Princeton University Press, 1964, *passim*.

sections of the Central Committee specifically responsible for substantive and operational propaganda activities are the important and secretive Foreign Section, specialized departments of science and culture and of economic affairs, a cadre section, and most interesting for the purpose of this chapter, the Department of Agitation and Propaganda (*Agitprop*). In addition, many Communist parties outside the Orbit have a clandestine apparatus organized on the "triad" principle. A "triad" consists of a political, a cadre, and a propaganda specialist to whom at times a technician is assigned. In both overt and covert propaganda activities, the Agitprop representative is part of the political-economic team. The activities of the Foreign Section are largely unknown, but experienced Sovietologists believe it to be the hub of control over foreign Communist parties, espionage planning, and propaganda activities. Probably directed by experienced area experts, it influences the work of the Foreign Ministry and the State Committee for Foreign Economic Relations, the latter being the spearhead of the Ministry of Foreign Trade. Thus the Foreign Section is perhaps the most important controlling factor in overt, semi-covert and covert international propaganda activities.

Agitprop is the executive office of the Party for domestic and foreign propaganda. As "a policy staff producing little propaganda material of its own", it "acts as a planner, director, and 'watchdog' of all communist media engaged in propaganda dissemination."[37] Internationally, the flow of propaganda seems to be organized simply. The Central Committee issues political directives which Agitprop, presumably supervised by the Foreign Section, processes into practical guidances. These set forth the lines to be followed in all propaganda media, including scores of lecturers and activists who spread the word throughout urban and rural centers.

Agitprop exerts influence over most media and organizations. Prior to 1957, it controlled VOKS, the All-Union Society for

[37] E. M. Kirkpatrick, ed., *Target: The World*, New York: The Macmillan Company, 1956, p. 26.

Relations with Foreign Countries. In 1957, VOKS was abolished and replaced by the State Committee for Cultural Relations with Foreign Countries, formed under the general aegis of the Ministry of Culture, but responsible directly to the Council of Ministers of the USSR. Although the governmental line of command appears clear enough, it is reasonably safe to assume that the new Committee will be subject to Agitprop recommendations since this Section, as well as the Foreign Section, is a Party organ and the Party exercises the real control. Similarly, the new "autonomous" All-Union Association of Friendship Societies, established in 1958, is undoubtedly controlled by the appropriate Party authorities.

The Friendship Societies afford a particularly interesting insight into the growing subtlety of Soviet propaganda under the slogan of the "new humanism." They are known to have existed in many countries since the Twenties. The new organization is a separate body; it has contact with the societies abroad, but its purposes for forming a rather ambitious organization in the USSR are different. The individual Friendship Societies are chaired by men noted for their artistic or scientific achievements. For example, the writer Ilya Ehrenburg is Chairman of the Soviet-French Society. There are now more than twenty such organizations in the USSR, not counting those in the Union Republics which in a sense are branch offices with special objectives. In a pretentious palace, called "House of Culture," visiting tourists and delegations are shown how the USSR honors the achievements of their countries. One might call this organized flattery—and it works: Visitors walk away impressed, since few of them look behind the facade of these organizations which consist of cultural "Potemkin villages." Nor is this all. The activities in the palace and the proceedings of the societies receive slanted coverage in the press and the Soviet radio. This provides additional effective propaganda.

Furthermore, communist parties throughout the world receive propaganda directives from the Foreign Section (while political interpretations of world events and the communist reactions thereto come from other sources). The parties, together with the front organizations, conduct direct and indirect propaganda operations on behalf of the Soviet Union, the base of world communism. Ostensibly non-communist front organizations, under the guise of their specific issues or interests, carry out communist business. Among the more important fronts are the World Peace Council, the World Federation of Trade Unions, International Union of Students, World Federation of Democratic Youth, and Women's International Democratic Federation. Most of them publish periodicals in several languages.

The successor magazine to the Cominform journal, called *Problems of Peace and Socialism,* or *World Marxist Review* in English and published in seventeen other languages will offer, as did its predecessor, political and propaganda guidance to communist-led nations. The domestic and foreign radio network of the USSR, directed to both communist and non-communist nations, is guided and partially serviced by Agitprop.

Diplomatic establishments and missions of the Soviet Orbit play an integral role in propaganda campaigns by tailoring their written and spoken statements to fit the Party Line. For example, if the Kremlin decides on a peace campaign, this topic will be pursued by all propaganda media, including diplomacy. Of all diplomatic establishments, only the communists fully understand how to merge diplomacy and policy with propaganda. Strategically, political objectives are aligned with propaganda campaigns; tactically, the communists seek to confuse their opponents by forcing them to speculate on which is the real and which is the alleged objective.

Psychologically Soviet-Communist propaganda aims at deluging the world with its words. Quantitative production of propaganda, regardless of its standards, is in itself regarded as desirable. Hitler's dictum that people will believe anything if they hear it often enough is not original; the communists knew it long before Goebbles' tenure as Nazi propaganda minister. Soviet propaganda has always tried hard to make the communist movement appear "respectable," secure support for it even from non-communists, and use that support to obtain popular endorsement of Soviet foreign policy. Beyond mass following, which Lenin regarded as of prime importance, the Party also attempts to win over the "intelligentsia." Being intelligent or professionally accomplished does not, unfortunately, prevent a man from being naive in matters of international relations. Western pacifists and "peace-at-any-price" defenders include some outstanding artists and scientists who neither understand the objective of communist propaganda nor are they acquainted with the devious ways in which such propaganda is presented as non-communist.

For valid reasons, propaganda has been assigned a major role in world politics. The communists realize that their ultimate objectives can only be reached by stages. The stages, in themselves broad and strategic, are implemented by tactical methods suited to the individual strategies. For example, among the strategic propaganda campaigns are those for peace, disarmament, and neutrality of uncommitted nations, disarray of Western defense and economic arrangements and, within the Communist Orbit, unity under the ideological guidance of the Soviet Communist Party. The tactics used to carry out these purposes vary greatly, but are applied in a coordinated and integrated fashion, engaging all propaganda media, including diplomacy, in the campaign.

Consider peace and disarmament. The reasons for attaining this strategic objective are neither humanitarian nor motivated by pacifism. Once it had been established (1) that war or a warlike situation was unproductive for communism in general and the USSR in particular, (2) that the risk of wholesale destruction could not be accepted unless the gains of the regime were to be gambled away, (3) that the rapid development of the USSR in technological and economic respects could still be matched or even surpassed by progress in the West and that violent attempts at revolution could boomerang, the Khrushchev regime determined that it needed many years to fulfill its ambitious economic planning and to reach the threshold of a new era from which to begin the "transition to communism." This would require an extended period of "peaceful coexistence," for which the Soviet leaders have clamored, with steadily increasing emphasis, since the twentieth Party Congress in 1956 made it an official policy.

But Khrushchev's unilateral announcement in January, 1960, that the Soviet armed forces would be cut one-third cannot be explained away as merely a demonstration of his desire for universal disarmament or increased investment in economic or social development. The new weapon technology obviously caused the Kremlin's military establishment to be modernized so as to strengthen its power potential and, at the same time, afford excellent propaganda for peace. In seeking nuclear disarmament, the Soviet government again has the advantage of world opinion, leaving the West to face a dilemma. For, even in the event of a nuclear agreement such as the test treaty of 1963 the possibility of deception cannot be ruled out. Very important factors in the disarmament campaign are the attempts to induce Western relaxation and complaisance and to stimulate assumptions that the changes in the Soviet system appear to augur well for an ultimate moderation toward democracy.

This double-headed campaign is both policy and propaganda. It is the motivating power behind the relaxation efforts that began to take distinct form in 1958. It became the subject of Soviet diplomacy as well as propaganda campaigns—which more often than not are one and the same. It has been taken up by all available media and all communist and crypto-communist organizations around the world, with the collaboration of neutralists and pacifists thrown in for good measure.

In surveying the means of propaganda-diplomacy at the disposal of the Soviet orbit, it becomes evident that the results have a powerful impact upon large areas of the world. For there is one point on which the communist propagandists far outstrip their opponents, namely, *to present basic issues of life in a manner that appeals to the fundamental aspirations of man in all climes.* Marxism in part appeals to the underdog by giving him a whipping boy accountable for the evils of social injustice and by shifting responsibility from the individual to society. The ideals of Western democracy feature values which are irrelevant to the underdog who needs food and shelter rather than a highly ethical and intellectual philosophy. The Western concept of freedom and the dignity of the individual means little to him.

In assessing the individual media of Soviet propaganda, it must be realized that the entire propaganda apparatus has been integrated into a fully coordinated, tightly knit system. To discuss the cultural media first, the Ministry of Culture plays an increasingly important role in the implementation of Soviet cultural policies. It is assisted by the State Committee for Cultural Relations with Foreign Countries and the new All-Union Association of Friendship Societies, both derivatives of the former VOKS.

Soviet propagandists have proved themselves extraordinarily skilled in using cultural media. They manipulate the arts and sciences—the most respectable among all media. Even more important, they operate under clearly defined policies which seek to establish as many cultural agreements and exchanges as possible. Such targets can be attained without necessarily engendering hostility. They use music and literature, drama and dance, the fine arts and the sciences to earn prestige in the West; they use technology and aid to impress the underdeveloped countries. They seek to gain the sympathies of artists and intellectuals everywhere. This type of propaganda remains quantitatively limited since it is directed to an educated minority. Nevertheless, it reaches the leaders and the intellectuals. It does not pretend to embrace the populace as do the mass media—radio, films, television, the printed word, and popular exhibits. In contrast, Communist China uses cultural media as primary propaganda weapons. In highly civilized countries, the level of cultural relations, based chiefly upon pre-communist achievements, is comparable to that of France; in Peking's main target area, the underdeveloped countries, the level is far lower and is geared to the more primitive minds of predominantly illiterate peoples.

Soviet international broadcasting has steadily increased its transmission time. Its output in 1959 was 975 hours weekly to which the Eastern European satellites added 1,060 hours. Communist China's radio propaganda output amounts to 512 hours weekly and that of the Far Eastern satellites to 220 hours. This indicates an output of 2,767 overt communist radio propaganda hours per week, an increase of about 400 hours over the 1958 output.[38] Since the propaganda budget is virtually unlimited, as many languages are used as deemed necessary. TASS, the Soviet News Agency, also broadcasts in Morse code, Russian, German, French and English; a Soviet Information Bureau "beams . . . background and feature material in Russian, French, Italian, English and Norwegian Hellschreiber."[39]

Little can be said concerning television for foreign consumption since its potentialities have yet to be developed; a few pre-censored taped programs may be hired for exchange. Much more important are the production of books, journals and special publications such as pamphlets and leaflets.

Every Communist party maintains either a daily or a weekly paper which probably could not remain solvent without the clandestine support of communist headquarters in Moscow. In addition, there are communist-sympathizing newspapers and magazines which by design or credulity foster Soviet objectives; most of them presumably receive help if only by the supply of free material. Of great significance are the communist news agencies, the most important of which are TASS and the New China News Agency (NCNA). Most East European states maintain their own news services, all of which are creatures of their parties and governments. TASS functions inside and outside the USSR. It is responsible for collecting foreign information and transmitting it to headquarters; exporting appropriately edited domestic news to foreign lands; collecting and disseminating domestic news to the Soviet bloc press.[40]

Dozens of communist periodicals are published by the Orbit in

[38] According to the U.S. Information Agency.
[39] Kirkpatrick, *op. cit.*, p. 80.
[40] Kirkpatrick, *op. cit.*, p. 79.

many languages and circulated in many parts of the world. Expected import difficulties often can be avoided by negotiations for reciprocal arrangements. Such agreements exist between the United States and the USSR, but they probably are not so effective as either party would wish. The Soviet publication *USSR* is of limited interest to American magazine readers; the American periodical *Amerika,* though valued highly by Soviet citizens eager for information from the West, is hard to obtain since publication is not advertised and rather few copies are put into public circulation. Yet many copies are returned as "remainders which could not be sold."[41] Some of the above mentioned "friendship societies" also publish journals in the languages of the countries in which they operate.

Book publishing is a very large operation in communist propaganda. In recent years the Foreign Languages Publishing House in Moscow alone has produced, and the international trade organization *Mezhdunarodnie Knige* (Foreign Books) has distributed more than 100 million copies of over 900 titles, each containing at least 50 pages. At the same time, Soviet State publishers disseminate annually 30 million books in the USSR alone. Thus one might say that Soviet book production reaches an annual high of at least 130 million copies.[42]

Peking's publishing activities are rapidly increasing. Books and journals are being disseminated at very low prices in many languages. Although no figures are available, the steady expansion of foreign-language production has been noticeable ever since the late fifties.

The book output of the Orbit nations is no less astounding. For example, during the first postwar decade, Poland published 500 books in 26 languages with a circulation of 12 million copies. Rumania, during the same period, published 42 million translations of 3,000 different book titles.[43] These figures do not cover

[41] For a list of foreign-language Soviet-satellite magazines, see Kirkpatrick, pp. 81-84.

[42] These are official Soviet figures, compiled from statistics in the periodical *Knizhnie Letopis* during an extensive period. They are probably correct.

[43] Kirkpatrick, *op. cit.,* p. 87.

the dissemination of pamphlets or leaflets; nor do they include such magazines as *International Affairs* or *New Times,* Soviet multi-language publications which are distributed in many millions of copies both inside and outside the communist orbit. Since importation of books and magazines from the communist orbit is relatively simpler than exportation of Western and Free World publications to the orbit countries, this medium of propaganda is far more advantageous to the communists than to the West, which is further hampered by fiscal restrictions. No such restrictions exist in the East, where unlimited funds are at the disposal of propaganda in any form.

The use of motion pictures produced in the USSR began most successfully in the twenties with the great classics of the silent films: *Battleship Potemkin, Mother, Storm over Asia,* and some of the first sound films: *Road to Life, Turksib, Shchors.* Not only were they extremely effective propagandistically, they also marked a high level of artistic accomplishment. However, throughout the thirties and forties, the Stalin repression caused a sharp deterioration in the quality of Soviet films and, in addition, contained blatant falsifications of history and contemporary life in the USSR, unacceptable to the West.

The Khrushchev relaxation policy and subsequent agreements on cultural exchanges have promoted a somewhat livelier film barter. It goes without saying that since film showings in public theaters are subject to reciprocity, the effectiveness and extent of such mutual propaganda is narrow. There has been a noticeable development toward more subtle propaganda, cloaked in well-made dramatic sequences.

So long as Khrushchev's policy of peaceful coexistence is continued by his successors, this trend is unlikely to change.

Exchange of delegations and, especially, participation in trade fairs, have become communist propaganda media of considerable proportions. The value of fairs is obvious; life and achievements in the Soviet Union can be pictured in every conceivable form and shape and demonstrated by prototypes. The propaganda value of delegations depends upon their mission and personalities. Not all of them travel for any other purpose than to gather information; others, particularly the high level leaders, combine their informational purposes with political or economic ones. Any statements they may make are propagandistically conceived.

This is by no means an exhaustive list of media. Owing to the integrated nature of communist propaganda and to the fact that it is permeated with potential subversive and espionage activities, other devices can and will be found whenever necessary for the implementation of policy. The economic field, for example, offers vast opportunities for propaganda, such as pressure by threat or enticement; technological successes have further enlarged the communist propaganda potential. Political statements and diplomatic correspondence, ideological campaigns, increase of economic and military power potential, and the "hope" offered to unsophisticated peoples—all these contribute to a powerful motivational force. Finally, if we add to these considerations the important fact that there are no budgetary impediments, we can only wonder how the West can expect to counter the gigantic communist propaganda campaign without radically changing its method of approach.

Parenthetically, it might be added that Communist China's propaganda apparatus differs from that of the USSR only in minor organizational aspects. Peking's propaganda policy and its implementation were more or less modeled after the Soviet example and then adapted to Chinese conditions.

8. National Foreign Policy and International Organization

THE GREAT DILEMMA

The problem of adjusting national foreign policy to international organization is relatively new. In the contemporary meaning of the term, it did not exist prior to the establishment of the League of Nations. There were, however, regional arrangements, comprising states which considered it wise to pool their strength better to safeguard their interests which were identical or similar. But such alliances can not be regarded as genuine international organizations, even though they have their acknowledged place in international politics as the United Nations Charter has clearly recognized.

When the League of Nations was founded, statesmen faced a new dilemma: How could a nation's foreign policy be independent and, at the same time, abide by the League's principles if national aims and objectives ran counter to those of the League? During the League's lifetime policy makers made little effort to solve this problem with unconventional methods except by introducing the international conference technique which survived the League and gradually became a common feature of modern diplomacy.[1]

[1] One of the earliest post-World War II studies on this new aspect of diplomacy was Lord M. P. Hankey's *Diplomacy by Conference*, London: Ernest Benn Ltd., 1946. See especially Chapter I.

The establishment of the United Nations was a step toward international community living. But although, as compared with the League, it increased the threat of sanctions against the breakers of peace, it did not abandon the principle of national sovereignty. It was this philosophy rather than that which would look upon the United Nations as a preliminary move toward world government that ruled the thinking of the framers of the Charter. Moreover, world government was unacceptable to the Soviet delegates, whose Marxist-Leninist doctrine could recognize no such government unless it professed a communist concept of classless societies, consisting of nationalities rather than nations. Thus the issue was, in 1945, whether the United Nations, like the League, was to be a forum of sovereign nations with all the members insisting upon their sovereign rights to the bitter end, or an association of member peoples, willing to make concessions to the point where the sacrifice of national sovereign rights might be accepted if the common good required it.

It is conceivable that, given time and peaceful development, many nations may be prepared to make such concessions for the sake of an enduring peace. There are definite indications to that effect; for example, the decision of numerous governments and parliamentary bodies to submit to the opinion and verdict of the International Court of Justice. (The United States Senate, creating a precedent in American history, ratified United States recognition of the Court and agreed to submit to its findings.) However, as was to be expected, this propitious development was severely impeded by the ideological dispute that has marred relations among the member states of the United Nations almost from the time it became apparent that the Axis powers would be defeated in the near future.

The contest of socio-political ideologies introduced a new dangerous element into international organization. More than *national* sovereignty, totalitarianism aspired to achieve worldwide *ideological* sovereignty. In other words, the sovereign rights of individual nations were to be subordinated to the international rule of an ideologically motivated organization. As a result, countries objecting to such an ideology kept insisting on their own sovereign national laws and prerogatives. In such circumstances, the process of adjusting national policies to international cooperation had already become obsolete by the time the United Nations decided to go to San Francisco and write the Charter. Thus sovereignty, once again, became the chief obstacle to productive international cooperation, that is, the adjustment of national to world politics.

An additional element of potential danger is the rapid multiplication of member states, many of which are still in the process of developing their national image after having been a colonized territory for decades or centuries. All these states are extremely jealous of their newly won sovereignty and therefore inclined to regard the United Nations as an exclusive club of sorts, membership in which is both a status symbol and an insurance policy, rather than as an international organization to preserve the peace even if it means the sacrifice of some elements of national sovereignty. In a sense, this is understandable. For those who formulate and execute foreign policy, considerations of national objectives are of decisive import. The question then arises as to what extent it is permissable or advisable to achieve these objectives by relinquishing sovereign rights. Obviously, participation in international organizations does not in itself constitute a violation of sovereign rights. But if there is to be actual cooperation with other nations, the problem of whether required compromises may conflict with sovereign prerogatives inevitably will have to be faced.

There can be no question that absolute sovereignty is detrimental to international peace. With the exception of General de Gaulle, non-totalitarian nations with political experience have acknowledged, openly or tacitly, that absolute sovereignty is no longer possible or profitable in a society of free and equal nations. The communist insistence on sovereignty is explainable in terms of their opposition to any societal organization that is not "socialist" controlled; the final goal of Marxist-Leninists includes the abolition of national frontiers which would automatically eliminate sovereignty altogether.

Thus adherence to an international organization of any strength presents non-communist policy makers with compounded difficulties. From time to time they will find themselves compelled to consider some relinquishing of their nations' sovereign rights if they really want to become a component of a society of nations. Representatives of totalitarian governments and parties realize the dilemma of their opposite numbers and exploit it for its propaganda value. While their membership in the UN seems in itself to be a proof of their willingness to cooperate, they are bound to find themselves in opposition to those powers whose ideologies are not theirs. They must, therefore, evade the issues; if the conclusion of an agreement cannot be prevented, they may later try to obstruct its implementation, dispute its interpretation or simply ignore it.[2] As they do not tolerate manifestations of individual freedom on the part of their citizens but prescribe their thinking and acting in accordance with strict over-all plans, so also do they wish to convert (or subvert) those nations which do not recognize the validity of their political and economic philosophy. Since in the majority of cases they cannot succeed in so doing, their main objectives are the creation of confusion and dissension among non-communist states and the use of the international forum as a propaganda platform. They, too, are unwilling to cede any of their sovereign prerogatives for that would mean giving up their aspirations to impose an ideological sovereignty of their own making. Thus the threat of ideological sovereignty fortifies rather than relaxes national sovereignty.

Yet sovereignty, whether absolute or relative, is unadaptable to genuine international organization. International cooperation is bound to remain superficial so long as international law does not supersede national law. No wonder policy makers find themselves in a precarious position when they try to formulate foreign policies for national security without being able to master collec-

---

[2] The refusal of the USSR to pay its part for the UN peacekeeping forces in the Congo is a good example; Moscow would probably prefer disorder permitting communist infiltration than orderly transition to democratic processes.

tive security. Under prevailing conditions, the most difficult of all
political problems—that of maintaining a workable and profitable balance between national interest and international cooperation—is virtually impossible to achieve, and the pressing of
attempts at ideological world sovereignty appears to rule out a
lasting solution of the problem. On the other hand, in both
formulation and execution of foreign policy it is no longer possible to ignore international organization. Indeed, the foreign
policy position of all countries is influenced by the existence of
the United Nations, and for this reason it is essential to survey
briefly the United Nations itself, the administrative apparatus in
the foreign offices dealing with UN affairs and the informational
activities of the UN.

ORGANIZATION OF THE UNITED NATIONS

The *Security Council* was conceived as the organization's most
important body and given "primary responsibility for the maintenance of international peace and security" (Art. 24, 1). But,
although on paper its power exceeds that of the League of Nations Council, in practice the Security Council has lost much of
its authority because of the ideological division between East and
West as expressed by the Soviet's indiscriminate use of the veto.
The powers conferring in San Francisco agreed to vest the Council with control over the UN organization; they also gave it the
right to enforce international peace. The Council was conceived
as a small, movable body, consisting of the Big Five permanent
members (the United States, United Kingdom, USSR, France,
and Republic of China) and six temporary members, to be
elected for two-year periods by the General Assembly. Its decisions must be approved by the Big Five, included in a majority
of seven. Perhaps in the future, the UN's failure to cope with the
problems of the ideological and nuclear age will be traced back
to the Yalta compromise on the veto. But, although the use of
the veto by the Soviet representatives in the Council has

obstructed much of the United Nation's business, it is true that the UN charter might not have been ratified by the U.S. Senate without the veto provision. Possibly the same is true of the other major nations since the veto was regarded as a safeguard for national sovereignty. It is ironic that the communist representatives, so opposed to what they call "bourgeois nationalism," should prove to be the ones most jealously guarding the security of their sovereign rights.

The *General Assembly* was not conceived as a powerful body. In fact, according to the Covenant, the League's Assembly had more authority. Consisting of representatives of all member nations, each having one vote, the UN Assembly's constitutional task is limited to advice, recommendations, and resolutions. In the case of important issues, decisions are reached by a two-thirds majority. (Art. 18, 2). Other questions require only a simple majority. In both contingencies, it makes no difference whether or not the majority embodies any of the great powers.

All components of the United Nations are required to submit annual reports to the General Assembly, which has considerable authority over some of them, notably the Social and Economic Council, and Trusteeship Council, and the Secretariat. Of great importance is its responsibility to elect part of the members of the Security Council, the members of the two above-named organs and (in consonance with the Security Council) the Secretary General. It also plays a role in appointing the judges of the International Court of Justice, must approve the UN budget and admit new members once they are approved in principle by the Security Council.

According to Article 10 of the UN Charter, the General Assembly may debate all problems of international security and submit recommendations except in issues which are simultaneously under discussion in the Security Council, but it can bring to the floor "any question or matters within the scope of the present Charter . . . and may make recommendations to the members of the UN or to the Security Council . . .". This Article, in combination with Article 11, has become a source of the Assembly's great influence on world opinion. Several times, when the Council was blocked by Soviet vetoes, the Assembly has been convoked to debate issues of gravity. One such convocation occurred as a result of the Soviet suppression of the Hungarian revolution, after the Security Council, hopelessly blocked by the Soviet veto, was prevented from intervening. The Assembly adopted a resolution condemning the Soviet action. However, there was no further sequence except the attempt by some of the members to keep alive the spirit of the resolution. The United Nations could not—and probably would not—use its combined power to retaliate for the Soviet action. Only the Security Council could make such a decision, but it is clear that an accused Council member would refuse to vote againt himself.

Thus, while the Assembly has become a world conscience of sorts, it cannot, like a parliament, demand and achieve action. But it "shall initiate studies and make recommendations" for the promotion of international cooperation in the political, economic, social, and cultural fields (Art. 13). The results of such studies are, again, subject to bipolar differences of opinion. Nevertheless, the General Assembly's influence on world opinion remains considerable and has increased in proportion to the Security Council's deadlocks.

The *Economic and Social Council* (ECOSOC), which originated in the 1944 Dumbarton Oaks Conference, consists of eighteen members of the United Nations who are elected by the General Assembly. The membership is organized in three "shifts," that is, six members "shall be elected each year for a term of three years" (Art. 61, 2). Decisions are made by a majority of the members present, each of whom has one vote (Art. 67). The tasks of ECOSOC are indicated by its name: It studies and reports on international problems concerning "economic, social, cultural, educational, health, and related matters" (Art. 62, 1) and, most important, "may make recommendations for the purpose of promoting respect for, and observance of, human rights and fundamental freedoms for all" (Art. 62, 2). Although it is to some degree "responsible to the General Assembly, in most areas it does things on its own initiative".[3] It is, of course, in close contact with the Specialized Agencies of the UN, such as World Health Organization (WHO), International Refugee Organization (IRO), UN Educational, Scientific and Cultural Organization (UNESCO), International Labor Organization (ILO), and Food and Agriculture Organization (FAO).

The *Trusteeship Council,* another of the six most important UN bodies, makes the UN a *de facto* supervisor over those "territories whose peoples have not yet attained a full measure of self-government" (Art. 73). This "International Trusteeship System" as it is called in Art. 75, applies to territories now held under mandate, those which may be detached from enemy states as a result of World War II and those placed *voluntarily* "under the system by states responsible for their administration" (Art. 77, 2). The Trusteeship Council consists of UN members who administer trust territories, as well as others who do not administer such territories. Since there must be as many members of non-administering nations as there are of nations in charge of trusteeship territories, the exact number of the members is indefinite and changes as mandated territories become self-administering. As in ECOSOC, each Trusteeship Council member has one vote and decisions are made by majority of members present.

Although responsible to the General Assembly, the Council's initiative is mainly its own. But its tasks are limited by the necessary caution exercised in supervising dependent territories.

The *International Court of Justice* "shall be the principal judicial organ of the UN" (Art. 92). It is the fifth of the principal organs of the UN enumerated in Art. 7 of the Charter. Its differences from the Permanent Court of International Justice are minor and more formal than substantive. The Permanent Court operated *within* but not *as a part of* the League of Nations; the International Court was incorporated into the UN. All members of the UN are "*ipso facto* parties of the Statute of

[3] E. P. Chase, *The United Nations in Action,* New York: McGraw-Hill Book Company, 1950, p. 72.

the International Court of Justice" (Art. 93). This Statute is annexed to the Charter and determines that the Court "shall consist of fifteen members, no two of whom may be nationals of the same state" (Art. 3 of Statute.). Members of the Court are elected currently by majority decision of the Security Council and the General Assembly. A judge's term is nine years, and he may be re-elected. The seat of the Court is The Hague; its administration is an independent one.

The effectiveness of the International Court was severely restricted by U.S. Senate Resolution #196 of 1946. The debate in the Senate concentrated largely on the question of sovereignty, and the Chairman of the Senate's Foreign Relations Committee, Tom Connally, was concerned primarily with possible outside interference in such domestic American problems as immigration, tariffs, and the Panama Canal. This reservation amended the Senate Resolution which authorized the President to accept, on behalf of the United States, the Charter of the International Court of Justice. The Resolution provided that the United States would not accept the Court's jurisdiction in the following matters:

(a) disputes the solution of which the parties shall entrust to other tribunals by virtue of agreements which are already in existence or which may be concluded in the future;

(b) disputes with regard to matters which are essentially within the domestic jurisdiction of the United States of America *as determined by the United States of America;*

(c) disputes arising under a multilateral treaty unless (1) all parties to the treaty affected by the decisions are also parties to the case before the Court, or (2) the United States of America specifically agrees to jurisdiction. [4]

The italicized insertion under (b), "as determined by the United States of America" contains the essence of the Connally

[4] Cf. S. S. Goodspeed, *The Nature and Function of International Organization*, New York: Oxford University Press, 1959, p. 319. See also U.S. Senate Resolution 19196, July 24, 1946.

Amendment. Accordingly, the United States could determine unilaterally whether or not it considered a case "essentially within the jurisdiction of the United States." Although the motives of the Amendment were determined to patriotic considerations, the Court's legal effectiveness was thereby greatly diminished and so, by inference, was the influence of the United Nations.

France, Mexico, and Pakistan followed the U.S. example. As an extenuating circumstance, the entire Resolution was conceived as a temporary one. It was to remain in force from its adoption in August, 1946, until August, 1951, "and thereafter until the expiration of six months after notice of abrogation." This qualification enabled lawmakers to submit resolutions to annul the 1946 amendment, and in 1959, such a resolution (94) was submitted by Senator Hubert Humphrey. "The Connally Amendment," the Senator wrote, ". . . added the words 'as determined by the United States' to the reservation of 'disputes which are essentially within the domestic jurisdiction of the United States.' These additional words had been specifically rejected by the Foreign Relations Committee . . . Since the administration of Franklin D. Roosevelt, the United States has consistently sought to support the principle of international organization. Yet our adherence to the World Court, one of the oldest and most fundamental organizations in the United Nations complex, is so qualified with reservations as to cast doubt on whether we are members at all . . . The Department of State has never approved of the Connally Amendment, and the American Bar Association has opposed it ever since its adoption. Last August (1958), Thomas E. Dewey, former Governor of New York, chairman of the American Bar Association Committee on International Law Planning, stated: 'The committee believes that the withdrawal of the United States reservation to jurisdiction of the International Court, to the extent that it allows the United States unilaterally to determine which disputes lie essentially within its own jurisdiction, would be a most salutary step. It would be a demonstration of faith in the rule of law, and a persuasive example to others' ".[5]

The *Secretariat*, the sixth basic UN body, is much more than an administrative agency. First and foremost, its chief, the Secretary General, appointed by the General Assembly on recommendation of the Security Council, plays a role whose importance cannot be overestimated, for the Secretariat is an "independent" agency in that it consists of international civil servants and not of nationals representing their country's interest. The Secretary General and his staff "shall not seek or receive instructions from any government or from any other authority external to the Organization" (Art. 100).

The Secretary General is "the chief administrative officer of the Organization" (Art. 97), but he also "may bring to the attention of the Security Council any matter which in his opinion may threaten the maintenance of international peace and security" (Art. 99). This phrasing indicates that the Charter deliberately left considerable initiative to the Secretary General as has been demonstrated by the incumbents of this post. Furthermore, the Secretary General and his organization are conceived to be the elements of continuity in the shifting and changing fortunes of the UN's organs and committees. "He is not a 'chief executive' . . . but he has powers unusual in a Secretary or even a Secretary General . . . The Charter does not prevent the Secretary General from being—indeed it invites him to be—the 'boss' of the General Assembly, the *Eminence Grise* of the Security Council, the elder statesman of the Economic and Social Council, and the great white father of the member states . . ."[6]

The Secretariat is organized as two large complexes, one chiefly administrative, the other dealing with substantive UN

---

[5] "Undercutting World Law," letter by Senator Hubert Humphrey in the *Washington Post* and *Times Herald* Washington, D.C., May 8, 1959. See also *Congressional Record*, Vol. CV, No. 48, March 24, 1959, pp. 4508-4513. At the time of this writing, five years have passed, but the Humphrey Resolution has never been acted upon.

[6] Chase, *op. cit.*, p. 338.

affairs. Among the administrative offices are those concerned with legal and personnel affairs, an Office of the Controller (fiscal) and the executive staff of the Secretary General. Seven offices and departments deal with UN affairs; the latter are headed by Under Secretaries, the former by Directors. The departments comprise Political and Security Council Affairs, Economic and Social Affairs, Trusteeship and Information from Non-Self-Governing Territories, Public Information and Conference Services. There is an Office of General Services and a Technical Assistance Administration, both of which are primarily logistical.

The Secretariat is staffed with international civil servants. This concept, first created by the League, was strengthened considerably in the UN Charter and the staff regulations. There seems to be a consensus that possible clashes between loyalty to the United Nations and to the country of origin are avoidable, thus insuring an efficient and faithful staff. Jurists, too, in examining this delicate problem, have concluded that there is no reason to believe there "is or should be any conflict whatever between the loyalty owed by every citizen by virtue of his allegiance to his own state and the responsibility of such a citizen to the United Nations in respect to work done by him as an officer or employee of the United Nations."[7]

A few words must be said about the *Specialized Agencies* which were established in Art. 57 of the Charter. Basically, these agencies are technical and highly specialized in "economic, social, cultural, educational, health and related fields." They are, in fact, too specialized to function strictly within the narrower framework of the United Nations, and, on the other hand, "the United Nations is not an administrative body in the same sense that the Specialized Agencies are." [8] In general, the Specialized

---

[7] *Report of the Secretary General on Personnel Policy*, January 30, 1953, pp. 21-33, as quoted in L. M. Goodrich, *The United Nations*, New York: Thomas Y. Crowell Company, 1959, p. 151.

[8] Goodspeed, *op. cit.*, p. 398.

Agencies exist by treaty and are, by their very nature, universally useful or necessary. They do not compete with private, national or international organs, but are the result of governmental agreements, negotiated with the United Nations.

The seats of these agencies are spread over a wide area: They may be found in Washington, London, Paris, Rome, Geneva and Montreal. Their organizations correspond approximately to that of the United Nations itself, in that they have a kind of assembly, a committee or council which has executive functions, and a director heading a secretariat. None of these agencies has any actual power. They merely dispense advice and specialized technical aid. The agencies may recommend legislative action to their members but can go no further. The statutes of the individual Specialized Agencies, although organizationally similar, are not necessarily identical. By the end of 1957, there were eleven permanent Specialized Agencies, with a twelfth in preparation. An Interim Commission for International Trade Organization had also been established.

According to Art. 63 of the UN Charter, the Economic and Social Council, under the General Assembly's over-all supervision, "may enter into agreements with any of the agencies referred to in Art. 57, defining the terms on which the agency shall be brought into relationship with the United Nations." The article further states that ECOSOC "may co-ordinate the activities of the Specialized Agencies through consultation with and recommendations to such agencies and through recommendations to the General Assembly and to the members of the United Nations." Thus, it would appear that the Specialized Agencies are regarded as organizations apart from the United Nations, although, through ECOSOC and the General Assembly, broad, if vague, organizational bonds are indicated. Unfortunately, the budgetary situation of the Specialized Agencies has never been good, since adequate funds are seldom allocated. Consequently, the agencies' solvency depends primarily upon the national interests of their members, who might contribute generously or skimpily, as they see fit.

THE UN AND REGIONALISM

Chapter VIII of the Charter deals with regional arrangements. Art. 52 states that "nothing in the present Charter precludes the existence of regional arrangements or agencies for dealing with such matters relating to the maintenance of international peace and security as are appropriate for regional action, provided that such arrangements . . . are consistent with the Purposes and Principles of the United Nations." Paragraph 2 of the Article goes on to express approval of arrangements which contribute to the "pacific settlement of local disputes" *before* bringing them to the attention of the Security Council. In fact, in paragraph 3 of the same Article, the Council encourages settlements through regional arrangements and, according to Art. 53, "where appropriate, utilize such regional arrangement or agencies for enforcement action under its authority." Art. 54 stipulates that the Council be "at all times kept fully informed of activities undertaken or in contemplation under regional arrangements or by regional agencies for the maintenance of international peace and security."

The significance of these stipulations of the Charter is very great. There is scarcely a regional arrangement in existence which does not state expressly that it considers itself to be under the auspices of the United Nations and that the treaty has been concluded within the stipulations of the UN Charter whose Chapter VIII provides the contractual framework. It is obvious that the founding fathers of the Charter, although progressing beyond the League, did not conceive of the UN as a universal organization which could decide world political issues by fiat. Rather, they seemed to envisage a roof organization, an international "holding company," under which sovereign nations could continue to associate in the interests of mutual security and peaceful arbitration.

This seems to demonstrate, first, a confirmation of the sovereign rights of member nations to ally themselves with any other nation regardless of whether the policies inherent in their agreements are to the liking of members outside the pact. Second, it admits implicitly that the power and influence of the United Nations, although considerable in many respects, still is not great enough to maintain universal peace without relying on the encouragement of regional pacts. Third, it anticipates the ideological schism between East and West, maintaining flexibility so as to remain maneuverable in the administration of world peace.

Thus, Chapter VIII was obviously a compromise. On the one hand, the authors of the Charter probably foresaw that the Security Council might be hampered by regional arrangements. On the other hand, the nations of the world were not yet ready, World War II notwithstanding, to sacrifice more than tokens of sovereignty so long as the schism between communism and capitalism continued to frustrate the One World concept. In addition, the framers of the Charter found themselves confronted by regional arrangements already in existence. The Inter-American Pact of Chapultepec had just been signed, the Arab League had been formed during the war, and the development of Western European political and economic pacts had begun.

The question of whether regional security pacts can be forged "which will be beyond the control of the Security Council and yet consistent with the Charter"[9] has not been conclusively answered. A genuine test case has not yet arisen. At least, such mutual security treaties as NATO or the Warsaw Pact have not been found inconsistent with Chapter VIII. The problem is still unsolved and probably will remain so.

The more complex question of how the United Nations can deal with the chasm between the "Commonwealth of Socialist Nations" and the free world is even further from a solution. The development of two antagonistic groups of states, led by super powers, can hardly be classified as regional arrangements. The Western groups were created for the purpose of defense against communist encroachment, the Eastern for the purpose of furthering its own aims of communist consolidation.

[9] Chase, *op. cit.*, p. 204.

It has been pointed out above that the United Nations is regarded by the communist leaders in Moscow and Peking as a propaganda platform from which to influence world opinion, statesmen, intellectual leaders, and organizations. Thus far, Moscow and Peking have had little opportunity to impose their views on the United Nations and its agencies. The Korean War, after all, was conducted under the UN flag; the Hungarian revolution was denounced; the United States was not condemned for the bloodless pacification of the Lebanon, and communist vituperation did not seem to make as much an impression on the world forum as the Soviet representatives had hoped. Even considering the abstentions of the neutralist countries in the voting battle between East and West, the United Nations as a whole has so far sustained the free world and has denied membership to Communist China.

It would be wrong to consider the United Nations a failure. Nor can the UN be overlooked as a strong moral force in the world. In the social, economic and cultural spheres, its record of achievement has been impressive, even though limited by the obstacles of the Iron Curtain. Also, there have been successes in the marginal fields of UN endeavor. But the major political issues have remained unresolved owing to the communist bloc's studied obstructionism. Moreover, the Soviet leaders have consistently tried to conclude agreements outside the international organization, notably in their efforts to hold "summit" meetings.

9. The United Nations and the Foreign Offices

ADMINISTRATION

The United Nations was established to make possible international cooperation. Ideally, it should become the focal point of organized international relations and maintain peace by collective action, enabling member governments to negotiate significant issues of their foreign relations within the framework of an international organization. The political and institutional aspects of UN activities have been outlined above. We now turn to the administration of international relations at the United Nations.

It has become an accepted rule that foreign officers are responsible for setting up and controlling policy in the United Nations. Since they guide foreign policies—or at least administer the conduct of international relations—they also supervise and guide national policy in the UN, subject to the same constitutional and political checks that shape the formulation of individual policies and the obligations agreed upon in the UN Charter.

Presumably most sovereign nations, certainly all member nations, have set up special offices whose exclusive concern is the UN. International and supra-national organizations other than the UN are dealt with in separate bureaus on both sides of the Iron Curtain. The U.S. Department of State is an exception; its Bureau of International Organization Affairs is responsible for

UN questions but also for certain problems of international organizations outside the sphere of the UN.

Prior to joining the UN, the United States had not participated in international peace and security organizations. But once a UN member, it made great efforts to contribute to the success of the organization. Soon after the writing of the UN Charter, the U.S. government established, within the Department of State, an Office for Special Political Affairs (SPA), which was charged with the responsibility for coordinating U.S. policies and actions regarding the UN. Rising tensions between the Western powers and the Soviet bloc increased the importance of the UN's role, and the need was felt for a more broadly planned bureau to help both the United States and the UN to carry out the task of safeguarding the peace. Therefore, in 1948, the SPA was reorganized into the Office of United Nations Affairs.

In the following years, international organization was not limited to the UN. NATO and other regional alliances and arrangements were set up in conformity with UN statutes which complicated and increased policy work, liaison, and support activities. As a result, the Office of United Nations Affairs gradually developed into the Bureau for International Organization Affairs. It is responsible for promoting "the most effective use of the machinery of international organizations in the conduct of foreign affairs" and "acts as the official channel between the United States and international organizations of an interregional character, except where official diplomatic channels are expressly provided for this purpose."[1] Its concern with the UN extends to political and security matters, social and human rights, freedom of information, questions of refugees and displaced persons, trusteeship and dependent area policies, and the development of the UN and its Charter. In addition, the Bureau deals with UN budgetary questions and technical advice, handles administration, looks out for the privileges and immunity of its own personnel, and works on problems of disarmament. In international but not necessarily UN matters, the Bureau is responsible for

[1] *Department of State Manual* #670.

U.S. participation in "governmental and non-governmental international organizations and conferences, congresses, and commissions, except for those of a bilateral nature." ² Specifically, it prepares technical, financial and substantive aid and advice for international meetings, serving as host to any such meetings that take place on American soil.

The Bureau's organization is simple. There are five Offices under the general supervision of an Assistant Secretary of State and the direction of an Executive Director and his Staff Assistant: Dependent Area Affairs; International Economic and Social Affairs; UN Political and Security Affairs; International Administration; and International Conferences. In addition, three Special Assistants handle UN Planning (long-range policy planning and organization); Public Affairs (all information media and intelligence); and American personnel for the UN.

The Office of Dependent Area Affairs is concerned with any problems arising from the United States' participation in the UN with respect to non-self-governing territories and the international trusteeship system. It ascertains, with the concurrence of other appropriate departmental offices, whether the United States' interests in such territories are consistent with the UN Charter and the agreed terms of trusteeship. The Office prepares studies and proposals on these issues for the regional advisory commissions dealing with trust territories. It arranges meetings for the Trusteeship Council and the Security Council to discuss matters concerning such areas, whether they be strategic or non-strategic. Paying close attention to the activities of both these bodies, the Office apprises those which affect US interests and is responsible for the preparation of reports on non-self-governing territories under United States administration. It especially provides work facilities for the Caribbean Commission and the South Pacific Commission and serves as a channel of communication between these commissions and appropriate federal agencies.

² *Ibid.* #671.

The activities of the Office of International Economic and Social Affairs are related to the Economic and Social Council (ECOSOC) and its subsidiary bodies and specialized agencies. It concentrates its efforts on the most effective use of international organization relative to such aspects of US foreign affairs as pertain to economic, social, and humanitarian programs. It coordinates the functions of ECOSOC with these policy-making bureaus of the State Department and other federal agencies which have a legitimate interest in economic and social matters. It also reviews substantive policies and programs relating to UN participation in UNESCO and assists in coordinating the technical assistance programs of the United States with those of the UN and other international agencies.

The Bureau of United Nations Political and Security Affairs formulates and coordinates United States political and security matters concerning the UN. It also "reviews responsibilities for related matters arising in other international bodies or regional organizations."[3] In carrying out these duties, the Bureau works not only with the political offices of the Department of State but also with the UN Military Establishment and the Atomic Energy Commission, specifically on matters of disarmament and the use of nuclear power for peaceful purposes. One of the Bureau's most important tasks is its concern with and facilitation of peaceful settlements of international disputes. Finally, the Bureau "co-ordinates and supervises the over-all preparations for each session of the General Assembly."[4]

The Office of International Administration's responsibilities are not limited to administrative functions such as management and fiscal policies of the UN and the coordination of budgetary problems. It also advises the geographic bureaus concerned with these policies. Similarly, it advises the European desks on budgetary questions regarding NATO and the Latin American desks on matters concerning the Inter-American organizations. Finally, the Bureau of International Conferences has inherited from the

[3] *Ibid.* #665.
[4] *Ibid.*

former International Administration and Information Staffs the maintenance of archives and documentation, and the publication of conference activities. The conference program staff works out details of international meetings and the Administration Staff not only implements the work efforts of the Conference Staff but also manages conference finances and maintains records.

The British Foreign Office formerly had two United Nations departments. The first was responsible for economic and social questions. The second, dealing with the UN itself, was primarily interested in political issues. Both departments were primarily envisaged as coordinating offices. The Foreign Office emphasized, as early as 1947, that the "co-ordinating role of the United Nations Department is of the greatest importance to ensure that His Majesty's Government's policy in relation to the various organs of the United Nations and the Specialized Agencies does not overlap, so leading to waste of effort."[5] The Foreign Office organization, as of March 1963, had only one United Nations Department which presumably is responsible chiefly for political issues; related problems are handled by various other departments dealing with economic and organization affairs.

The United Nations Department is the link between the Foreign Office and the British delegation to the UN and is primarily responsible for the composition of the delegation. In cooperation with such departments as the Western Organization and Planning Department or the Economic Relations Department, the United Nations Department coordinates Foreign Office business vis-à-vis the UN as well as the work of various government departments dealing with the United Nations or other international organizations. Thus, the United Nations Department represents the Foreign Office views on a number of "interdepartmental panels dealing with particular aspects of the work of the United Nations or the Specialized Agencies."[6] The

---

[5] *Foreign Office Guide*, Second Edition, April 1947, pp. 22-23.

[6] *Ministère des Affaires Etrangères: Administration Centrale*, Paris: Imprimerie Nationale, 1963, pp. 20-22.

Department's extensive competence implies that the British government attributes great importance to UN activities, and its relatively small size does not reduce its effectiveness.

In the French Foreign Ministry, the small staff of the Sub-Directorate for the UN and International Organizations is charged with the following formidable tasks: (1) examination of questions concerning the UN and its subsidiary bodies especially the Security Council, the General Assembly, ECOSOC, the Trusteeship Council and the International Court of Justice; (2) participation in the commissions for disarmament, international law and other commissions and committees set up by the General Assembly; (3) technical and economic assistance for Europe, the Far East, and Latin America; (4) cooperation with the UN International Fund for Children, refugee organizations and relief for Palestine and Korea; (5) collaboration with the UN Food and Agriculture Organization, health and labor organizations, the International Atomic Energy Commission and nearly all other international bodies of UN concern. The Sub-Directorate coordinates its work with the specialized offices in the Ministry itself as well as with other government agencies. It also studies general questions concerning France's attitude toward international organizations outside the UN.[7]

The Soviet Ministry of Foreign Affairs has three bureaus responsible for work on International Organizations, International Economic Organizations and the United Nations. Information on the division of labor among these three offices is not available but it may be assumed that, at least in the United Nations Division, the type of work resembles that of similar bureaus in other foreign offices. In view of the Soviet outlook on world politics, the Party's interest in the UN is not necessarily consistent with the philosophy expressed in the UN Charter. Rather, it tends to exert all possible influences upon world opinion, using the UN components as sounding boards and platforms. One might go a step farther and submit that all

[7] *Ibid.* pp. 20-22.

international meetings and conferences are used in this way by the Kremlin and those satellite states which are represented in the UN. For this and related reasons, the UN bureaus in the *Minindel* can have little influence and most likely are chiefly service offices.

Since Communist China is not a member of the United Nations, its interest in international organization is theoretical. Two bureaus are concerned with international cultural and economic relations but no branch of the state government lists an office dealing with UN affairs. Should the United Nations eventually accept Communist China as a member, it is to be expected that an office charged with UN affairs would be established in Peking's Ministry of Foreign Affairs.

REPRESENTATION IN THE UN

Upon signing the Charter, member nations bound themselves to be represented properly in the United Nations. Specially appointed emissaries, envoys who usually carry the rank of ambassador, were sent to serve the interests of their respective countries. As a rule, they need not be confirmed by their parliamentary bodies but are nominated and chosen by their heads of state or foreign ministers. Nor does the United Nations have to give them an *agrément*. Possible consultations with the UN Secretariat concerning the appointee are entirely at the discretion of the appointing power.

Although designated to coordinate their country's interests with those of the international organization, they are first and foremost agents of their own government and accountable strictly to it. They remain representatives of their foreign offices under whose jurisdiction UN affairs fall. No important decisions can be made by the delegates without consulting their governments. This is particularly evident in sessions of the Security Council and the General Assembly, which deal with essential matters of foreign policy or international relations. Only in exceptional cases, when a delegate to the Security Council or a delegation leader in the General Assembly happens to be the chief of his own government, for example a prime minister, does he make his own decision, perfectly aware, however, that he must defend such action before his cabinet and parliament at home.

Whether UN delegates are to be regarded as having diplomatic status and whether they are to have all those prerogatives which international law has accorded to regular diplomats has not been stated unequivocally. In defining the status of delegates and officers of the League of Nations, its Covenant was more articulate than is the Charter of the United Nations. Article VII, paragraph 4, of the Covenant held that "Representatives of the Members of the League and officials of the League when engaged on the business of the League shall enjoy diplomatic privileges and immunities." The Swiss government concurred and helped make this provision a reality.

In contrast, Article 105, paragraph 2, of the Charter of the United Nations provided that representatives of the members are granted "such privileges and immunities as are necessary for the independent exercise of their functions in connection with the organization" and leaves it up to the General Assembly to determine "the details of the application . . . of this article" or to "propose conventions to the members of the United Nations for this purpose." Paragraph 1 of the same Article determines that the "Organization shall enjoy in the territory of each of its Members such privileges and immunities as are necessary for the fulfillment of its purposes." This is hardly a generous allowance of diplomatic privileges when compared with those of the League. Yet there can be little doubt that the United States, elected host to the United Nations, would have accepted a broader interpretation of the status of delegates and officers of the UN just as Switzerland once recognized the agents of the League "as having first class diplomatic status."[8]

It is possible that the chief delegates have been given high

[8] P. B. Potter, "Permanent Delegations to the League of Nations," *Geneva Special Studies of the League of Nations Association of the U.S.*, Geneva, November 1930, Vol. I, No. 8, p. 5.

diplomatic titles to compensate for their ambiguous diplomatic status. Naturally, every sending government is concerned that its representative be accorded the honors all envoys expect, not so much for himself but rather for the government he symbolizes. Many states have named their leading representatives ambassadors, possibly assuming that such rank carries with it privileges, granted not by the Charter but by international courtesy.

Just as a delegate's liaison agency with his government is his foreign office, so the Secretariat is his liaison agency with the United Nations. The personnel of the Secretariat consist of international civil servants, supposedly pledging loyalty to the United Nations rather than to their own country. Although their status does not quite measure up to the peculiarities of their position, there is at least one indication that they are held to be "above" the nations, namely, their exemption from taxes. Usually only regular diplomats are given such privileges. However, there is no provision in the Charter to make international civil servants extraterritorial. It is interesting to note that "efficiency, competence, and integrity" are not the sole factors to be considered in the selection of the staff of the secretariat. Article 101 determines that "due regard shall be paid to the importance of recruiting the staff on as wide a geographical basis as possible."

The permanent delegates at the UN, representing the members of the Security Council, usually possess ambassadorial rank and are advocates of their respective governments' foreign policy as it tends to contribute to and take advantage of global security under the principles of the Charter of the UN. Each of the five permanent members is represented by one delegate. So are the six non-permanent members, who are elected to serve a term of two years (Art. 23). While there is only one representative for each member state serving on the Council, a delegate may transfer his responsibilities temporarily to an alternate of his government's choice. The advisory staff to the members of the Security Council, which is not limited in numbers by the Charter, has no special standing in the organization.

To reiterate, the delegates of the Security Council are strictly executing their national foreign policies. They are not policy makers and their authority is less than that of a chief of a diplomatic mission.

Similarly, the representatives of all members of the UN in the General Assembly are emissaries of their respective governments. The maximum representation of each member is five delegates. However, more generous than the League Covenant, the Charter does not forbid the use of alternates, political and technical advisors, and experts on special problems. In view of the extensive work on many committees of the Assembly, where national representatives must be delegated by their chiefs, the delegations are rather substantial bodies, reflecting individual national policies in the political, economic, social and cultural fields. While it is obvious that these delegates must try to coordinate and correlate their government's policies with the overriding requirements of global harmony, they remain the spokesmen for their prescribed national policies. They can only carry out these policies, not make them. The same is true of the Trusteeship Council or the Atomic Energy Commission, whose members are obviously bound by the decisions of their governments. This procedure is somewhat less stringent in the case of the Economic and Social Council, or in certain instances, of the General Assembly, if the resolutions adopted are advisory rather than legislative.

The importance that national governments attach to the United Nations is further indicated by the fact that many members have found it necessary to appoint delegates other than their regular diplomatic representatives. At the beginning of UN meetings, ambassadors and ministers were designated to represent their countries at UN functions. Very soon, the pressure of business made this double assignment impossible except at special occasions. However, a number of smaller states, mainly for reasons of economy, have assigned their envoys to represent them at the UN.

Membership in the various organizations of the United Nations, including the commissions, committees, and subcommittees, is determined by the respective countries and not by the

UN. Generally, it is up to the chief delegates to see that their governments are properly represented. Frequently, governments appoint outstanding citizens or specialists for particular jobs.

Since there is no *corps diplomatique* at the UN and delegations do not necessarily have contact with each other, except that of working together in the UN, the Secretariat is the center where international information converges, and where universal trends and tendencies are most noticeable. Being a "neutral" meeting ground, it is conceivably the main source of UN "intelligence"—if this term can be applied at all.

UN INFORMATION SERVICES

The technique of persuasion has been adopted also by the United Nations. Its philosophy is clearly stated in the (revised) principles, subscribed to by the General Assembly in 1952:

> The United Nations cannot achieve the purpose for which it has been created unless the peoples of the world are informed of its aims and activities. The basic policy of the United Nations, in the field of public information, is therefore to promote to the greatest possible extent, within its budgetary limitations, an informed understanding of the work and purposes of the Organization among the peoples of the world. To this end, the Department of Public Information should primarily assist and rely upon the services of existing official and private agencies of information, educational institutions and non-governmental organizations. It should not engage in "propaganda"; it should undertake, on its initiative, positive informational activities that will supplement the services of existing agencies. In so doing it should pay particular attention to the special problems and needs of those areas where, in relation to other areas, information media are less fully developed, with a view to ensuring the most effective use of facilities and resources available . . . [9]

The principles further state that the Department of Public Information (renamed Office of Public Information in 1958)

[9] *UN General Assembly Resolution 595* (VI), February 4, 1952.

"should provide services in the following main fields: press, publications, radio, television, graphics and exhibitions, public liaison and reference." The work is planned along regional and language lines, giving emphasis to whatever media are most effective in any given territory.

Since 1952, when these principles were issued in a revised form, the General Assembly's consensus seems to have been that information activities should be increased. Accordingly, an "Expert Committee on United Nations Public Information" was set up in November, 1957, and the results of its studies were submitted to the Secretary General in August, 1958. The report which completely outlines UN information activities, probably is the most comprehensive document available on the UN concept of information.[10] Briefly, the media are used as follows.

Press services are provided for several hundred correspondents permanently accredited to UN headquarters. Services are also extended to radio, television, and newsreel correspondents, cameramen and photographers. The UN offices in Geneva are covered by almost 200 correspondents of all media. The most substantial part of the UN Central and Editorial Press Services consists of press releases.

Radio Services, about 20 percent of the entire information budget, have six geographic-language sections: Middle Eastern Service, Southeast Asian and Transpacific Service, Latin-American-Iberian Service, European Service, English Language Service, and General Service. The services are divided into relayed and unrelayed broadcasts, the latter having been found rather ineffective.

Television services produce feature and documentary programs for use over national broadcast facilities. They cover major meetings of the General Assembly and Security Council, and provide facilities enabling national broadcasting organizations and their correspondents to originate programs from the United Nations.[11] The investigating Expert Committee pointed

---

[10] General Assembly, A/3928, September 1958, 13th Session, Agenda Item 55.
[11] UN General Assembly, A/3928, September 20, 1958, p. 42.

out that television programs received in the United States and Canada are the most significant and that to assess their effectiveness outside the North American continent is difficult. Interestingly, these programs were initiated by the demands of the North American market.

A number of documentary motion pictures have been produced by the Film Services, mainly to further the purposes of UN Specialized Agencies. In a sense, this program is comparable to that of USIA in connection with the US technical assistance (Point Four) program. The cost of producing these films is surprisingly low; for example, a six-reeler, "Blue Vanguard," dealing with the Suez crisis, cost only $34,000, excluding staff salaries and common staff costs.

Graphic Services produce photographs, film strips (projected as a series of still pictures similar to slides), wall sheets, photo posters, and exhibits. Being primarily educational, these are used most profitably in underdeveloped areas.

The Publications Service publishes the *United Nations Review* in English, French, and Spanish. There is also a comprehensive program offering booklets, pamphlets, leaflets, and reprints for free distribution in various languages. *A Yearbook of the United Nations* is published by the Columbia University Press at no expense to the UN Information Office. Other publications include such books as *United Nations Postage Stamps, Ten Year Catalogue of United Nations Publications, Charter of the United Nations, Everyman's United Nations,* and *Basic Facts.*

The Public Liaison Division is subdivided into sections for non-governmental organizations, educational groups, visitors (including speakers, guided tours, public inquiries), sales and circulation. Of the 227 non-governmental organizations with which liaison has been established, no less than 178 were United States national organizations. Great importance is attached to the Educational Section which strives to imbue children with the underlying principles of the Charter of the United Nations. However, "the primary responsibility for such education rests on the Member States themselves, with their Ministries or Departments of Education and, most important of all, on their teachers."[12] An interne and fellowship program, which supports studies of various duration, is extended to civil servants, students, and special internes or guide-internes.

As is evident, the UN Information services use the same media as do the national propaganda agencies. The policy of avoiding "propaganda" is well meant, and certainly there are many aspects, such as the international supervision of the programs, which render difficult any attempt at propaganda. But the UN needs to advertise its organization and objectives. This is both necessary and understandable, and to shy away from the word "propaganda" seems unrealistic. There is nothing evil in propagandizing United Nations aims; in fact, the information budget of the UN permits far too little dissemination of information.

In the context of this examination, propaganda is demonstrably a part of international relations which even the supranational UN cannot eschew. Propaganda is needed and world politics without it is as unthinkable as was foreign affairs without diplomacy in the nineteenth century. Diplomacy and propaganda are as inseparable as ideology and nationalism, or nuclear missiles and modern military strategy.

[12] *Ibid.*, p. 61.

Summary

The formulation and carrying out of foreign policy is the result of a wide variety of factors, attitudes, and circumstances. The process of developing policy and the functional aspects of what one may call policy machinery are bound to influence the nature of policy and therefore affect the character of international relations. Our understanding of foreign policy as a national or world political phenomenon cannot be complete without knowledge of the processes of its making, attention to the ideological and psychological aspects influencing the relations between nations, and realization of the intangibles which render political foresight so hazardous.

Is it possible to deepen and broaden insight into the decision-making organs by resorting to mechanistic expedients in order to come up with more correct predictions or solutions, based as they are on "exact science" such as mathematical interpretation of content analysis and computers? The answer is yes—but only if these techniques are used for purposes of corroboration or fact-finding in the sphere of ascertainable statistics. To believe that future policy makers will be able to rely for the solution of their problems on such scientific auxiliaries as quantification and cybernetics is a dangerous illusion.

In view of the innumerable complexities and pitfalls of foreign policy making for which solutions cannot be mathematically determined, it may be useful to highlight those aspects that must be kept in mind by policy officials and students of foreign affairs.

1. Foreign policy is not only an international problem. It is inextricably tied to domestic issues. It is not only a political problem but has social, psychological, and economic implications as well. It is not only related to the internal conditions of the country that creates it but is also influenced by currents and pressures from within other countries, whose foreign policies are, in turn, influenced—if not determined—by their own domestic conditions. The myth that international relations can be maintained without interest in or interference with other countries' domestic affairs has long since been refuted. A statesman who still believes that he can divorce foreign from national affairs is out of date and may be a danger to his country.

2. Foreign policy is as strong as the relative defensive or offensive potential at its disposal. Included in this consideration is the speed with which this potential can be mobilized. The degree of effective cooperation between policy and strategy profoundly influences the character of political and military organization, and planning is a premise for successful policy formulation and implementation. Lack of such coordination among the political, economic, and defense agencies and failure to maintain unity of purpose inevitably leads to disastrous consequences.

3. Foreign policy inevitably reflects the economic beliefs of nations. It will be shaped in accordance with the economic status of the policy-making governments, that is, their own material and potential wealth and their relative economic solvency. Further points at issue are the economic conditions in a country's general area and the political, ideological, and economic pressures brought to bear upon it by powerful neighbors. But however strong economic considerations may be, they must be seen in the light of political conditions and ideological trends. Even though it might appear that economy shapes foreign policy, this is rarely so. Finance, commerce, international trade, or currency

questions may influence political decisions but are—certainly in the communist orbit—predominantly manipulatory and not the sole rationale behind ultimate policy objectives.

4. Foreign policy is only as sound as the information it uses. The quality and practicability of a policy is closely related to the accuracy of the intelligence material, the lucidity and objectivity of its analysis, and the experience, erudition and intuition to be found in its evaluation. Certainly the wisest foreign policy will be created by a government that has spared neither effort nor expense to secure the best intelligence, the finest analysts and researchers, and the ablest interpreters of informative material, all of whom should be free to express their opinion and be given the opportunity to be heard—and heeded. A policy maker who pays insufficient attention to such information and who believes he knows better than his qualified advisers is likely to plot a hazardous international course for his ship of state.

5. Foreign policy is as effective as its implementation or enforcement permits it to be. For this reason, it must cope first of all with two developments that make the contemporary world so different from all past eras: ideology and technology. It must adopt ways of reasoning to deal with these problems. It must, in both formulation and execution, consider the scientific advancement of the twentieth century, which has seen the growth of the revolutionary new aspects of civilization—promising and mortally dangerous at the same time. It is essential that foreign policy develop adequate techniques in all branches of its endeavors, be able to change quickly when necessary, and be versatile in order to meet new problems with alternate policies and a wide choice of tactics.

6. Foreign policy and propaganda are interrelated. With the disintegration of traditional diplomacy, direct and indirect propaganda have become the chief media of communication, especially between the East and West. The techniques of persuasion have, in many ways, replaced those of diplomacy and, although diplomacy also tried to persuade, it did so by way of reasoning and not, as propaganda does so often, by appeal to mass instincts.

More often than not a foreign policy that cannot at the same time be used as a propaganda policy has little practical value. Quite frequently policies are announced precisely because of their propaganda value. Thus propaganda has become an integral part of the policy machinery.

Since the fate of nations and of the world depends largely upon the principles which underlie the relations between them, there can be little doubt that the machinery of foreign policy is the crux of world politics. This machinery is no mere mechanical process but a reflection of political objectives and designs. To know the machinery is to understand its products.

Foreign policy making is a complex and delicate task. Its formulation involves almost every aspect of the lives of nations and citizens. Its creation demands more of experts and statesmen than does any other task in government. Its processes require close cooperation among heterogeneous elements.

There are no quick and easy decisions. Even those of a tactical or temporary nature must be thoroughly reasoned. Basic policies can only be developed slowly and deliberately, with the nation's best minds aiding the professionals, with more than usual understanding on the part of parliamentary bodies, and with the support of the people. A nation must provide facilities for adequate policy planning and prepare for contingencies and alternatives of a long-range nature, but it must also be able to meet rapidly moving events with swift countermeasures. Most of all, the men responsible for creating policy must realize that nineteenth-century techniques of international relations radically changed when ideological aggression polarized the world and nuclear deterrents virtually eliminated large-scale war.

Where citizens are well informed on international affairs, where lawmakers provide the means for first-rate foreign relations agencies, and where statesmen are most able to take a reasonably long-range view—in such a country will foreign policy machinery be most effective and the national future most secure.

Selected Bibliography

INTERNATIONAL RELATIONS IN A DIVIDED WORLD

Brogan, D. W., and D. V. Verney, *Political Patterns in Today's World*, New York: Harcourt, Brace and World, 1963

Duchacek, I., and K. W. Thompson, *Conflict and Cooperation among Nations*, New York: Holt, Rinehart and Winston, 1960

Herz, J. H., *International Politics in the Atomic Age*, New York: Columbia University Press, 1959

Kaplan, M. A., ed., *The Revolution in World Politics*, New York: Wiley, 1962

———, *System and Process in International Politics*, New York: Wiley, 1957

Kulski, W. W., *International Politics in a Revolutionary Age*, New York: Lippincott, 1964

London, K. L., *The Permanent Crisis*, New York: Walker and Co., 1962

Morgenthau, H. J., *Politics among Nations: The Struggle for Power and Peace*, New York: Knopf, 1960

Schelling, T. C., *The Strategy of Conflict*, Cambridge: Harvard University Press, 1960

Seton-Watson, H., *Neither War Nor Peace: The Struggle for Power in the Post-War World*, New York: Praeger, 1960

INTERNATIONAL LAW

Bishop, W. W., Jr., *International Law*, Boston: Little, Brown and Co., Second edition, 1962

Brierly, J. L., *The Law of Nations*, New York and Oxford: Oxford University Press, Sixth edition, 1963

Carlston, K. S., *Law and Organization in a World Society*, Urbana: University of Illinois Press, 1962

Jacobini, H. B., *International Law, A Test*, Homewood, Ill.: Dorsey Press, Inc., 1962

Jessup, P. C., *A World Law of Nations*, New York: The Macmillan Co., 1948

Kaplan, M. A., and N. de B. Katzenbach, *The Political Foundations of International Law*, New York: Wiley, 1961

Larson, A., *When Nations Disagree: A Handbook on Peace through Law*, Baton Rouge: Louisiana State University Press, 1961

Lauterpacht, Sir Hersch, *The Development of International Law by the International Court*, New York: Praeger, 1958

Nogee, J. L., *Soviet Policy towards International Control of Atomic Energy*, Notre Dame, Ind.: University of Notre Dame Press, 1961

IDEOLOGY AND FOREIGN POLICY

Bereday, G. Z. F., W. W. Brickman, and G. H. Read, eds., *The Changing Soviet School*, Boston: Houghton Mifflin Co., 1960

Berg, A. I., *Kiberneticu ma Slughlu Kommunizimu (Cybernetics in the Service of Communism)*, Gosenerqoizdat, Moscow, 1961. Translated into English by the Joint Publications Research Service, U.S. Department of Commerce, Washington: JPRS: 14, 592, July 25, 1962

Brzezinski, Z. K., *Ideology and Power in Soviet Politics*, New York: Praeger, 1962

Cohen, A. A., *The Communism of Mao Tse-tung*, Chicago: The University of Chicago Press, 1964

Haskins, C. P., *The Scientific Revolution and World Politics*, New York: Harper and Row, 1964

Lawrence, M. W., ed., *Neutralism and Nonalignment*, New York: Praeger, 1962

Orleans, L. A., *Professional Manpower and Education in Communist China*, National Science Foundation, Washington: Government Printing Office, 1960

GEOGRAPHY: PHYSICAL, POLITICAL, ECONOMIC, HUMAN

Alexander, J. W., *Economic Geography*, Englewood Cliffs, New Jersey: Prentice-Hall, 1963

American Assembly, The, *The Population Dilemma*, Englewood Cliffs, New Jersey: Prentice-Hall, 1963

Carlson, L., *Geography and World Politics*, Englewood Cliffs, New Jersey: Prentice-Hall, 1958

Cohen, S. B., *Geography and Politics in a World Divided*, New York: Random House, 1963

Cole, J. P., *Geography of World Affairs*, 2nd ed., Baltimore: Penguin Books, 1963

Demiashkevich, M., *The National Mind*, English-French-German, New York: American Book Co., 1938

Gregor, H. F., *Environment and Economic Life: An Economic and Social Geography*, Princeton: Van Nostrand, 1963

Jones, S. B., *Geography and World Affairs*, New York: Rand McNally, 1962

Mudd, S., *The Population Crisis and the Use of World Resources*, Bloomington: University of Indiana Press, 1964

Murphy, G., *Human Potentialities*, New York: Basic Book Publishers, 1958

Pounds, N. J. G., *Political Georgraphy*, New York: McGraw-Hill, 1963

PUBLIC OPINION AND FOREIGN POLICY

Albig, W., *Modern Public Opinion*, New York: McGraw-Hill, 1956

Almond, G., *The American People and Foreign Policy*, New York: Praeger, 1960

Bailey, T. A., *The Man in the Street*, New York: Macmillan, 1948

Buchanan, W., and H. Cantril, *How Nations See Each Other, A Study in Public Opinion*, Urbana: University of Illinois Press, 1953

Hero, A. O., *Americans in World Affairs*, Vol. I.; and B. C. Cohen, *The Influence of Non-Governmental Groups on Foreign Policy-Making*, Vol. II. Boston: World Peace Foundations, 1959

Irion, F. C., *Public Opinion and Propaganda*, New York: Crowell, 1950

Key, V. O., Jr., *Public Opinion and American Democracy*, New York: Knopf, 1961

Lasswell, H. D., *Public Opinion in War and Peace; How Americans Make up Their Minds*, Washington: National Education Association, 1943

Markel, L. J., et. al., *Public Opinion and Foreign Policy*, New York: Harper, 1949

Truman, D. B., *The Governmental Process, Political Interests and Public Opinion*, New York: Knopf, 1955

INTERNATIONAL TRADE AND FOREIGN AID

Asher, R. E., *Grants, Loans, and Local Currencies: Their Role in Foreign Aid*, Washington: The Brookings Institution, 1961

Feis, H., *Foreign Aid and Foreign Policy*, New York: St. Martin's Press, 1964

Henderson, W. O., *The Genesis of the Common Market*, Chicago: Quadrangle Books, 1962

Humphrey, D. C., *The United States and the Common Market*, New York: Praeger, 1962

Isaiah, F., *The European Common Market: An Analysis of Commercial Policy*, New York: Praeger, 1961

Jensen, F., and Walter, I., *The Common Market: Economic Integration in Europe*, Philadelphia: J. B. Lippincott, 1965

Linder, S. B., *An Essay on Trade and Transformation*, New York: John Wiley and Sons, 1961

Shanks, M., and J. Lambert, *The Common Market Today and Tomorrow*, New York: Praeger, 1962

Vanek, J., *International Trade: Theory and Economic Policy*, Homewood, Ill.: Richard D. Irwin, Inc., 1961

NATIONAL SECURITY AND THE BALANCE OF TERROR

Brodie, B., *Strategy in the Missile Age*, Princeton: Princeton University Press, 1959

Dinerstein, H. S., *War and the Soviet Union: Nuclear Weapons and Revolution in Soviet Military and Political Thinking*, New York: Praeger, 1959

Gallois, P., *The Balance of Terror: Strategy for the Nuclear Age*, Boston: Houghton Mifflin Co., 1961

Garthoff, R. L., *Soviet Strategy in the Nuclear Age*, New York: Praeger, 1962

Gulick, E. V., *Europe's Classical Balance of Power*, Ithaca: Cornell University Press, 1955

Hsieh, A. L., *Communist China's Strategy in the Nuclear Era*, New York: Prentice-Hall, 1962

Kahn, H., *On Thermonuclear War*, Princeton: Princeton University Press, 1961

Kissinger, H. A., *The Necessity for Choice*, New York: Harper Brothers, 1961

Liska, G., *International Equilibrium, A Theoretical Essay on the Politics and Organization of Security*, Cambridge: Harvard University Press, 1957

———, *Nations in Alliance, the Limits of Interdependence*, Baltimore: Johns Hopkins Press, 1962

Lowe, G. E., *The Age of Deterrence*, Boston: Little, Brown, 1964

Committee on Government Operations, U.S. Senate, *Organizing for National Security*, Subcommittee on National Policy Machinery, Washington: U.S. Government Printing Office, 1960

Sokolovsky, V. D., *Soviet Military Strategy*, analyzed and annotated by H. S. Dinerstein, L. Goure, and T. W. Wolfe, Englewood Cliffs, New Jersey: Prentice-Hall, 1963

Strausz-Hupé, R., et. al., *Protracted Conflict*, revised ed., New York: Harper, 1963

PROTECTIVE ALLIANCES AND ORGANIZATIONS

Cottrell, A. J., and J. E. Dougherty, *The Politics of the Atlantic Alliance*, New York: Praeger, 1964

The European Free Trade Association—Today and Tomorrow, prepared by Business International, Inc., distributed by McGraw-Hill, Inc., New York, 1964

Knorr, K., ed., *NATO and American Security*, Princeton: Princeton University Press, 1959

Modelski, G., ed., *SEATO*, Vancouver: Publication Centre, University of British Columbia, 1963

Munk, F., *Atlantic Dilemma: Partnership or Community?* Dobbs Ferry, N.Y.: Oceana Publications, 1964.

Riker, W. H., *The Theory of Political Coalitions*, New Haven: Yale University Press, 1962

Thomas, Ann Van Wynen, and A. J. Thomas, Jr., *The Organization of American States*, Dallas: Southern Methodist University Press, 1963

Wilcox, F. O., and H. F. Haviland, Jr., *The Atlantic Community*, New York: Praeger, 1963

Wolfers, A., ed., *Alliance Policy in the Cold War*, Baltimore: Johns Hopkins University Press, 1959

INTELLIGENCE AND ESPIONAGE

Dallin, D. J., *Soviet Espionage*, New Haven: Yale University Press, 1955

Deriabin, P., and F. Gibney, *The Secret World*, New York: Doubleday and Co., 1959

Dulles, A. W., *The Craft of Intelligence*, New York: Harper and Row, 1963

Foote, A., *Handbook for Spies*, Garden City: Doubleday and Co., 1949

Hilsman, R., *Strategic Intelligence and National Decisions*, Glencoe, Ill.: Free Press, 1956

Hutton, J., *School for Spies: The ABC of How Russia's Secret Service Operates*, New York: Coward-McCann, 1962

Kent, S., *Strategic Intelligence*, Princeton: Princeton University Press, 1951

Platt, W., *Strategic Intelligence Production*, New York: Praeger, 1957

Ransom, H. H., *Central Intelligence and National Security*, Cambridge: Harvard University Press, 1958

Wolin, S., and R. M. Slusser, *The Soviet Secret Police*, New York: Praeger, 1957

FOREIGN OFFICE ORGANIZATION

Bailou, J., and P. Pelletier, *Les Affaires Etrangères*, Paris: Presses Universitaires de France, 1962

Chatelain, J., *La Nouvelle Constitution et la Régime Politique de France*, Paris: Editions Berger Heurouet, 1959

DeConde, A., *The American Secretary of State*, New York: Praeger, 1962

Fainsod, M., *How Russia Is Ruled*, rev. ed., Cambridge: Harvard University Press, 1963

Price, D. K., ed., *The Secretary of State*, Englewood Cliffs, New Jersey: Prentice-Hall, 1960

Robinson, J. A., *Congress and Foreign Policy-Making*, Homewood, Ill.: Dorsey Press, 1963

Stout, H. M., *British Government*, New York and London: Oxford University Press, 1955

Strang, Lord, *The Foreign Office*, New York and London: Oxford University Press, 1955

Tang, P. S. A., *Communist China Today*, 2nd revised ed., Washington: Research Institute on the Sino-Soviet Bloc, 1961

Westerfield, H. B., *The Instruments of American Foreign Policy*, New York: Crowell, 1963

FOREIGN POLICIES EAST AND WEST

Barnett, A. D., ed., *Communist Strategies in Asia*, New York: Praeger, 1963

Beloff, M., *Foreign Policy and the Democratic Process*, Baltimore: Johns Hopkins Press, 1955

Boyd, R. R., *Communist China's Foreign Policy*, New York: Praeger, 1962

Conquest, R., *Power and Policy in the USSR*, London: Macmillan and Co., 1961

Dallin, A., ed., *Soviet Conduct in World Affairs*, New York: Columbia University Press, 1960

Dallin, D., *Soviet Foreign Policy after Stalin*, Philadelphia: J. B. Lippincott, 1961

Goodman, E., *The Soviet Design for a World State*, New York: Columbia University Press, 1960

Mackintosh, J. M., *Strategy and Tactics of Soviet Foreign Policy*, New York and Oxford: Oxford University Press, 1963

Northedge, F. S., *British Foreign Policy*, New York: Praeger, 1963

Perkins, D., *The American Approach to Foreign Policy*, revised ed., Cambridge: Harvard University Press, 1962

Shulman, M. D., *Stalin's Foreign Policy Reappraised*, Cambridge: Harvard University Press, 1964

POLICY FORMULATION AND DECISION MAKING

Elder, R. E., *The Policy Machine: The Department of State and American Foreign Policy*, Syracuse, N.Y.: Syracuse University Press, 1960

Frankel, J., *The Making of Foreign Policy: An Analysis of Decision Making*, New York and London: Oxford University Press, 1963

Lerche, C. O., Jr., and A. A. Said, *Concepts of International Politics*, Englewood Cliffs, New Jersey: Prentice-Hall, 1963

Modelski, G. A., *A Theory of Foreign Policy*, New York: Praeger, 1962

U.S. Senate, Committee on Government Operations, *National Policy Machinery in Communist China*, Washington: Government Printing Office, 1960

———, *National Policy Machinery in the Soviet Union*, 1960

Snyder, R., et. al., eds., *Foreign Policy Decision-Making*, New York: Free Press of Glencoe, 1962

Sorensen, T. C., *Decision-Making in the White House*, New York: Columbia University Press, 1963

Truman, D. B., *The Governmental Process*, New York: A. A. Knopf, 1960

DIPLOMACY THEN AND NOW

Kertesz, S. D., and M. A. Fitzsimons, *Diplomacy in a Changing World*, Notre Dame, Ind.: University of Notre Dame Press, 1961

Klineberg, O., *Human Dimension in International Relations*, New York: Holt and Rinehart, 1964

Nicholson, H., *The Diplomat*, New York: Harcourt, Brace and Co., 1939.

———, *The Evolution of Diplomatic Methods*, London: Constable and Co., 1954

———, *Diplomacy*, New York and London: Oxford University Press, 1964

Plischke, E., *Conduct of American Diplomacy*, Princeton: Van Nostrand, 1963

Seabury, P., *Power, Freedom, and Diplomacy*, New York: Random House, 1963

Wallace, L. P., and W. C. Askew, eds., *Power, Public Opinion and Diplomacy*, Durham: Duke University Press, 1959

Wriston, H. M., *Diplomacy in a Democracy*, New York: Harper, 1956

PROPAGANDA IN INTERNATIONAL POLITICS

Barghoorn, F. C., *Soviet Foreign Propaganda*, Princeton: Princeton University Press, 1964

Barrett, E., *Truth Is Our Weapon*, New York: Funk and Wagnalls, 1953

Carroll, W., *Persuade or Perish*, Boston: Houghton Mifflin, 1948

Hargrove, J., *Words Win Wars*, London: Wells, Gardner, Darton and Co., 1940

Holt, R. A., *Radio Free Europe*, Minneapolis: University of Minnesota Press, 1958

Joyce, W., *The Propaganda Gap*, New York: Harper and Row, 1964

Kirkpatrick, E. M., ed., *Target: The World*, New York: Macmillan Co., 1956

Lerner, D., *Propaganda in War and Peace*, New York: George W. Stewart, 1951

Lifton, R. J., *Thought Reform and the Psychology of Totalism: A Study of "Brainwashing" in China*, London: V. Gollancz, 1961

Martin, L. J., *International Propaganda*, Minneapolis: University of Minnesota Press, 1958

McMurray, R., and M. Lee, *The Cultural Approach: Another Way in International Relations*, Chapel Hill: University of North Carolina Press, 1947

Passin, H., *China's Cultural Influence*, New York: Praeger, 1963

Schramm, W., ed., *Mass Communications: A Book of Readings*, Urbana: The University of Illinois Press, 1960

Whitaker, U. G., ed., *Propaganda and International Relations*, San Francisco: Howard Chandler, 1960

Whitton, J. B., *Propaganda and the Cold War: A Princeton University Symposium*, Washington: Public Affairs Press, 1963

Yu, F. T. C., *Mass Persuasion in Communist China*, New York: Praeger, 1964

THE UNITED NATIONS AND FOREIGN POLICIES

Bloomfield, L. P., *The United Nations and American Foreign Policy*, Boston: Little, Brown and Co., 1960

Chade, E. P., *The United Nations in Action*, New York: McGraw-Hill, 1950

Claude, I. L., Jr., *Swords Into Plowshares: The Problems and Progress of International Organization*, 2nd ed., New York: Random House, 1961

Goodrich, L. M., *The United Nations*, New York: Thomas Y. Crowell Co., 1959

Goodspeed, S., *The Nature and Function of International Organization*, New York: Oxford University Press, 1959

Hankey, Lord M. P., *Diplomacy by Conference*, London: Ernest Benn Ltd., 1946

Index